Politics in
Southeast
Asia

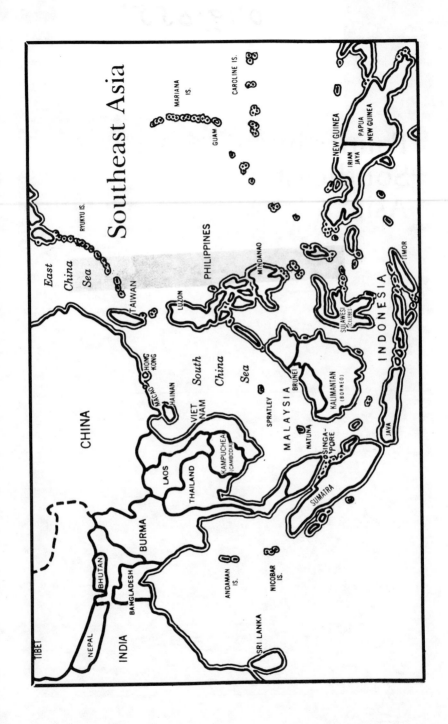

Southeast Asia

Politics in Southeast Asia

Clark D. Neher

SCHENKMAN BOOKS, INC.
Cambridge, Massachusetts

Copyright © 1987

Schenkman Books, Inc.
P.O. Box 1570
Harvard Square
Cambridge, MA 02138

Library of Congress Cataloging in Publication Data

Neher, Clark D.
  Politics in Southeast Asia.
  Bibliography: p.
  Includes index.
  1. Asia, Southeastern—Politics and government.
I. Title
DS526.7.N43   320.9′59   79-19263
ISBN 0-87047-010-8
ISBN 0-87047-011-6 pbk.

Printed in the United States of America.

Contents

Contents

Preface

The authors of a recent distinguished text, *In Search of Southeast Asia*, note that on the island of Mactan in the Philippines a monument was erected by the Spanish colonialists "to glorify God, Spain, and Ferdinand Magellan." In 1941, during the period of American rule in the Philippines, a marker was placed in the same area which stated: "On this spot Ferdinand Magellan died on April 27, 1521, wounded in an encounter with the soldiers of Lapulapu, Chief of Mactan Island." The inscription further noted the first successful circumnavigation of the earth by one of Magellan's ships.

Following independence from the United States, the Philippines erected its own monument, entitled "Lapulapu," which reads: "Here, on 27 April, 1521, Lapulapu and his men repulsed the Spanish invaders, killing their leader, Ferdinand Magellan. Thus, Lapulapu became the first Filipino to have repelled European aggression."[1]

The diversity of perspectives shown by these markers illustrates the problem any author faces in attempting to analyze foreign societies, or indeed, one's own society. By definition, a Westerner has a Western bias if he assumes it is almost impossible to "escape" his past. But then, can an Asian scholar objectively understand the diverse traditions of even his or her geographical birthplace? Can the urban Indonesian analyze the rural Javanese, Sumatran, or Ambonese? There is no definitive answer to these questions. Instead, one can only heed the admonition to be aware of one's values and biases and make every effort to overcome one's propensity for ethnocentric analysis.

A second kind of Western ethnocentric bias refers to the tendency to see the Western impact on Southeast Asia as primary and to ignore the continuity of the indigenous culture. This

---

[1] David Joel Steinberg, ed., *In Search of Southeast Asia* (New York: Praeger, 1971), p. xi.

second problem is also one of perspective. The eminent historian of Southeast Asia, D.G.E. Hall, wrote of the importance of presenting Southeast Asia as "an area worthy of consideration in its own right, for its history cannot be safely viewed from any other perspective until seen from its own."[2]

The term "Southeast Asia" is relatively new and perhaps is more meaningful to scholars and diplomats than to the people who live in the area. The term was first used during World War II by the Allied powers to describe the region commanded by Britain's Admiral Mountbatten. Even during the war, the term referred to a slightly different configuration of nations than now. The Southeast Asia Command (SEAC) included Burma, Ceylon (Sri Lanka), Thailand, the Malay peninsula, and Sumatra. Today there is wide acceptance among scholars that "Southeast Asia" includes the Philippines, Indonesia, Malaysia, Singapore, Vietnam, Cambodia (Kampuchea), Laos, Thailand, Brunei, and Burma.[3]

There is great presumption in writing a textbook on Southeast Asia, given its historical, political, economic, and cultural diversity. As a geographic entity, Southeast Asia makes sense as that area east of India and south of China. Certainly, the people of Southeast Asia do not identify themselves as Southeast Asians. There is little sense of a shared civilization. On the contrary, relations between Southeast Asian and the Western nations have been more frequent than relations among the Southeast Asian nations themselves.

The great diversity of Southeast Asia should not preclude the attempt to find common analytical themes. Indeed, it is in the heterogeneous nature of the area that similar patterns and themes are manifested. Moreover, Southeast Asian nations have shared a set of common historical experiences that continue to influence contemporary political activity. Chapter 1 of this book focuses on diversity; at the same time, the common patterns found throughout Southeast Asia contribute to the book's overall integration.

[2] D. G. E. Hall, *A History of Southeast Asia* (3d ed.; New York: St. Martin's Press, 1968), p. xxii.

[3] To avoid confusion the name Cambodia will be used throughout the text. Following the Communist takeover in 1975, the government changed the nation's name to Kampuchea.

Chapter 2 emphasizes those aspects of history that affect the area's political life, including the adaptation of Hinduism, Islam, and Buddhism and the assimilation of Western ways, stemming from colonialism. The Southeast Asian experience in nation-building constitutes the theme of Chapter 3, which describes the postindependence search for a political format. Each Southeast Asian society has faced the challenge of bringing order to the conflict between the retention of traditional patterns and the adaptation of new ideas. Much of the conflict and turmoil in the area's politics during the postindependence period has resulted from the struggle between tradition and modernity (most recently in the form of Westernization) and the attempt to find a balance between the two which is appropriate to each nation's particular conditions. Considerably more attention is paid to Thailand in this and subsequent chapters, reflecting the author's particular interests and the desire to provide more depth of analysis for at least one Southeast Asian nation.

Chapter 4 studies how political ideas and behavior patterns become a part of a society. The pattern of individual attitudes, beliefs, and values toward the political order of a society, that is, the political culture, constitutes an important part of Southeast Asian political life. In this chapter the reader will find an analysis of Buddhism, Islam, and animism as they relate to political activity. Various political ideologies will be discussed. Because the character of authority relations is particularly important for understanding Southeast Asian political life, that theme is emphasized in this political culture chapter.

Over 70 percent of the Southeast Asian people live in rural areas, and Chapter 5 presents an overview of these villagers' political role. Thailand is featured as a nation with a peasantry that in recent times has not rebelled against the established forces—in contrast to the Philippines, where rebellion was carried out first against the Japanese during World War II and then against the established government.

The nations of Southeast Asia exhibit exceedingly diverse political systems. Chapter 6 looks at military rule, civilian dictatorial rule, Communist rule, and quasi-democratic rule. This chapter analyzes the political dynamics of each Southeast Asian nation.

The final chapter places Southeast Asia in an international

context by indicating how the various nations interact with their neighbors and the superpowers. This chapter assesses the prospects for stability and change in Southeast Asia.

This book is written for students and laymen who do not already have considerable background in the study of Southeast Asia. Its purpose is to present highlights and provide order for the study of politics in Southeast Asia. The book makes no attempt to be encyclopedic by including a dizzying array of details. Instead, the reader is presented with information and interpretation that seek to emulate D.G.E. Hall's standard: viewing Southeast Asia as an area worthy of consideration in its own right.

Acknowledgments

The contents of the first edition of this book were drafted in 1976–78 following three lengthy stays in Southeast Asia. The second edition was written in 1980 following a fourth research project in the Philippines, and the third edition was completed in 1986 during a sabbatical leave in Thailand. I am grateful to the National Science, Ford, and Fulbright Foundations for their generous assistance and to the faculty and staff of Chulalongkorn University, Chiang Mai University, and Payap University in Thailand, and the University of San Carlos in the Philippines for their intellectual counsel and use of their facilities.

Although final responsibility for errors and misinterpretations is mine, I have over the years assimilated the views of many others, and incorporated their interpretations in this book. I am grateful to a number of outstanding graduate students who have helped shape *Politics in Southeast Asia*. During each state of this book I received every possible assistance from the Department of Political Science at Northern Illinois University. My colleagues James Banovetz, M. Ladd Thomas, Dwight King, and Brantly Womack, in particular, provided scholarly support.

Throughout the years my interest in and knowledge of Southeast Asia has been sustained and broadened by many scholars. Among these, especially, are David Wilson, Michael Moerman, Charles Keyes, Donn Hart, M. Ladd Thomas, Dwight King, Herbert Rubin, Ansil Ramsay, Prasert Bhandachart, Bidhya Bowornwathana, Kusuma Snitwongse, Somsakdi Xuto, Suchit Bunbongkarn, Gary Suwannarat, Proserpina Tapales, Ronald Provencher, and Arlene Neher. Their scholarly insights vastly improved the quality of *Politics in Southeast Asia*.

1
Diversity and Commonality

Those areas of the world that are designated "regions" usually have a dominant landmass or a contiguous border that clearly distinguishes the area. However, a person looking at a world map would have little reason to group together the ten disparate nations of Southeast Asia, which are characterized more by their island or peninsula nature than by a shared territoriality. The major integrating feature of the area is the dominance of the oceans, which act as important communication channels for every Southeast Asian nation except landlocked Laos.

The region is generally divided into two major categories: mainland and insular Southeast Asia. The former consists of Burma, Thailand, Laos, Vietnam, and Cambodia; the latter includes Indonesia, Singapore, Malaysia, Brunei, and the Philippines. The mainland states share the Buddhist religion in common, while the island nations of Brunei, Malaysia, and Indonesia are Muslim, the Philippines Christian, and Singapore Taoist. The patterns of development have differed enormously in these two categories, largely as a result of geographical configurations and access to waterways.

The themes of diversity and commonality in Southeast Asia might well be introduced with comparative statistical data that cover a wide spectrum of information. Table 1[1] presents demographic, economic, and political data that are important for assessing similarities and differences in Southeast Asia. It makes clear that a proper analysis of Southeast Asia must include separate treatment for each individual nation. The ten societies are so culturally diverse and politically and economically varied

[1] Far Eastern Economic Review, *Asia 1986 Yearbook* (Hong Kong, 1986).

1

Table 1 SOUTHEAST ASIA

	Population (million) 1984–85	Population Growth Rate %/year 1977–84	Years till Population Doubles	Life Expectancy years	Per Capita Income $ U.S. 1984	Urban Population %
Brunei	0.2	2.4	29	71	22,000	64
Burma	39	2.2	32	55	180	24
Cambodia	6.2	2.1	33	43	n.a.	16
Indonesia	168	2.2	32	55	566	22
Laos	3.8	2.3	30	45	140	16
Malaysia	15.7	2.2	32	67	1,996	32
Philippines	56.8	2.5	28	64	603	37
Singapore	2.6	1.1	64	71	6,922	100
Thailand	52.7	1.9	36	63	794	17
Vietnam	60.5	2.5	28	66	n.a.	20 (approx.)
Japan (for comparison)	120	0.6	110	77	9,714	76

that serious doubts arise as to whether the area constitutes a meaningful entity at all.

Most of the world's great religions are found in Southeast Asia. The mainland is dominated by the Theravada and Mahayana schools of Buddhism. Buddhism, which entered Southeast Asia partly as a result of the reaction against the elaborate rituals of Hinduism, has influenced every aspect of life of the mainland inhabitants for centuries. Fully 90 percent of the Thais, Burmese, Cambodians, and Laotians are Theravada Buddhists; the other ten percent profess Hinduism, Islam, Chris-

Political System 1986	Predominant Religion	Ethnic Groups (% of total population)
Absolute Monarchy	Muslim	
Military Authoritarian	Theravada Buddhist	Burmese, 75; Indians, 9; Karens, Shans, Kachins, 7; Chinese, 5
Communist Authoritarian	Theravada Buddhist	Khmers, 85; Annamese, Laos, Chinese, 15
Military Authoritarian	Muslim	Javanese, 45; Sundanese, 17; Madurese, 10; Others, 28
Communist Authoritarian	Theravada Buddhist	Laos, 95; Others, 5
Controlled Democracy	Muslim	Malays, 47; Chinese, 34; Indians, 9
Civilian Democracy	Catholic	Filipino, 95; Chinese, 2; Others, 2
Controlled Democracy	Taoist Confucianist	Chinese, 79; Malays, 12; Indians, 9
Controlled Democracy	Theravada Buddhist	Thais, 85; Karens, Khmers, 3; Malay, 3; Chinese, 9
Communist Authoritarian	Mahayana Buddhist	Annamese, 88; Khmers, 4; Chinese, 6; Others, 2
Democracy		

tianity, or animism. The overwhelming majority of Vietnamese are Mahayana Buddhist, although there is an important Christian and Taoist minority.[2]

Islam became the principal religion of the Indonesians and Malays in the 13th and 14th centuries. Sustained by a common devotion to the "five pillars" of the Muslim faith, Islam has exerted a major impact on the lives of well over half of all Southeast Asians during the past five centuries. Muslims com-

[2] See Chapter 4 for a discussion of Theravada and Mahayana Buddhism.

prise about 90 percent of the Indonesian population. Scattered throughout the archipelago are smatterings of Buddhists and Christians, while the island of Bali has the distinction of remaining the only Hindu locale in all Southeast Asia. Approximately half of the Malaysian population is Muslim. The Chinese and Indian minority groups in that country comprise 34 and nine percent of the population, respectively.

The Catholic religion was introduced to the Philippines over 400 years ago when the Spanish colonized the country. Much of the hierarchical political and social structure of the Philippines reflects the role of the priesthood. The southern islands of the Philippines contain a large Muslim community, consisting of about five percent of the Filipino population.

The presence of several major religious traditions in Southeast Asia, while indicative of diversity at one level, should not give the impression of totally different religious belief systems from one society to another. Indeed, each of the religions enumerated is more properly seen as a syncretic adoption and adaptation of numerous traditions that have resulted in new, unique religions. For example, it is more proper to speak of the "Javanese religion" than the "Indonesian Muslim religion."

Moreover, most of the Southeast Asian peoples have assimilated earlier animistic beliefs into the more formal religious doctrines. At every level of society, from peasant to aristocrat, worship of magicoreligious spirits is an integral part of daily life. Throughout Southeast Asia over the centuries, there has been a continuing interaction of indigenous and new religions that has given a dynamic quality to religious life and that, despite the various mixes and manifestations of the different religions, has provided a degree of religious similarity in the area.

Southeast Asia's geographical position as a link between the great Indian, Chinese, and Australian civilizations has contributed to a succession of migrations, immigrations, and invasions that have resulted in great ethnic diversity. Ethnic heterogeneity, which is common to all the Southeast Asian nations, is a source of both strength and weakness. The varied ethnic, cultural, and linguistic patterns have infused the area with new ideas and a dynamic quality that are lacking in more homogeneous societies. At the same time, the ethnic diversity has resulted in crises of integration and divisions that even today continue to threaten the stability of the area.

As with colonized regions throughout the world, the ethnic makeup of an area is not necessarily congruent with national borders. The Western colonialists arbitrarily drew boundary lines that often separated a particular minority group into two nations. In Thailand, for example, in the mountain areas of the north live the Shans and Karens. Yet the bulk of the Shan and Karen populations is found in Burma. Similarly, northeast Thailand is predominantly composed of Laotian ethnic groups, while the southernmost provinces are populated by Malay Muslims.

In Indonesia there are an estimated 100 ethnic groups, and more than 200 distinct languages are spoken. Indonesia's national motto, "Unity in Diversity," reflects a common theme that is found throughout Southeast Asia: the need to bring unity and to promote nationalism among minority groups. Thus far, the Southeast Asian nations have been dominated politically by the majority ethnic groups of the plains and deltas, while urban economic life has been dominated by minority groups, in particular the Chinese.

Perhaps the most salient division in Southeast Asia is between the plains people and those who live in the hills and mountains. The hill groups remain economically impoverished and politically powerless. The hill people have practiced *swidden,* or slash-and-burn agriculture, for centuries, with the result that their political forms developed in fundamentally different ways from the plains people, who practiced irrigated agriculture. The hill people are more nomadic, with weaker, less integrated political structures, whereas the lowlanders developed tightly structured village communities, often ruled by feudal or bureaucratic chiefs.

Notwithstanding the diverse and heterogeneous nature of Southeast Asia, certain similarities can be enumerated that provide a general framework for analyzing Southeast Asia as an entity. Most striking has been the postindependence movement from diffuse feelings of nationalism into strong nationalist loyalties. The movement corresponds to the common task of nation-building and the quest for modernization. The nationalist movement has manifested itself in various ways; but the roots of the movement lie in the common colonial history experienced by all the Southeast Asian nations, as well as their common subjugation by the Japanese during World War II.[3] Many of the problems faced by the Southeast Asian leaders today in economic and political development can be traced to common historical patterns.

Southeast Asian nations also are characterized by the agricultural base which is at the heart of the nations' economic life. The major activity of the overwhelming majority of Southeast Asians is agriculture. Almost three-fourths of the cultivated land in Southeast Asia is in rice crops; two-thirds of that land is devoted to subsistence farming and one-third involves commercial agriculture.[4] The basic economic unit is the family-operated farm, with most of the farm products being consumed by the family itself, or used to pay for the additional farm labor required, or for barter.

The village is the major unit of identity for the rural population. It acts as the educational, religious, cultural, political, economic, and social center for most Southeast Asians. Villages are usually organized hierarchically, with a village headman (often the largest landowner) serving as the major focus of power.

The hierarchical structure at the village level is found at all levels of Southeast Asian political and social life. Essentially, these societies are organized into networks of superior-subordinate (patron-client) ties, which form the basis of the political structures of the society. These patron-client bonds act as an integrating grid of relationships that hold the society together, and as linkages between the state and the citizenry.

Patron-client bonds, which pervade most of Southeast Asia, are found in most societies that have only a few institutionalized structures that link the citizenry with the state. Moreover, such bonds tend to prevail in areas of Southeast Asia where there are marked inequalities in wealth, status, and control. Where re-

---

[3] Only Thailand was never formally colonized by Western powers. Nevertheless, the Western imperialist countries informally exerted pressure which was not unlike a colonized status.

[4] Ashok K. Dutt, ed., *Southeast Asia, Realm of Contracts* (Dubuque, Iowa: Kendall/Hunt Publishing Co., 1974), pp. 49, 51.

sources are insufficient, those with limited access to the resources form alliances with individuals of a higher
socioeconomic level. The relationship is one of mutual benefits,
where the patron expects labor, protection, defense, or some
other reward in return for dispensing benefits to the subordinate. The mutual interests provide a security that the state itself
cannot provide.

The discussion of differences and similarities concludes by
noting the difficulties the Southeast Asian nations face in achieving stable, viable governments. Since the postindependence
period following the end of World War II, each of the ten
nations has undergone numerous fundamental changes. Burma
has moved back and forth between civilian nationalist rule and
military rule, and now emphasizes the "Burmese way" to socialism. Cambodia has evolved from the charismatic rule of
Prince Sihanouk to military rule to a Communist government.
Indonesia was ruled by nationalist civilian President Sukarno
until 1965, when the military took over all power. Laos has
undergone countless changes, which culminated in the Communist victory in 1975. The absolute monarchy of Brunei became
independent from Great Britain 1 January 1984. Malaysia has
been relatively stable, although its democratic government was
interrupted for a short period in 1969–70 by martial law, following severe race riots. The Philippines, once considered Southeast Asia's showcase of democracy, moved to civilian dictatorship
when President Marcos abrogated the constitution in 1972. Lee
Kwan Yew has continued to rule Singapore under a system of
controlled democracy. Thailand, on the other hand, was ruled
by the military almost continuously until 1973, when a student-
led revolt resulted in an unstable democracy with elections and a
return to civil liberties. The democratic period lasted only three
years. In October 1976 the military carried out a coup d'etat and
returned the nation to authoritarian rule. Since 1976 the political system has evolved toward a controlled democracy with the
formal trappings of representative rule and the continued domination of the military. The Socialist Republic of Vietnam became
one nation in July 1976, following several decades of constant
war. Vietnam was divided at the 1954 Geneva Conference, creating two "independent" entities, North and South Vietnam.

The pervasive instability of the Southeast Asian nations is

characteristic of societies undergoing rapid and fundamental change. The forces of development and modernization, both from within and without the area, are unprecedented in scope and intensity. These forces act in fits and starts, and hence there does not appear to be any unilinear or inevitable direction to the changes. All the Southeast Asian societies are in a state of flux, with changing demographic, economic, and political patterns. To understand these changes it is important to have a broad historical perspective.

2
Political Background

One significant feature of Southeast Asian history is the continual interaction with external societies from the earliest civilizations to the present day. Even the various names associated with the area throughout history reflect the importance of foreign influence: Further India, Indo-Chinese Peninsula, Indian Archipelago, Netherlands India, and the like.

Just as it would be naive to ignore the pervasive impact of foreign cultures on the Southeast Asian societies, one must also be careful not to underestimate the indigenous forces that have shaped the area. The continuity of Southeast Asia is, in the main, a result of the capacity to retain the integrity of the native culture by choosing certain aspects of foreign cultures to assimilate.

Southeast Asian history has exhibited a vitality and distinctiveness that can be traced back many thousands of years. Recent scholarship has revised the conventional wisdom that portrayed ancient Southeast Asian cultures as largely borrowed from more civilized neighbors. It now seems clear that the original inhabitants of the area had developed an autonomous civilization and had established an indigenous societal order long before the first migrations into the area by outsiders from China and India. Indeed, there is evidence that the movement of technologies may have been from Southeast Asia to China as much as the other way around.

> Clearly, without the requisite material and institutional infrastructure, aspects of higher cultures could not have been so successfully transplanted to the region. Nor would so much that is neither Indian nor Chinese have endured had indigenous

cultures not possessed vitality and been both receptive to enrich-
ment and able to maintain distinctiveness.[1]

Before the migrations from the north and west, Southeast
Asians engaged in wet-rice cultivation that did not differ appre-
ciably from that of today. Dry swidden agriculture was practiced,
mostly in the hill areas. Where wet-rice agriculture was practiced, control over water became a source of power and contributed to the organized and highly structured political order. The
inhabitants raised pigs, cattle, chickens, and buffalos, the latter
domesticated for work in the fields. The rivers served as the
main means for transportation, so that many became highly
skilled in the arts of navigation. The family was based on a
married couple and children living in one household. The spiritual life of the people revolved around the propitiation of spirits
and ancestor worship.

These characteristics have remained an important part of
Southeast Asian life even today. The subsequent influence of the
various external forces did not displace the indigenous culture,
but rather added to it in ways that make Southeast Asian culture
unique.

In general, migration patterns into Southeast Asia have been
from north to south, from the regions now known as western
and southern China and Tibet. The river valleys were the main
arteries of transportation. Initially, Australoid and Negrito peoples migrated to as far as Australia, Indonesia, Malaysia, and the
Philippines. They were followed by Indonesian peoples during
the second and third millennia B.C., who now constitute the
bulk of the population in Indonesia and Malaysia.[2]

The Mons moved down the river valleys of present-day
Burma and Thailand, the Shans or Thai people dispersed over a
wide area of the mainland, while the Khmers migrated to the
Mekong Valley, and the Vietnamese to the Red River delta.[3] As
these groups moved southward, many of the original inhabitants

---

[1] Lea A. Williams, *Southeast Asia: A History* (New York: Oxford University Press,
1976), p. 25.

[2] John Bastin and Harry J. Benda, *A History of Modern Southeast Asia* (Englewood Cliffs, New Jersey: Prentice-Hall, 1968), p. 2.

[3] Ibid., p. 2.

were forced out of the valleys into the hills, where they became nomadic. The conflict between the hill and valley peoples remains a salient problem of integration in the nations of Southeast Asia.

The inhabitants of Southeast Asia were first influenced by the process of Indianization (sometimes called Hinduization) during the centuries immediately preceding the Christian era. There is some difference of opinion regarding the means by which Indian culture was disseminated. One theory suggests that it was transmitted by traders who established marketing centers in Southeast Asia that evolved into important towns. Others note the importance of Brahman priests who were attached to local courts and who proselytized Hindu beliefs.[4] It is clear that no Indian armies were sent to subjugate the Southeast Asians. Indians never colonized the area, nor were there ever large numbers of Indians present in Southeast Asia.

Perhaps no outside culture has played as important a role in the shaping of Southeast Asia as the Indian, whose impact can be found in the realms of government and culture. The ruling classes were the first to adapt those Indian forms that enhanced their positions of power. The Brahman influence was especially fitting for a court culture, with its emphasis on the concept of the god-king, whose magical powers were seen as the basis for political authority.

> Kings, their secular commands strengthened with religious weapons, replaced earlier local chieftains. The Southeast Asian king was not proclaimed to be merely an intermediary between man and divine beings; he claimed to be an incarnation of a bodhisatva or a Hindu deity . . .[5]

The political order was seen as a microcosm of the cosmic order. The king was to his kingdom as God to the cosmos. Kings began to deify themselves as the reincarnation of Shiva, Vishnu, or Indra. Great monuments were built to the glory of the rulers; this glorification culminated in the great Khmer kingdoms between the sixth and fifteenth centuries at Angkor, and the Srivijaya and Majapahit empires in island Southeast Asia from the

---

[4] See Bastin and Benda (p. 4) for a discussion of these views.
[5] Williams, p. 30.

seventh to the thirteenth centuries. The principles of absolutism and hierarchy, introduced during the process of Indianization, are principles that remain today an essential aspect of Southeast Asian politics. Only northern Vietnam and the Philippines were not touched by Indian culture.

Theravada (Hinayana) and Mahayana Buddhism were the second important foreign influences exported from India, though these stemmed also from Ceylon. By about 500 A.D. Theravada Buddhism had been established in Burma and was moving eastward across mainland Southeast Asia. Mahayana Buddhism traveled a more northern route through China and eventually became the dominant religion of Vietnam.

In contrast to Indianization, Buddhism was introduced directly to the people rather than indirectly through the ruling classes. Buddhism created a quasi-egalitarian religious community of which even the monarchs became members. Buddhist cosmology was similar to that of Hinduism, although it included no belief in an all-powerful God. No series of gods existed which might compete with the worship of local spirits. Hence Buddhism was more easily assimilated than Hinduism.

In addition, the monks could exercise a measure of restraint on the monarchs. In contrast to Hindu beliefs, the monkhood practiced the principles of otherworldly simplicity and frugality. The monks became the teachers in the village and the organizing leaders of the peasantry.[6] In this way Buddhism was able to permeate all classes of people, from the royal court to the most isolated village.

Clearly, the impact of Theravada Buddhism was great, with its emphasis on egalitarian relationships, on undermining the god-king concept, and on the link forged between the peasantry and the rulers. Buddhism was absorbed into the Indianized Angkor kingdom and, with its emphasis on equality, helped to bring about the downfall of the kingdom.

The ages of Hinduism and Buddhism coincided with the era of Sinicization in Vietnam. China ruled over Vietnam for about 1,000 years, from 111 B.C. to 939 A.D. In contrast to the administration of the Indianized area of Southeast Asia, the

---

[6] Harry Benda, "The Structure of Southeast Asian History: Some Preliminary Observations," *Journal of Southeast Asian History, 3(1),* March, 1972.

Chinese Confucian administrative system was structured secularly, without an absolute ruler. Instead, the emperor was seen as a guardian, whose position was based more on his institutionalized role than his personal charisma. The hierarchical, structured bureaucracy which became the basis of authority, stability, and continuity, was administered by a mandarinite of classical education. Examinations determined which persons could serve in the distinctive ranks. Since education was limited to the sons of the wealthy, a self-perpetuating elite rule was created. These mandarin bureaucrats wielded the political power in Vietnam even more than the emperor, whose power was more ritual than political.

Although dominated for ten centuries by the Chinese, the Vietnamese resisted being absorbed totally into the Chinese culture. The Vietnamese waged their struggle against the Chinese at every opportunity; in subsequent centuries they were often to revive the nationalist struggle.

As with Buddhism, the spread of Islam in Southeast Asia was relatively free from violence. Islam came to Southeast Asia via the trade routes, so that its first adherents were the urban traders. Rulers of the port cities converted to Islam at least partially for economic reasons. Muslim merchants were more prone to attach themselves to a port where an Islamic sultan ruled than a Hindu king. Conversion to Islam brought the trader into an international community of Muslims, the *unmat*, which became a significant aspect of economic life in Indonesia. The greater sense of community and trust among Muslim traders extended their entrepreneurial advantage.

Like Buddhism, Islam stressed an egalitarian creed: all persons are equal before Allah. By the fourteenth century Islam dominated the Malay peninsula, Indonesia, and the southern Philippine islands, although not in the purer form found in other predominantly Islamic societies. Islam meshed well with animism and Hinduism, so that the final product was syncretic and unique to each separate area.

By the sixteenth century the forces of Indianization, Buddhism, and Islam had shaped every aspect of life in Southeast Asia. The area consisted of numerous small kingdoms that were neither unified, nor distinguished by boundaries. These kingdoms repeatedly clashed as they vied for land and power. Some kingdoms exhibited a degree of stability, although instability was more usual. Some kingdoms shared common political forms based on Hindu-Buddhist conceptions of statehood, while others had become Islamic, or Confucian mandarinite states. The Western imperialists arrived at a time when the map of Southeast Asia bore little if any resemblance to the nation-state configurations found today. There were no formal, stable boundaries between one principality and the next. Instead, the bounds of sovereignty were determined by constantly shifting power relations. Western colonialism, which began in 1511 when the Portuguese captured Malacca, not only changed the map of Southeast Asia but drastically altered the elite sociopolitical systems. But at the same time, continuity and autonomy prevailed among the majority of people. One historian has pointed out that despite the many changes that have taken place, "a century from now the colonial experience will be seen as having merely disturbed, not diverted, the flow of Southeast Asian history."[7]

The Southeast Asian nations were subject to varied colonial experiences; hence it is difficult to generalize about the area as a whole. In the four centuries of colonial rule, from the early 1500s to the post-World War II era, the British conquered the areas now called Malaysia, Brunei, Singapore, and Burma, while the French controlled present-day Laos, Cambodia, and Vietnam. Indonesia was incorporated into the Netherlands Indies, and the Philippines were colonized initially by the Spanish and subsequently by the United States. The Portuguese were the first colonialists to conquer parts of Southeast Asia, but their empire dwindled as the Western imperialists fought among themselves for power. Only Thailand escaped formal colonization.

The motivations for the imperialists varied from one area to another. Primarily, the private corporations and governments were seeking overseas empires for economic gain through exploiting cheap labor and resources. Merchants went abroad to make fortunes in trade; politicians and militarists arrived to consolidate the holdings of the business classes, to "bring civilization" to the natives, and to add to the power and glory of the motherland.

Despite the varied manifestations of colonial rule in Southeast

---

[7] Williams, p. 51.

Asia, several common elements can be discerned. First, colonial rule eventually resulted in the formation of separate nation-states with viable boundaries. The imperialists guaranteed these boundaries (mainly to separate competing colonial spheres), thus introducing a sense of stability and order to the region. At the same time, these boundaries often cut through ethnic groups, isolating the nonintegrated ethnic minority groups of today. For example, the inhabitants of northeast Thailand are ethnically Lao; the southernmost provinces of Thailand are populated by Malay Muslims, and the northern provinces are peopled with Shans, Karens, and other hill groups with affinity to Burma. The colonialist-inspired map of Southeast Asia shows the somewhat arbitrary demarcations of Europeans more concerned with their empire than with the ethnic makeup of the region.

Colonialism was responsible also for the growth of economic structures. Ports, railways, and roads were built as the infrastructure for the movement of goods and resources. Hospitals, which improved health conditions, and schools for the children of the aristocracy (many of whom, ironically, became anti-Western nationalist leaders), were established by the colonialists. A money economy was introduced and large-scale industries were established. The new factories required large numbers of skilled and unskilled laborers. The Southeast Asian peasant found such labor crude and antithetical to traditional values. Consequently, the colonialists imported Chinese and Indians to work in factories, tin mines, and rubber plantations. The Chinese and Indian communities, through their connections with Western imperialism, have enjoyed and continue to enjoy economic power in Southeast Asia far beyond their numbers.

The rise of industry and increased trade brought about the rapid growth of cities. There emerged a plural economy, with a gulf between urban and rural citizens, the former a part of a money economy, the latter retaining a subsistence form of agriculture. Both groups were exploited as their resources were depleted. Although the urban centers were most profoundly influenced by colonialism, the money economy also affected rural subsistence areas. With the growth of plantation agriculture, a new agricultural proletariat arose that was dependent on money-lenders and urban landowners for survival.

A plural economy developed with the minority of the inhabitants tied to the flourishing colonial economy and the majority dependent on subsistence agriculture. The plural economy became "a monumental Western skyscraper on Eastern soil, with the natives in the basement; all [inhabiting] the same country, but the building was of a different world, the modern world to which the ordinary native had no access."[8] Colonialism exacerbated disintegrating relations between the rural and urban peoples, and between the rich and the poor. This problem was particularly acute in areas where the imperialists ruled by "indirect" means.[9] The Dutch East Indies Company, for example, utilized the indigenous Indonesian power structure in the company's outer islands to administer that area. The peasantry was systematically exploited both by Dutch colonialists and the Indonesian aristocrats whose primary loyalty became the mother country of the East Indies Company. The consequent antipathy and distrust between the peasantry and aristocracy subsequently played an important destabilizing role in Indonesian history.

One effect of colonialism was the discrediting of the indigenous symbols of government authority. John Cady notes:

> The forced pace of centralized government administration required the implementation of unfamiliar legal codes and court procedures, the detailed assessment of all land for taxation purposes, and the multiplication of other services generally associated with a capital investment economy. Such changes placed foreigners in complete control of all colonialized areas and left the mass of the indigenous populations socially disrupted as well as politically helpless.[10]

Perhaps the most important consequence of colonialism was its direct impact on the rise of nationalism throughout Southeast

[8] J. S. Furnivall, quoted in Guy Hunter, *Southeast Asia: Race, Culture, and Nation* (New York: Oxford University Press, 1966), p. 61.

[9] Direct rule of Europeans over Southeast Asians was carried out by the Dutch in Java, the British in Burma, the French in Vietnam, and the Spanish in the Philippines. Indirect rule occurred when local leaders were retained in a governing capacity, as in the outer islands of the Dutch East Indies Company, the sultanates in Malaya, and in the hill areas of Laos, Cambodia, and Burma.

[10] John F. Cady, *The History of Post-War Southeast Asia* (Athens, Ohio: Ohio University Press, 1974), p. xix.

Asia. The colonial nations became unified territorial states, whereas their predecessors had been nonintegrated dynastic principalities. By the late nineteenth century, the major national boundaries had been demarcated and the entire area of Southeast Asia, except Thailand, was in European hands. The colonialist dominance was a result both of superior force and repression, and of a set of attitudes on the part of the Southeast Asians themselves, including deference and a lack of self-esteem.

Nationalism is a sense of strong identification and feeling toward the nation. It is also an anticolonial sentiment and a desire to emphasize indigenous traditional ways. Nationalism arose in Southeast Asia as a result of the colonialist conception of the nation-state and was led principally by indigenous intellectuals who had been trained in the West or in colonially established schools. That these intellectuals were Western trained and inculcated with Western values only to become the spokesmen for an anti-Western nationalist doctrine is one of the major ironies of Southeast Asian history. Rupert Emerson has noted that the paradox of Asian nationalism is that it is the import of the West that brought to fighting consciousness societies that derived wholly from non-Western sources.

> . . . in the future, a great part of the inner dynamics of nationalism in Asia must result from this profound contradiction within nations that derive from an ancient Asian past and yet have been brought to national awareness not only by the Western impact but by the revolutionary appeal of their own native Westernizers.[11]

The intellectuals articulated the importance of a broad perspective that transcended narrow primordial identities. Steeped in the environment of Western technology, they had argued that industrialization was the only path to eventual independence. The intellectuals had contempt for the land-owning aristocrats who had fared well under colonialism, and helped to undermine

---

[11] Rupert Emerson, "Paradoxes of Asian Nationalism," in Robert O. Tilman, ed., *Man, State, and Society in Contemporary Southeast Asia* (New York: Praeger, 1969), pp. 250–251.

their power and to offer alternative leadership. The intellectuals learned how to organize people from their observations of the colonialists.

This latter point is important because for the first time an organized, effective leadership group emerged in Southeast Asia that could mobilize the peasantry. In Indonesia, for example, the nationalist movement began in the early 1900s, not as a product of oppressive rule by the Dutch, but, again ironically, as a response to the more enlightened Dutch policy to open and liberalize the political system. New indigenous socioeconomic classes emerged precisely at the time the Dutch policy of encouraging economic and educational development programs was at its height. The new class of intellectuals adopted Dutch ways and became the vanguard of the nationalist movement.

The Dutch Ethical Policy after 1900 increased the scope of government and required more and more indigenous administrators. A generation of trained civil servants arose who eventually became the leadership of new independent nations. John Legge, a scholar of Indonesian history, writes that Dutch rule in the Indies was not particularly harsh. He notes that nationalism was not the product of oppressive rule but of deeper forces of social change that accompanied the new economic development. The disruption of the social patterns of the village and the undermining of many of its customary certainties aroused broad dissatisfaction, and produced a new awareness of the outside world.[12]

Dutch rule, then, had established a national boundary—had increased the scope of government so that Indonesians became aware of the Dutch preserve—and set in motion the forces of modernization. The result was a heightened nationalism that led to the subsequent struggle for independence. The Indonesian experience is not dissimilar from the experience of other nationalist movements throughout Southeast Asia.

The leadership of the Indonesian nationalist movement consisted of Western-educated persons who were caught between their native culture, for which they had little appreciation, and Western culture, which they were not allowed by the Dutch to

[12] John D. Legge, *Indonesia* (Englewood Cliffs, New Jersey: Prentice-Hall, 1964), p. 116.

join. These leaders sought some form of synthesis between the two cultures that would be uniquely Indonesian. Indonesian aristocrats generally were not a part of the nationalist movement because they feared they would lose their high position and the perquisites they enjoyed under Dutch rule. The peasantry was mobilized by the fiery oratory of Sukarno, a revolutionary leader of Indonesia who led the nation to independence and became the state's president.

The nationalist revolt in Vietnam grew out of the colonial era, when the French concentrated their economic interests in certain areas while allowing an upper-class Vietnamese elite to become landowners of huge estates at the expense of the peasantry, who lived in poverty. The traditional society had been badly shaken by the colonialists; corvee labor was forced on the peasantry; and prisons were overflowing with Vietnamese nationalists.

Vietnamese nationalist resistance to French rule was initially led by "mandarins" who viewed the French as usurpers of their power. French colonialism had destroyed the essence of the political and economic system in Vietnam and replaced it with a system that was exploitative and designed to serve French economic interests. However, as French rule was consolidated and French economic interests dominated urban life, the mandarins found they could profit from closer ties with the colonialists. Soon the peasantry was forced to toil for both its French and its elite Vietnamese masters. Peasant taxes were increased to pay for the huge colonial budget. Land was forcibly taken from the peasantry and given to wealthy landholders to assure a large surplus of rice for export. In the Tonkin region of Vietnam, for example, 500 large landowners, both French and Vietnamese, came to own 20 percent of the land. In South Vietnam, 70 percent of all landowners owned only 15 percent of the arable land. Fifty-seven percent of the rural population in the south were landless.[13] The peasants' life was worse under French rule than under the previous feudal regimes.

To replace the mandarin leadership, a new group of nationalist leaders emerged, drawn from every socioeconomic and

[13] Eric R. Wolf, *Peasant Wars of the Twentieth Century* (New York: Harper and Row, 1969), p. 166.

religious class. In the early 1900s the nationalist movement merged with Communist groups, and the latter eventually took over leadership under Ho Chi Minh. In 1939 he brought a number of groups into a single organization, the Viet Nam Doc-Lap Dong Minh Hoi (League for the Independence of Vietnam), which became known as the Vietminh. This group succeeded in ousting the Japanese occupation forces and then the French, when the latter attempted to regain control over their former colony in 1945. The war against the French, which lasted eight years, ended with the defeat of the French in 1954 and the coming to power in North Vietnam of a Communist-nationalist government led by President Ho Chi Minh. In 1976 the Communist government declared a united Vietnam, ostensibly free from all foreign influence.

The Japanese conquest during World War II had brought all of Southeast Asia under a single authority for the first time in history. The Japanese interregnum accelerated the nationalist movements by placing more Southeast Asians in administrative positions, by shattering the myth of Western invincibility, by presenting new value systems to replace Western values, and by facilitating economic change. The Japanese defeat in 1945 opened the floodgates of nationalistic spirit and demands for total independence.

The Southeast Asian nations emerged from World War II with their economic and political structures in shambles. Except for Thailand, each Southeast Asian nation had to cope with the attempts of the Western colonialists to regain their lost colonies. The local leadership was in discord over the most effective way to secure independence and the best type of society to establish.

The first problem concerned the struggle for independence from the Western colonialists. Burma and Indonesia were involved in wars for independence immediately following the world war. For the Indonesians, the war for independence continued for four years, until in 1949 Indonesia won its sovereignty. Burma became independent in 1948. Vietnam's war for independence lasted even longer, until the French withdrew in 1954. (Laos and Cambodia's transitions to independence were smoother than Vietnam's.) Malaysia did not engage in a war for independence; instead, the country negotiated with the British over a period of twelve years, until 1957, when the Malayans proclaimed the independent Federation of Malaya. The Philippines, which had been prepared for eventual independence by the Americans prior to the war, moved peacefully into independent status in 1946.

Southeast Asia in the postindependence era was led by nationalists who attacked Western dominance; at the same time they adopted Western methods and outlooks to proclaim and exhibit their independent, sovereign status. Nationalism was the ideology used to integrate disparate peoples. In Vietnam, Laos, Cambodia, Indonesia, and Burma, nationalism as a unifying force was manifested in violent struggles for independence. In the Philippines, Singapore, and Malaysia, the struggle was relatively nonviolent. In all cases the nationalist leaders were constantly confronted with the problem of reconciling the desire to retain traditional values, the desire to be independent of the West, and the desire to adopt the nationalism, technology, and secularism of the developed Western societies.

Nationalism was not an ideology shared by all Southeast Asians. For the overwhelming majority of peasant-farmers, the adoption of a nationalist ideology required a fundamental shift in value systems and expectations. The state had to become the object of the peasantry's sentiments and it had to demonstrate that it could better fulfill spiritual, economic, social, and political needs than could the traditional institutions. For most Southeast Asians, the traditions and expectations of the villagers were alien to the often indirect and intangible rewards modern states offer. For centuries the rural people had been socialized into a pattern aimed at close identification with primordial institutions, namely, the family, clan, or village. All of a citizen's needs including that for self-fulfillment could be met at these levels in a direct, effective, and spontaneous manner. The nation-state, on the other hand, was a psychologically distant unit which for much of the citizenry symbolized exploitation, alien rule, and oppression.

Nationalism, then, was essentially a phenomenon of the intellectuals, most of whom had Western education and Western experience. The intellectuals had wider horizons, over and above primordial identities. They were highly skilled people in an environment that was not receptive to such skills. Their professional skills were not relevant in societies whose institutions were based on traditional values and procedures. The intellectuals foresaw that their own survival depended on the growth of industrialization and the process of modernization, which, in turn, would foster professional positions. Modernization became identified with nationalism in the minds of the educated sector in Southeast Asia. The nationalist leaders argued that without modernization the Southeast Asian nations would be swallowed by imperialist forces.

Intellectuals favored modernization not only to provide themselves with high-level positions but also to undermine the power of the indigenous aristocrats who posed a threat to their power. The power of the aristocrats was based on land ownership and their close ties with the colonial rulers. Intellectuals ingratiated themselves with the peasantry by launching land-reform programs in the name of nationalism and modernization. The intended result was the mobilization of the peasantry, the reduced influence of the aristocracy, and the consequently strengthened position of the intellectuals.

To carry out their goals in the postindependence period, the nationalist leaders needed to legitimate their position vis-à-vis the citizenry. Because the governmental institutions had been compromised during colonial and Japanese rule and had been devastated during the post-World War II independence struggles, the nationalist leaders did not find authority in government positions per se. Instead, authority was largely a product of the charismatic relationship that developed between the nationalist leadership and the citizenry.

Charismatic authority is inherently unstable. The lack of systematic political institutionalization in the years following World War II was symptomatic of the emphasis on ideology and personality. As leaders, Prince Sihanouk of Cambodia, President Sukarno of Indonesia, and President Ho Chi Minh of Vietnam succeeded brilliantly in heightening the sense of national identity among their countrymen. As pragmatic leaders involved in the day-to-day business of running an effective government, their success was limited.

The euphoria that accompanied the success of the independence movements did not last long. The nationalist leaders were concerned primarily with building the unity and pride of their citizenry and only secondarily with the day-to-day administrative and economic development problems. The chaos of the independence period stimulated expectations among the citizenry which could not possibly be met by governments that were in the process of attempting to establish viable political structures. Increasingly throughout Southeast Asia there were tensions between the different generations of leaders: the older "solidarity makers" and the younger, more pragmatic "administrators."

The long-term result of the frenzied independence period was authoritarian regimes. By the 1970s military regimes ruled in Thailand, Cambodia, Burma, Indonesia, and South Vietnam. Laos and the Philippines were ruled by civilian dictatorships, while only Malaysia and Singapore boasted quasi-democratic governments. In 1975, Laos, Cambodia, and Vietnam were ruled by Communist governments. Perhaps the most important accomplishment of the postindependence period was that all of the Southeast Asian nations enjoyed a good measure of territorial integrity, although even that accomplishment was compromised by the Vietnamese invasion and subjugation of Cambodia and Laos.

At the end of the war, Southeast Asia had to pursue the two goals of national sovereignty and identity and political development simultaneously. These goals were attained with varying degrees of success, depending on the policies of the colonial power, the abilities of the nationalist leaders, the resources available to them, and the relative homogeneity of the country ethnically, politically, geographically, and economically. An overview of the political situation today in each of the Southeast Asian nations provides a perspective for analysis of these goals.

3
Postindependence Southeast Asia

THAILAND

Thailand emerged from World War II considerably more stable and secure than any other nation of Southeast Asia. Although the government, led by Prime Minister Phibun Songkram, had acquiesced to a virtual Japanese occupation during the war, the people suffered few if any real social, economic, or political hardships. The Thais maintained control over the country's internal administration. The mainstay of the economy, rice, was in abundant supply. Damage caused by the war was slight. Finally, unlike other countries of the region, Thailand's stability and security were not threatened by a debilitating struggle for independence.

In 1944, when it became evident that Japan would lose the war, the military regime of Phibun Songkram was forced to resign in favor of civilians. Among them the most important were Pridi Phanomyong, the brilliant head of the pro-Allies underground Free Thai movement, and Khuang Aphaiwong, an opposition leader who was later to preside as prime minister over four governments. The military was stripped of all effective power, political parties were organized, and the first elections in almost a decade were held. Thailand appeared to be headed toward a constitutional system of parliamentary democracy under Pridi's leadership. Pridi's alleged involvement in the tragic and unexplained shooting of Thailand's young King Ananda Mahidol in June 1946, however, precipitated his downfall. On 8 November 1947, ranking military officers, charging the Pridi regime with failure to cope with severe postwar economic problems, carried out a bloodless coup d'etat. Pridi fled the country; Khuang Aphaiwong was made prime minister of a caretaker government.

Following elections in January 1948, Khuang again formed a government, this time on the basis of a parliamentary majority. Four months later, however, the military once more seized power and the government was turned over to Phibun Songkram. Civilian government in Thailand ended.

Despite a number of attempts to oust him from power, Phibun managed to retain leadership of the government for nine years. His search for a wider base of popular support in the mid-1950s, however, proved to be his undoing. Proclaiming a new "era of democracy" in which freedom of speech and press were encouraged, political parties flourished, and plans were laid for new elections in 1957, Phibun unwittingly unleashed a flood of criticism against his regime, which paved the way for another coup d'etat. Capitalizing on Phibun's involvement in the fraudulent February 1957 elections, General Sarit Thanarat, army commander-in-chief, seized power in September of that year, suspended the constitution, dissolved the National Assembly, and declared martial law. Phibun fled into exile.

To give an aura of legitimacy to his coup d'etat, General Sarit assigned prominent civilians to cabinet posts until the elections in December 1957. He then mobilized a parliamentary majority and set up General Thanom Kittikachorn as prime minister while he went to the United States for extended medical treatment. Thanom's regime, however, was weakened by recurring crises, and when Sarit returned in October 1958 he again seized power. An interim constitution was promulgated giving him unlimited power and establishing an appointive Constituent Assembly with power to legislate and to draw up a new constitution. Sarit died in December 1963 and was succeeded by General Thanom Kittikachorn.

General Thanom Kittikachorn succeeded Sarit in 1963 as Thailand's eleventh prime minister since the 1932 coup. Thanom, in personality, seemed a striking contrast to the decisive, ambitious, ruthless Sarit. Indeed, Thanom's reputation as a soft-spoken man of high integrity caused most commentators to assume his regime would be short lived. However, by assimilating potential rivals for power into his own clique, by using the enormous prestige of the throne, by pursuing a vigorous economic development program, and by retaining the military and economic support of the United States, Prime Minister Thanom held and strengthened his position for a decade. Moreover, General Prapat Charustiara, who was then number two man in the official hierarchy but was clearly the major power in the kingdom, was content to allow Thanom to hold the top position.

The Thanom government proved no more immune to venality than its predecessor. However, Thanom and Prapat's extraordinarily high degree of involvement in graft and corruption did not preclude some impressive accomplishments. Thailand achieved a position of leadership in Southeast Asian affairs and its rulers, at least initially, loosened the reins that were strangling citizens' liberties under Sarit. They promulgated the June 1968 constitution, reinstated political parties, and reintroduced provincial, municipal, and national elections.

The promulgation of Thailand's eighth constitution, in 1968, and the national elections in February 1969 for the House of Representatives did not substantially change the bureaucratic-elitist system of government. As in the past, the new constitution served the regime in power by strengthening its position. The political scene after the elections provided abundant material for viewing Thai politics as a struggle among various elite factions for power, wealth, and status. The politics of factionalism were manifested within the cabinet, within political parties such as the progovernment United Thai People's party (UTPP), and within the National Assembly.

The factional infighting among members of the UTPP centered on a struggle for the scarce resources of money and position. A group of government party members who had been elected to the lower house of the bicameral National Assembly demanded that large sums of money be spent in their provincial constituencies in return for their support of government policies. Moreover, the clientele of Prime Minister Thanom, which fell into disarray as he came closer to retirement age, began moving toward leaders who appeared to be in the ascendancy. Cabinet members vied among themselves for a larger share of the budget. In 1971 factionalism continued to be the dominant trend of Thai politics until the ruling elite was threatened by the possibility of losing its power to competing groups. To prevent this, Generals Thanom and Prapat—in a coup against their own government—seized complete control.

In the past when opposition groups have threatened to block a government's program, the regime in office has summarily taken all power into its own hands, or, through a coup d'etat, a new faction has assumed the dominant opposition. Thus in November 1971 Thai history repeated itself when a revolutionary council, headed by Thanom and Prapat, dissolved the parliament, abrogated the 1968 constitution, banned political parties, restricted civil liberties, and declared martial law. Absolute rule returned.

Although factionalism was the dominant variable in the 1971 crisis, there were substantive issues that provided additional impetus for the military's seizure of power. In 1970 and 1971 the National Assembly had delayed approving the government's budget requests. Moreover, the government had felt hampered by national assemblymen who demanded personal and material gains for themselves at the expense of the military budget. The government also claimed that its economic development program, as well as national security, were endangered by the delays of the recalcitrant legislature. Prime Minister Thanom said that if the country was to pursue the constitutional process, the government must be able to act swiftly to cope with internal and external problems, and the delays were felt to exacerbate the precarious economic situation, which featured a negative balance of payments and a growing trade deficit. As the American military investment continued to decrease, with the United States withdrawing its troops from Thailand, Thailand's balance of payments was adversely affected, and members of the government warned that the economic problems could be exploited by insurgents.

Another factor that the government claimed was important in the decision to overthrow the constitutional order was the admission of the People's Republic of China to the United Nations. The government's fear of Thailand's indigenous Chinese was expressed by Thanom after he seized power, when he voiced concern about the loyalty of the Chinese. Moreover, the new prominence of China increased the regime's dismay at the withdrawal of American troops from Southeast Asia. Thanom argued that the new foreign policy considerations would precipitate uncertainties with which only a strong, centralized government could cope.

Thai politics has rarely involved disputes over ideologies, and despite Thanom's allegations, the 1971 coup was no exception; ideological considerations were not significant ingredients. Notwithstanding allusions to anticommunism, development, and national security, the 1971 seizure of power was essentially an attempt to perpetuate power and to secure the leaders' vast financial fortunes.

The seizure of power by Thanom, against his own constitutional government, was bloodless, swift, and without apparent opposition, although the king, instead of issuing a legal royal pardon to the coup leaders as he had in previous coups, simply issued a proclamation requesting support for the new regime. The 1972 fiscal budget was immediately promulgated with the military's share larger than that agreed to by the House budget committee. In an action intended to deter would-be criminals, summary executions of criminals by a government execution squad were carried out. Thai newspapers reported on the rapid decrease in crime throughout the nation following the overthrow.

The new leaders decided to merge the twin cities of Bangkok and Thonburi into the "Greater Bangkok Municipality" and began to focus attention on urban rather than rural problems. During the legislative period from 1969 to 1971 the rural areas had become of paramount interest, but after the coup the government's attention shifted to problems of urban pollution, slums, foreign investment, crime in the streets, and urban planning. The new regime did not, however, move swiftly to legitimize its status through constitutional means. An "interim" constitution was not promulgated until December 1972, more than a year after the coup.

Under the 1972 constitution, Marshal Thanom retained his positions as prime minister and minister of defense, and in addition he assumed the foreign affairs portfolio. The constitution provided that the prime minister may take any steps "appropriate for the purpose of preventing, repressing or suppressing actions which jeopardize the national security, or the throne, or the economy of the country, or the national administration, or which subvert or threaten law and order of the good public morals or which damage the health of the society." Thanom's power was strengthened also by the provision that the new "legislative body" of 299 National Assembly members be handpicked by the regime in power. Thanom appointed 200 military officers and 99 civilians. The legislature's functions were closely circumscribed to ensure executive dominance in all matters.

The periodic returns to absolutism are reminders that the history of Thai politics is rich in general patterns that have remained consistent throughout the centuries. The paternalistic and autocratic kingdoms of Sukhothai and Ayuthaya are prototypes of the usually benevolent, yet authoritarian leaders of more recent times. Given the fact that politics in Thailand has occurred almost exclusively at the highest levels among elite cliques vying for power, with little effect on the citizenry and without the people's interest or involvement, the Great Tragedy of 14 October 1973 *(Wan Maha Wipayok)* stands as an extraordinary event. Through the efforts of a large sector of the citizenry, including some 65 persons who died and nearly 1,000 persons who were injured in the accompanying violence, the military government was overthrown and the top leadership forced into ignoble exile. King Phumipon Adunyadet, whose own power and position were greatly enhanced by the October incident, appointed Thailand's first civilian government since the immediate post-World War II era. Sanya Thamasak, the rector of Thammasat University, former chief justice, and close advisor to the king as privy councillor, became prime minister. The new government moved to promulgate a democratic and "people-oriented" constitution and to initiate elections for a new government.

A multitude of planned and accidental events, none of which separately would have been a sufficient motivating force, converged to bring about the momentous change. The major underlying causes of discontent leading to the overthrow of the military included the political and economic mismanagement of the military regime itself, the perception that the military was increasingly ruling in their own self-interest, factionalism within the military, and the rise of an organized and aroused student population supported by the citizenry and the king. In addition a number of fortuitous and unforeseen incidents occurred which contributed to the overthrow.

Since the 1971 coup d'etat when the Thanom government abrogated the constitution and took all power into its own hands, the political and economic situation in Thailand had deteriorated. The economic problems were not entirely attributable to the rule of the military, but rather resulted from a combination of factors including extreme weather conditions (both droughts and flooding) and an increased balance-of-payments deficit stemming from the gradual reduction of American troops throughout the country and unbalanced trade agreements, notably with Japan. A steep rise in inflation made the Thai farmers as well as the salaried middle-class bureaucrats worse off economically than in the previous decade. The Thanom government seemed unable to cope with the worsening situation and the reports of the regime's leaders' personal wealth and corruption exacerbated the rising discontent of the citizenry and in particular that of the students. In the months preceding Wan Maha Wipayok the Thai citizenry became aware of the regime's involvement in numerous scandals.

The military itself was becoming factionalized as various cliques maneuvered to be in the best position once Marshals Thanom and Prapat retired. The rapid rise in power of Colonel Narong Kittikachorn was disconcerting to a number of top-ranking generals who objected to the perpetuation of the Thanom-Prapat dynasty. Colonel Narong, as the son of Thanom and the son-in-law of Prapat, was being groomed to succeed to the office of prime minister to insure the continuation of the family monopoly of power and wealth. The October incident brought the intra-military rifts into the open so that the military was not able to present a united stand against the students. In addition, a number of military and police personnel refused to obey the orders to put down the October riots. The king, who was appalled by the violence and who provided active moral support to the students, disillusioned many in the military and police who revered the king's word and who were therefore reluctant to use force against the students.

The students of higher education in Thailand have long been described as passive and apolitical. Hence, the emergence of the

National Student Center of Thailand (NSCT) consisting of university and college students throughout the kingdom was not initially deemed to be significant. However, as a result of coordinating a series of minor demonstrations against government corruption and Japanese "economic exploitation," the NSCT became a highly organized and visible lobby for reform. The NSCT was more conservative than radical. The student members supported the monarchy and called for a return to the traditional Thai values. Although they abhorred the excessive corruption and self-interest of the military regime, they did not call for the overthrow of the government.

The military government's arrest of 13 people, including students, university lecturers, and former politicians (all of whom were charged with treason for demanding the promulgation of a constitution), provided the NSCT with a cause célèbre to motivate and mobilize large numbers of students. The initial demands of the students were limited: freedom for the 13 people arrested and a new constitution within six months. Some 200,000 persons marched in support of the demands. The king called for restraint and compromise on all sides, and large sectors of the police and military as well showed reluctance to use force. Early on the morning of 14 October, Wan Maha Wipayok, one section of the riot police used force, despite the fact that the demonstrators were dispersing and returning home satisfied that their demands had been met. As word of the forced dispersal spread, the students regrouped at Thammasat University to plan their response. The rapid escalation of the violence continued as certain elements of the police and military began firing indiscriminately on the thousands of demonstrators. In revenge for the deaths of their colleagues, the students rampaged through the streets burning those buildings that were the most hated symbols of the military regime. Prime Minister Thanom and Deputy Prime Minister Prapat no longer could depend on the support of the various military and police factions and therefore fled the country. The demonstrators had achieved a victory they had not sought or expected.

The king and Prime Minister Sanya appointed a generally conservative cabinet of well-known and established bureaucrats and scholars. In addition King Phumipon established and appointed the members of a national convention of over 2,000 people from every walk of life. These bureaucrats, professors, farmers, businessmen, and politicians in turn elected a 299-member National Legislative Assembly whose duties were to promulgate a constitution and to act as the legislative body until nationwide elections could be carried out. The Assembly was notable for its small number of military personnel, and the wide array of occupations represented by its members.

Prime Minister Sanya's government was immediately besieged by severe problems. Laborers, having been oppressed for decades by low wages and an increased cost of living, took advantage of the new freedom by demanding higher wages and by staging strikes, almost all of which were settled in the laborers' favor. Crime and acts of violence and insurgency increased during the interim period when the government was concentrating on bringing administrative order to the kingdom. Inflation continued unabated. Students, heady with the success of their demonstrations, began to participate actively in, and to criticize, every facet of governmental affairs, often angering officials and citizens who called for support of Sanya's interim government.

During the transitional period of Sanya's rule the Thai economy was subjected to unprecedented problems. Thailand, together with most nations of the world, suffered from the combined forces of inflation and recession. The increase in oil costs and imports in conjunction with rising rice costs were the major causes of the estimated 20 percent inflation rate for 1974. Inflation, in turn, reduced the demand for various goods, reduced the amount of spendable money available, and led to uncertainty and reduced investments. Overall industrial profits decreased, resulting in rising unemployment and falling expansion rates.

Thailand's remarkable decade of rapid growth terminated at least temporarily in 1973. Following the overthrow of the military, labor strikes, which had been banned under military rule, increased enormously. There were over 2,000 labor strikes in 1973, almost all following the October uprising, and some 1,500 strikes were counted in the first six months of 1974. In contrast, during the years 1969 to 1972 just over 100 labor strikes occurred. In most cases the labor strikes forced the managers to pay higher wages, but the pay scale still remained low. In 1974 the government raised the minimum daily wage from 60 cents to $1.00.

The post-uprising period also saw thousands of farmers traveling to Bangkok to demonstrate for reforms. The farmers complained of increased indebtedness to landlords and moneylenders. In the 1960s and early 1970s, in far greater numbers than ever before, wealthier citizens from Bangkok and the provincial capitals bought land from indebted farmers and then rented out the land. By 1974 in the Central Plains, the number of farmers renting land surpassed 50 percent, an unprecedented percentage with ominous implications. Traditionally, Thai farmers have owned the land they till.

All of these problems arose during an administration which perceived its role as that of a caretaker. Sanya Thamasak was reluctant to take any concerted action or promote any long-range policy. His major goal was to oversee the promulgation of a new permanent constitution to be followed by elections. Hence, programs to counteract the worsening economic situation were deferred until the new constitution was drafted, followed by the election of a "legitimate" government.

Thailand's ninth constitution, which went into force in October 1974, called for a bicameral legislature with an appointed Senate and elected House of Representatives. The prime minister was to be an elected member of the House. The president of the Privy Council appointed the Senate, presumably with the king's concurrence. Compared to the 1968 constitution the document gave more power to the elected representatives and less to the appointed senators.

The election, Thailand's eleventh since the 1932 revolt, took place 26 January 1975. As in the past, personalities were more important than issues, although once again the Democrat party slate, traditionally the leading opposition group, won overwhelmingly in Bangkok. The Democrats led by Seni Pramoj won 72 of the 269 National Assembly seats, more than any single other of the 42 parties that campaigned. About 110 seats were won by persons formerly aligned with the military rule of Thanom and Prapat, now split into several parties.

Seni Pramoj was elected prime minister by the House of Representatives, but he could not form a coalition. His elevation to the office of prime minister marked the second time Seni had held that position. In 1945, having served as minister to the United States and having been a leader of the anti-Japanese Free Thai movement, Seni became prime minister for four months. His main accomplishment was to negotiate a postwar settlement with the Allied powers. Subsequently, Seni, who was 69 at the time of the 1975 election, has been the nominal leader of the opposition forces, and has enjoyed a reputation for the highest intellect and integrity.

Until the 1975 election the Democrats were the major conservative opposition. During the campaign, however, the Democrat party platform called for mild socialism, thus breaking with the party's long-standing support of a pure capitalist system. Following the election, while Seni was attempting to form a coalition, the Democrats adopted a program calling for the withdrawal of American forces from Thailand according to a specific timetable and the repeal of the anti-Communist act, with emphasis on preventive measures instead of suppressive counter-insurgency programs. In addition the Democrats called for constitutional amendments abolishing the appointed Senate, and allowing for a minimum voting age of 18 instead of the present minimum age of 20. Urgent land reform was a key platform in the Democrats' program, as well as the establishment of diplomatic relations with the People's Republic of China.

Seni Pramoj submitted his cabinet and program to the National Assembly on 6 March 1975, but he lost a vote of confidence and the government was forced to resign. The conservative parties agreed to support Kukrit Pramoj, the younger brother of Seni Pramoj and leader of the Social Action party, for prime minister. Kukrit was a close confidant of the king, was active in conservative political circles for several decades, and was considered Thailand's leading newspaper publisher. By April 1975 the newly elected government was functioning. However, promises of patronage were the glue holding the coalition together. In this situation, where the coalition depended on the loyalty and satisfaction of a number of divergent parties, and where self-interest largely prevailed over the public interest, the eventual downfall of Kukrit's government had to be expected.

To strengthen his slight parliamentary majority and to keep from facing a defeat on a vote of confidence, Kukrit dissolved the National Assembly in January 1976 and called for new elections. The election campaign was particularly violent with numerous terrorist acts and political assassinations. The major issues of the campaign included law and order, the role of the United States in Thailand, the economic recession, and the price of rice.

On 4 April 1976, 40 percent of the Thai adult population voted, and a new government came into power. Kukrit himself was defeated for a parliamentary seat in his Bangkok constituency and therefore was not eligible to form the government. The Democrat party increased its plurality to 114 of the 279 seats. The largest share of seats went to centrist and conservative parties. The left-wing Socialist and liberal New Force parties won a total of only six seats. The election results were interpreted as a move to the right in Thai politics, and a concern on the part of the electorate about the increase in internal insurgency and the intentions of Thailand's neighbors, Laos, Cambodia, and Vietnam, all of which had changed to Communist governments during the preceding year.

Seni Pramoj, at age 71, once again became prime minister, leading a strong coalition of conservative parties. The size of the majority indicated a higher degree of stability than Kukrit's government had enjoyed. However, as with all previous governments since 1932, the role and intentions of the military still remained crucial in assessing the ultimate impact of this new government on modern Thai politics.

Those intentions became clear in October 1976, when the military again overthrew the democratic government, proclaimed martial law, and abrogated the constitution. The precipitating event was the return from exile of former Prime Minister Thanom Kittikachorn. Because Thanom symbolized the long era of military dictatorship in Thailand, thousands of university students demonstrated against his return. However, an equally large number of vocational students, supported by certain military factions, opposed the university students' demonstration. The two groups, who in the past three years had broken into opposing factions, clashed in a violent, riotous scene at Thammasat University. The riot, which was instigated at least partly by the military's support for right-wing student and youth groups, provided the military with a pretext for declaring a state of emergency and ending the three-year democratic period.

The reasons for the October 1976 coup go back much further than Thanom's return. The 1973 student revolt which began the democratic period raised the expectations of many Thais that fundamental economic reforms would be carried out, as happens with any change of government. This three-year period, however, coincided with a worldwide recession and with inflation that temporarily ended the nation's rapid economic growth. The rise in the price of oil, in particular, caused an inflationary spiral, so that the real income of Thais declined. Hence the hopes of many Thais that democracy would improve their lives were dashed by an economic situation over which the new government had no control.

The civilian government's inability to cope with economic problems was paralleled by its incapacity to establish land reform, urban development, and reform programs designed to decrease the gap between the rich and poor. Prime Ministers Seni and Kukrit Pramoj recommended such programs but could not move them through the bureaucracy or the conservative parliament. The one exception was Kukrit Pramoj's $125 million program to provide funds to local-level communes for projects which the local leaders themselves chose. The commune program was a striking break from the traditional Thai approach of centralized policy-making, directed from the top down. For the most part, however, the bulk of the Thai people perceived nothing but deterioration in their economic position.

The civilian government was also faced with an international and regional situation over which they had little control. The change to Communist governments in Vietnam, Laos, and Cambodia and the rise in insurgency throughout the Thai countryside shocked many Thais, who felt that only an authoritarian, military-dominated government could deal effectively with these threats. Under the military, the Thai government had relied mainly on the United States for its defense needs, but under the civilian government, the decision was made to formulate a more even-handed, pragmatic foreign policy that provided flexibility and featured renewed ties with the Communist nations. The state of flux was destabilizing and added to the uncertainty felt by many Thais, especially the military and financial elite.

The civilian government initially was united in opposition to the military and in determination to make democratic government work. As they were forced to make decisions, however, and to choose how scarce resources should be allocated, the civilian leadership factionalized. The Democrat party, in particular, broke into left, center, and right groups, with none willing to support the others. Members of the cabinet and parliament sought self-serving ends rather than ends compatible with stable government. The result was stagnation, instability, and a reputation as an inept administration.

The weakness of the civilian government was paralleled by consolidation among various military factions. Following the student revolt, the Thai military was humiliated and in disarray. In the next three years, the military cliques readjusted and finally united as they waited for an opportunity to reassert their dominant political position. The student riots in October 1976 provided that opportunity. In addition, the death of the moderate General Kris Sivara several months before the October coup removed the one military leader with the prestige and power to prevent a military coup.

The military was concerned that the civilian government could not adequately defend the country against the threats stemming from the new Communist governments in Southeast Asia. Second, they desired to regain the power they felt was taken from them when Seni Pramoj appointed a civilian to the defense ministry post. In addition, the military sensed that the civilians were vulnerable and that public opinion increasingly supported a return to strong, effective government.

The new military government was led initially by Admiral Sangad Chaloryu. He established an Administrative Reform Council consisting of the prominent military leaders, and then set up a civilian, Thanin Kraivichien, as prime minister. Thanin was a supreme court justice and close confidant of the king. The military requested his appointment largely because he lacked a political base and could therefore be controlled, and because he was staunchly anti-Communist. Thanin, in turn, appointed a largely civilian cabinet made up of persons loyal to him. The Administrative Reform Council was to remain the primary power in the kingdom.

Thanin proved to be less pliable than the military had expected. He moved forcefully in a number of areas, particularly in the repression of suspected dissidents. His foreign policy was based on an anti-Communist ideology that precluded improved relations with Cambodia, Laos, and Vietnam. Thanin's policies proved too rigid even for the military, and after months of unsuccessful attempts by the military to moderate his views, a group of military leaders carried out another coup in October 1977, ousting Thanin and placing General Kriangsak Chamonond in the position of prime minister.

The military could now rule directly rather than indirectly through a civilian front man. In his first months of leadership, Kriangsak showed a moderate and pragmatic view. He quickly won the support of intellectuals, students, labor, the bureaucracy, and the peasantry, after the stifling and repressive Thanin period. Kriangsak moved to promulgate a new constitution and called for elections on 22 April 1979. The constitution called for the appointed Senate and elected House of Representatives jointly to choose the next prime minister. Because Kriangsak himself appointed the senators he was assured of continued rule. The election was characterized by a low voter turnout (19.5 percent in Bangkok), the defeat of the Democrats in Bangkok, the victory of right wing parties, and the defeat of democratic socialist candidates. Kriangsak was believed by most Thais to be more moderate than his civilian predecessor. He established diplomatic relations with neighboring Communist countries. However, despite his proclamation of the Year of the Farmer, he did not institute fundamental reforms that might have improved the lot of the rural Thais.

By the end of 1979, Kriangsak's administration was beset by serious economic and foreign policy problems that eventually led to his downfall on 28 February 1980. As with other Third World nations, Thailand faced a growing need for oil that constantly increased in price. The result was an accelerated inflation rate that reached 20 percent in 1979, a shortage of petroleum products, and an increasingly high deficit. Kriangsak's decision to increase oil prices some 60 percent precipitated the public's and elites' dissatisfaction with his administration.

Defense Minister General Prem Tinsulanond was named Thailand's seventh prime minister in as many years. With the strong support of the army leadership and the backing of the revered King Phumipon Adunyadet, Prem's position was enviable. He succeeded in gaining the support of three major political parties: Social Action, Chart Thai, and Democrat. He managed to have his military position as commander-in-chief extended despite having reached the mandatory retirement age of 60. Moreover, he was successful in keeping support of key military leaders through his adroit reshuffling of the senior military officers.

Prime Minister Prem has managed to hold power since 1979. His moderate image, ability to mobilize civilian politicians into a broad-based parliamentary majority, support from important military factions, and backing from the king, have strengthened his position.

Despite these assets, Prem has faced serious problems. The perception of Prem as "indecisive" by certain army groups led to a 1 April 1981 coup attempt, which raised concerns about Thailand's political stability. The coup, Thailand's 14th since 1932, began when a group of army officers established a revolutionary council, seized key positions in Bangkok and, for a short time, controlled radio communications. The attempt was led by regimental commanders with the rank of colonel, who were known as Young Turks.

The coup collapsed in two days after Prem mobilized his army supporters, in particular General Arthit Kamlang-ek, and the royal family announced its support for the Prem government. General Arthit's major role in putting down the coup attempt earned him fame and rapid promotion to army commander-in-chief.

Prem strengthened his position in April 1983 when he called for parliamentary elections. In a trouble-free election with 53 percent of the population voting, the Democrat, Chat Thai, and Social Action parties won 56, 73, and 92 seats respectively in the 323 seat lower house of the National Assembly. A new coalition was formed made up of the SAP, Democrat, Prachakorn Thai, and National Democracy parties, while the Chart Thai became the major opposition.

The 1983 election continued the trend of the 1979 elections, when far-left and far-right parties were rejected in favor of moderate parties. More voters voted along party lines than in the past. Thus, the major parties became more institutionalized and less reliant on famous personalities.

Prem did not join a political party nor was he a candidate for the National Assembly. He was chosen prime minister largely because he was acceptable both to the military and to liberal and conservative politicians. After the elections he resigned from his position as prime minister, then "bowed" to the entreaties of party leaders who viewed him as the only hope for a stable regime. As a retired general, Prem no longer held a military position. The most important military leader in Thailand was General Arthit, who held the positions of army commander-in-chief, supreme commander of the armed forces, chief of the Bangkok peacekeeping force, director of the internal security operations command, and chairman of Thailand's telephone organization. He emerged as Prem's most likely successor, although his rapid rise to power alienated some military officers. His image as a "strongman" and his reputation for asserting his opinions on major political issues made him a controversial figure.

In 1985 Prem's position seemed especially stable after General Arthit's status was lowered following his defeat on a series of controversial issues designed to augment the power of the military. Nevertheless, on 9 September 1985 a group of military leaders attempted to overthrow the government of Prem. Allegedly led by Colonel Manoon Roopkachorn, this coup had the support of former military generals including former Prime Minister Kriangsak, former Deputy Army Commander Yos Thephsadin na Ayuthaya, and former Supreme Commander Serm na Nakhon. Except for Colonel Manoon, who was allowed to flee the country, the suspected coup leaders were put on trial.

The major reason for the coup attempt was factionalism within the army among leading generals who were vying for power. Moreover, Manoon, a leader of the Young Turks, was frustrated at being ousted from the army after his involvement was confirmed in the 1981 coup attempt.

Colonel Manoon's followers saw him as a charismatic leader. He apparently believed that his followers as well as his patrons in the army would rally behind his move. There was some indication that active duty high ranking generals gave Manoon advance approval for the coup, but that allegation was not substantiated. Another factor precipitating the coup attempt concerned a large number of armed forces leaders who had lost fortunes in a chit fund scandal. A successful coup might have allowed these leaders to limit their financial losses and their embarrassment.

Colonel Manoon claimed that the coup attempt was made to

solve economic problems throughout the nation. However, army factionalism, personal ambition, and conflict over promotions appeared to be more likely reasons. Rather than indicating political instability in Thailand, the 9 September coup attempt reflected a strong, stable, and institutionalized regime. The complete failure of the coup, despite leadership and support from high ranking individuals, may act as a lesson to potential plotters that successful coups are a part of Thailand's past.

When the Thai National Assembly met 1 May 1986, Prime Minister Prem met an unexpected defeat of a royal decree which resulted in the immediate dissolution of the elected House of Representatives and a call for elections to be held 27 July 1986. The dissolution occurred almost a year before his four-year term was completed.

The defeat of the decree (a relatively minor bill regarding fees for diesel fueled vehicles), and the consequent call for new elections for 347 representatives could have been interpreted as both a vindication of more stable political institutions, and as a reversion to the personal politics of the past. The first interpretation reflected the smooth and normal practices of the democratic process in a parliamentary system. The army formally pledged neutrality and Army Commander-in-Chief Arthit promised that the elections would be held without military interference.

The second interpretation stressed the view that the decree defeat was based not on disagreement with the issues, but on personal factionalism. Over 40 members of the government coalition who broke ranks were led by former party leaders who had lost their positions in the Prem administration and wanted revenge. The dissidents were thought to prefer a "strongman" leader such as General Arthit to replace the more mild mannered Prem. Prem's dismissal of Arthit prior to the July 1986 election removed Arthit from his position of power and provided Prem with a new aura of decisiveness. Prime Minister Prem's administration was viewed as "boring" and uncreative, unable to solve the nation's economic problems. These problems had become especially acute in early 1986 as the export price of rice dropped precipitously, leaving farmers in debt.

Reports of vote buying increased the public's already negative view of the members of parliament. Thai newspapers reflected the public's dismay at those members of parliament who precipitated the government's downfall because of personal grudges, and who were susceptible to bribes in return for voting a particular way. The "new" Thai politics was seen to include major aspects of the "old."

The 1986 elections confirmed Prem's leading role. Although he was not a parliamentary candidate himself and did not belong to any political party, he fashioned a coalition of four major parties including the Democrats who won 100 of the 347 seats, the Chart Thai party with 63 seats, the Social Action party with 51 and the Rassadorn party with 18. Once again the Thais chose moderate party candidates and rejected those representing the far right or left. The 61.5 percent voter turnout nationally and the 37 percent turnout in Bangkok were the highest in history. Prem became the longest-serving prime minister of an elected government.

INDONESIA

The problems for Indonesia in its search for national identity were fundamentally different from those which Thailand faced. Whereas Thailand was spared the destruction of its cities and economy in World War II, Indonesia was devastated. Moreover, Thailand did not face a struggle for independence against a colonial power, whereas Indonesia endured a four-year war with the Dutch between 1945 and 1949. Thailand also enjoyed the advantage of a relatively homogeneous society, while Indonesia was characterized by extraordinary geographical, linguistic, ethnic, and social heterogeneity. The nationalist leaders of Indonesia were faced with the challenge of fashioning a nation-state out of some 3,000 islands spread throughout a 3,000 mile-long archipelago, inhabited by over 100 ethnic groups, speaking over 200 languages. Nationalist ideology played a far more important role in the evolution of contemporary Indonesia than in Thailand.

Postindependence unity in Indonesia relied mainly on the leadership of President Sukarno, who dominated Indonesian politics for two decades until 1965 when he was overthrown. Sukarno was born of Javanese parents in 1901. Early in his life he inherited a commitment to the anticolonial struggle. His patron, Tjokroaminoto, a wealthy newspaper editor and political activist, introduced Sukarno to nationalist organizations and ideas. Sukarno became a brilliant orator with the power to deeply move his audiences by explaining his political aims in the language of Javanese mythology. He was imprisoned and exiled by the Dutch on a number of occasions but when released returned to his role as spokesman for the anticolonialist revolution. Sukarno used his martyrdom and his superb energy as an organizer of nationalist groups, including the Indonesian Nationalist party (PNI), to unite the nation. But his greatest strength came from his oft-repeated proclamations: "Give me 1,000 old men, and with them I shall have confidence to move Mt. Semeru. But give me ten youths who are fired with zeal and with love for our native land, and with them I shall shake the earth!"

During World War II Sukarno was brought out of exile by the Japanese and given a high administrative post. He was accused of collaborating with the Japanese occupation forces although he defended himself by arguing that only by taking an administrative position could he influence Japanese policy vis-á-vis Indonesia. In 1945, following Japan's defeat, Sukarno proclaimed Indonesian independence, a goal not reached until December 1949, when the Dutch yielded to world (mainly United States) pressures and negotiated a treaty of independence for Indonesia.

In 1949 Sukarno, the nationalist, became president, and Hatta, the administrator, became vice president and later prime minister. The close relationship of these two men helped strengthen the fragile stability that followed the fight for independence. However, with the struggle against the Dutch no longer a unifying force, and with Sukarno and Hatta moving in different directions, stability again became tenuous.

For Hatta, the main postindependence concerns were economic stabilization, protection of Dutch investments, nonalignment in foreign affairs, and administrative reorganization.[1] For Sukarno, on the other hand, the main concern was national

---

[1] Herbert Feith and Alan Smith, "Indonesia," in Roger M. Smith, ed., *Southeast Asia: Documents of Political Development and Change* (Ithaca, New York: Cornell University Press, 1974), p. 166.

unification and solidarity. A classic struggle arose between two groups: the "administrators," who concentrated on the problems of economic restoration, and the "solidarity makers," who were committed to ideology and nationalism.[2] Whereas the administrators did not mobilize the support of the Indonesian people, the solidarity makers, relying on ideological messianic oratory and calling for the "new Indonesian man," mobilized the citizenry and in 1953 took over the government.

The period 1949–1956 was characterized as the era of liberal democracy. Political parties flourished, parliamentary government was established, and a relatively responsive election was held in 1955. Herbert Feith argues that the decline of liberal democracy resulted from the failure of the Hatta group of administrators to keep public support. The administrators, with their concern for legality, ran afoul of the predominant nationalist sentiment. They were replaced by the "solidarity makers," who were less committed to parliamentary democracy and less inclined to cope with the day-to-day administrative problems.

Feith suggests that the revolutionary transition to independence created a high level of political unrest, which the administrators attempted to dam rather than to channel.[3] Moreover, in 1949 Indonesia had adopted Western constitutional forms to show the Western powers and the Dutch that Indonesians could govern themselves in a modern and democratic manner. These Western institutions did not "fit" a culture which traditionally placed little value on representation or group formation. Indeed, as the economic plight of the people continued to worsen, the political parties and the parliament were increasingly blamed. Western forms were found to be less than panaceas. The political parties actually were more destructive of national unity than they were constructive. The parties tended to articulate (and thereby exaggerate) the political, religious, and ethnic differences among Indonesians.

Clearly, liberal democracy did not live up to expectations.

---

[2] See Herbert Feith, *The Decline of Constitutional Democracy in Indonesia* (Ithaca, New York: Cornell University Press, 1962).

[3] Ibid., p. 608.

President Sukarno himself suggested that liberal democracy's Western forms were a sham and that only a truly Indonesian political pattern, reflecting Indonesian traditions and values, could resolve the chaotic situation.

Sukarno's panacea was "guided democracy." Instead of the trappings of Western parliamentary democracy, Sukarno in 1956–57 moved toward uniquely Indonesian forms based on traditional village procedures of making decisions by consultation and discussion (*musjawarah*) and searching for unanimous agreement (*mufakat*). He had only contempt for "50 percent plus 1 democracy," which he saw as a polarizing method. Instead, he called for a return to the spirit of *gotong rojong* (mutual benefit), where, in an environment of cooperation and tolerance rather than competition, decisions could be arrived at with unanimous approval.

Sukarno made nationalism (i.e., the submergence of regional and ethnic loyalties in favor of national ones, including total allegiance to Sukarno himself) the cornerstone of his Indonesian ideology. In the name of nationalism, Sukarno called for revolutionary change from Western forms toward indigenous patterns. The old order was to be replaced with a revolutionary new order—a new Indonesian culture, free from the mentality of colonialism.[4] Nationalism meant the annihilation of "neo-colonialism" and the building of a socialist society.

Under guided democracy, most political parties were banned. The Communist party of Indonesia (PKI) and the Indonesian Nationalist party (PNI) retained a vigorous organization. Parliament's power was steadily reduced, and finally it was dissolved. At the same time, Sukarno established, appointed, and headed various councils and national front groups. He periodically proclaimed martial law and suspended civil liberties, thereby ensuring that the opposition was minimized.

One important feature of the guided democracy period was the growing political significance of the Indonesian army, and also of the Communist party. The army inherited a new, higher

---

[4] See Herbert Feith, "Indonesia," in George McT. Kahin, ed., *Governments and Politics of Southeast Asia* (2nd ed.; Ithaca, New York: Cornell University Press, 1964), p. 234.

status from its role as the principal agent of the independence struggle. As in Thailand, the army was and is the most effectively organized and closely knit institution in the country. The PKI emerged as an articulator of the revolutionary-nationalist ideology proclaimed by Sukarno. Like the army, the PKI is tightly and hierarchically organized. Most importantly for Sukarno, the PKI acted as a counterbalance to the increasing power of the army, and hence he supported the party's activities. When, on the other hand, the PKI position was dominant, President Sukarno reacted by strengthening the army's position.

President Sukarno's role as a balancing agent suggests that the era of guided democracy was not totalitarian in the sense that the government had total control over the society. On the contrary, Sukarno's rule was often tenuous and superficial. He constantly had to balance the demands of numerous groups. Sukarno could not treat the army, PKI, Chinese business groups, students, rightist Muslims, outer-island groups, or Javanese as subordinates. Rather, he had to treat these groups as either rivals or partners, depending on the situation and accordingly bargain, manipulate, cajole, or persuade.

Guided democracy was presented as the logical outcome of the failure of a discredited Western system and as a return to traditional political patterns, congruent with Indonesian culture and therefore more stable and effective. However, many scholars have argued that guided democracy was essentially a mask to disguise the true aims of the Indonesian leadership.[5] The emphasis on *gotong rojong, musjawarah,* and *mufakat,* it is argued, reflects rhetoric more than reality. Under guided democracy the Indonesian people did not participate in government policymaking. The kinds of procedures used at the village level could not be transferred to the national political scene. One author noted that "put bluntly, [guided democracy] is a cloak for a power struggle, a facade built out of myths and slogans to shield a system of autocratic personalized rule."[6]

In the early 1960s guided democracy was confronted with

---

[5] See Jeanne S. Mintz, *Mohammed, Marx, and Marhaen, The Roots of Indonesian Socialism* (New York: Frederick Praeger, 1965).

[6] Ibid., p. 225.

increasing economic and political problems that resulted in fer-
ment among various groups in Indonesia. In 1963 Sukarno set
forth his "Crush Malaysia" (*Konfrontasi*) campaign to direct attention away from the severe internal discontent and to unify the
country against "neoimperialism." The confrontation policy was
directed against the imminent establishment of Malaysia, which
consisted of a merger of Malaya, Singapore, Sabah (North
Borneo), and Sarawak. The policy was supported by the army,
whose budget was increased during the confrontation, as well as
by the PKI, which stressed the anti-imperialist theme and which
saw confrontation as contributing to further economic deterioration and the consequent discontent of the peasantry.

By 1965 Indonesia faced economic chaos and political instability at both the peasant and elite levels. The most striking
problem was the disruption of the economy. Because of economic mismanagement by Sukarno's regime, flagrant corruption at every level of the bureaucracy, and the confrontation
policy which drained the budget, the government lost control of
the economy. The cost of living index rose from a base of 100 in
1957 to 36,000 in 1965. The transportation industry collapsed.
Unemployment in the cities was rampant.

In addition to the economic problems, Sukarno was moving
Indonesia in radically new directions in foreign policy. He identified himself with the goals of the PKI and formed an alliance
with the People's Republic of China. Moreover, Sukarno sided
with the PKI in its policy of building a "fifth force" by arming the
peasantry with guns supplied by China and engaging in unilateral action in Java to seize land and distribute it among the
landless peasantry.

The tensions arising from the political and economic problems were heightened by the state of Sukarno's health, which
deteriorated severely in August 1965. During this period a
group of dissident army officers apparently met to plan a purge
of the army high command. These plotters ostensibly believed
that the army's highest leadership, the Council of Generals,
planned to seize power (allegedly with the support of the American Central Intelligence Agency) and that therefore a preventive coup was necessary. The result was one of the most significant and far-reaching events in contemporary Southeast Asian
history. For the 1965 Gestapu coup (an acronym derived from

the Indonesian words meaning 30 September movement) fundamentally changed Indonesia's political structure, decimated the Indonesian Communist party, led to one of the worst bloodbaths in history, and brought into power a military government that has ruled ever since.

The precise role of the PKI, the Council of Generals, the dissident army rebels, and President Sukarno himself in the abortive Gestapu coup may never be known. The evidence is inconclusive and contradictory, and almost all of the leading participants in the coup were murdered, executed, or brought to trial after months in prisons. Two basic interpretations of the Gestapu coup have been presented. The first suggests that young rebels in an internal army affair attempted to overthrow the army high command by kidnapping the Council of Generals. According to this interpretation, neither the PKI nor President Sukarno conspired in the plot. This interpretation suggests that Sukarno and the PKI were the victims rather than the initiators of events.

The second interpretation suggests that the army rebels, in collusion with Sukarno and the PKI, plotted the overthrow of the army high command with the eventual goal of setting up a socialist state, led at least initially by Sukarno. The immediate goal was to avert the mobilization of the army in the event of Sukarno's death and to remove the one organized group that stood in the way of their goals. Proponents of this view cite the presence of Sukarno and PKI groups at the coup headquarters at the Halim Air Force Base as evidence of their complicity.[7]

Both versions agree that the coup leaders kidnapped most of

---

[7] For varied views of the Gestapu coup see Benedict Anderson and Ruth T. McVey, *A Preliminary Analysis of the October 1, 1965 Coup in Indonesia,* Interim Report Series, Modern Indonesia Project (Ithaca, New York: Cornell University Press, 1971); Arnold C. Brackman, *The Communist Collapse in Indonesia* (New York: W. W. Norton, 1969); Peter J. Dommen, "The Attempted Coup in Indonesia," *China Quarterly,* No. 25 (January/June, 1966), pp. 144–170; John Hughes, *Sukarno: A Coup that Misfired, A Purge that Ran Wild* (New York: McKay, 1967); Justus van der Kroef, "Origins of the 1965 Coup in Indonesia: Probabilities and Alternatives," *Journal of Southeast Asian Studies, 3* (September, 1972), 277–298; Tarzie Vittachi, *The Fall of Sukarno* (New York: Frederick A. Praeger, 1967); W. F. Wertheim, "Suharto and the Untung Coup—The Missing Link," *Journal of Contemporary Asia, 1(2)* (Winter, 1970), 50–57.

the Council of Generals, although General Nasution, the defense minister and chief of staff of the armed forces, escaped. The captured generals were murdered in a particularly hideous manner and buried at Halim Air Base. There is some evidence that Sukarno and PKI leader Aidit believed that the generals would be detained, confronted with charges of treason, and found guilty at a later trial. However, the brutal deaths suggest that events got out of hand.

The coup attempt was blocked when General Suharto (who was not a member of the Council of Generals but who commanded the Strategic Army Reserve) assumed command of the army and within hours captured the leading coup participants. Members of the PKI who were at the air base, where the coup headquarters was set up, were accused by the military of complicity in the coup. Inexplicably, the PKI newspaper *Harian Rakjat* published an editorial on 2 October expressing "sympathy and support" for the purge of the generals, despite the fact that the coup had clearly failed. Sukarno himself had been present at the base, but left for his palace at Bogor before the plotters were captured, when he realized the coup might not succeed.

The coup attempt failed because the bulk of the army opposed the goals of the rebels and moved swiftly under General Suharto. Second, neither the PKI nor any other group had prepared the population to rise in support of the coup. Moreover, the murders of the generals caused revulsion among much of the population. Indeed, those murders set the scene for one of the most far-reaching bloodbaths in history as members and suspected supporters of the PKI were themselves murdered. Sukarno's vacillation, once he heard of Nasution's escape from the kidnappers, undermined the movement's aims too. Without Sukarno's strong endorsement, the coup leaders were not able to mobilize the masses in support of the plot against the army generals.

The bloodbath lasted almost two years and resulted in the deaths of an estimated 500,000 persons. The army sanctioned and even encouraged the killing of suspected Communists. Gradually, the violence expanded in scope as racial, religious, ethnic, social, economic, and political differences became cause enough for mass killings. Soedjatmoko, a leading Indonesian diplomat, noted that what took place was a psychological and historical breakdown where tolerance and consensus vanished overnight, and passion replaced compassion. What began as a "political cleansing" ended in an indiscriminate orgy of death. Following the abortive coup, Suharto was named army chief of staff by a reluctant Sukarno. With each passing month, Suharto took on more power at the expense of Sukarno. Suharto moved deliberately as he slowly reduced Sukarno's power. Suharto banned the PKI, arrested pro-Sukarno officials, ended the confrontation policy, rejoined the United Nations, and finally in 1967 removed Sukarno from what had become the ceremonial office of president.

President Suharto proclaimed a new order for Indonesia, with emphasis on industrial development, economic stabilization, and reconstruction. By 1970 inflation had been brought under control and foreign investment, exports, and oil earnings increased significantly. At the same time, the military government moved to limit political freedoms. Political freedom was not to be extended to Communists, nor was it to lead to disruption, nor to the questioning of the actions of the military government.

Indonesia's first elections since 1955 were held in 1971 as the citizenry chose representatives in the newly established parliament. One hundred of the 460 representatives were chosen by the president, thus assuring the army's control over the parliament. The government's power was also strengthened by the stipulation that antigovernment statements were prohibited. Hence effective campaigning was banned. Moreover, the military had established its own party group, Sekber Golkar, a federation of members from numerous organizations representing diverse economic groupings. Sekber Golkar was the only party with access to large quantities of material resources. More importantly, the large Indonesian civil service was mobilized into Sekber Golkar. The officials, in turn, exercised influence over the voting of rural people. The Sekber Golkar party also enjoyed the advantage of representing a group, the military, that had brought a relatively high degree of economic stability to Indonesia, in contrast to the economic chaos under Sukarno. The government party won 63 percent of the votes, overwhelming the other parties and assuring Suharto and the military continued, and now legitimate, rule.

Suharto's success in the 1971 elections provided encouragement to the Golkar to repeat the election process in May 1977. As in 1971, the purpose of the election was to strengthen and legitimize Suharto's rule through "democratic" means. The election processes and results were similar to those of the previous election. Golkar controlled the bureaucracy down to the village levels and had use of unlimited funds. Golkar officials intimidated voters and at the same time offered substantial financial inducements. The opposition Unity Development party (PPP) comprised an amalgamation of the Islamic parties. The PPP had neither the official clout nor the financial resources to compete on an equal basis.

As in 1971, Golkar received just over 62 percent of the vote. The PPP gained 29 percent and minor parties accounted for the rest. Because the parliament also consisted of 100 government-appointed persons, Suharto's power remained incontestable vis-á-vis opposition parties. On 22 March 1978 President Suharto was unanimously reelected to a third five-year term by the Indonesian Congress (MRP). Adam Malik, chairman of the Congress and former foreign minister, was elected vice president. The new cabinet contained eleven generals, reflecting the continued importance of the military in his administration.

Despite the military government's initial successes in some areas, the Suharto regime had several major problems. Corruption at all levels remained rampant. Oil revenues, which at one time brought in some $5 billion per year, declined precipitously in 1975 when Pertamina, the state oil company, nearly went bankrupt. However, in the 1980s oil revenues again became an important source of development funds. Political repression has continued, with the taking of many thousands of political prisoners and the banning or merging of most political parties. At the end of 1977 student demonstrations broke out against Suharto's questionable business activities and the slow pace of development, particularly in the rural areas. Suharto had several hundred students arrested. The most prominent newspapers were temporarily banned and allowed to reopen only after their editors agreed to censorship.

In 1979, in response to international pressures, Suharto ordered the release of the bulk of political prisoners, many of whom had languished without trials in prisons for 14 years. At the same time Suharto ordered that the new economic plan

(1979–84) focus on "economic justice" for all Indonesians. Specifically, the plan called for a large financial investment in the areas of production, distribution of food, comprehensive education and health programs, and support for small businesses.

Despite these serious problems, the May 1982 election was a striking success for President Suharto and his Golkar party. Through skillful political management, selected repression of oppositionists, a workable economic program, and unlimited access to revenue, Suharto's party won 64 percent of the vote with the Muslim PPP garnering 28 percent and the Nationalist PDI only eight percent. Suharto thus had five more years as president, making him one of the longest ruling leaders in the world. He will be 67 in 1987 when once again elections will be held. At present, there is no clear successor or rival to Suharto, because he has managed to dominate political life in Indonesia.

The basic problems which have beset Indonesia for decades remain largely unresolved. The gap between the military elites and the civilian populace, between urban and rural services, and between landlords and peasants has widened rather than narrowed. Urban unemployment and slum conditions have spread rapidly in the past decade. At the same time a semblance of political order exists that is unprecedented in postindependence Indonesian history. This political stability is based both on fear of repression and on a relatively more effective bureaucracy than existed under Sukarno.

VIETNAM

Vietnam's search for national identity received its greatest impetus during the thousand-year period of Chinese domination (111 B.C. to 939 A.D.). The ability of the Vietnamese to emerge from that period with many of their traditions intact symbolizes the nationalist urge which has pervaded Vietnam's history. Similarly, the struggle against French colonialism, Japanese occupation, and most recently American intervention, reflects the importance of Vietnamese nationalism.

That is not to say that Vietnam has always been united. During the era of French colonialism, Vietnam was divided into three areas: Tonkin in the north, with Hanoi as the capital; Annam in the middle region, with Hue as the capital; and in the south, Cochin China, where Saigon served as the capital. This division

was congruent with a traditional geographic regionalism beginning in the 10th century A.D., when the Vietnamese began their
southern movement.

> Those who moved south were pioneer souls, adventurous,
> risktaking, and hardy, differing sharply from their sophisticated
> cousins who stayed behind in Hanoi and their tradition-minded
> cousins who remained in Hue.[8]

Traditionally, the northerners have seen themselves as modern, progressive, and efficient, while they have seen the southerners as lazy. The Annamese see themselves as highly cultured,
the northerners as grasping, and the southerners as rustic. On
the other hand, southerners regard themselves as pacifistic and
their northern neighbors as aggressive and violent.[9]

Besides these differing cultural perceptions, national unification also had to overcome the cultural and political dichotomy
between the rural areas and the cities. Communication between
the cities and villages scarcely existed; such interaction as there
was consisted largely of the exploitation of the peasantry by the
mandarin class. Moreover, Vietnam is populated by minority
groups who have traditionally been treated with disdain by the
Vietnamese majority.

Despite the divisiveness which has characterized much of Vietnamese history there has remained a nationalist continuity in the
form of anticolonialism and antineoimperialism. Following the
Japanese defeat in World War II in 1945, Ho Chi Minh, the
leader of the League for the Independence of Vietnam, known
as the Vietminh, proclaimed the independence of Vietnam and
set up a provisional government headed by himself. In March
1945, the French and the representatives of the newly established Democratic Republic of Vietnam led by Ho agreed that a
new independent state existed. However, agreement broke
down, and a series of clashes led to the French-Indochina War
that lasted eight years.

The Vietminh succeeded in controlling most of the land area,

---

[8] Douglas Pike, *War, Peace and the Vietcong* (Cambridge, Massachusetts: Massachusetts Institute of Technology Press, 1969), pp. 52–54.
[9] Ibid.

but the French kept control of major cities and much of Cochin China. The French were generously supported during the war by the United States, which contributed approximately $2.6 billion to the French, or about 80 percent of the entire cost of the war. Despite the technological superiority of the French, their cause collapsed in 1954 following a major military defeat in the northern area near Dienbienphu. Although opposed by a large sector of the important urban-elite groups, the Vietminh claimed to embody the spirit of Vietnamese resistance against all foreigners and to enjoy the support of the overwhelming majority of the people. The Geneva Agreements of 1954 sought to separate the rival French and Vietminh forces by setting up a temporary military demarcation line at the 17th parallel. This line was not intended to be a political or territorial boundary. In addition, the Geneva Agreements called for eventual national elections for the purpose of unification.

Following the French defeat there was agreement that the Vietminh could most effectively represent Vietnamese interests at Geneva. Indeed, the Geneva Agreements were negotiated by Vietminh and French officials. The Vietminh presented itself as a national front group representing diverse interests. Communist doctrine, which was an important element of the Vietminh's essentially nationalist ideology, was not stressed.

During the period of the Geneva Conference, there emerged in Saigon an anti-Vietminh administration initially led by the former Annamese emperor Bao Dai and subsequently by the strongly anti-Communist Ngo Dinh Diem. On 26 October 1955 Diem proclaimed the Republic of Vietnam with himself as the first president. One of his first acts was to repudiate the Geneva Agreements, specifically the provision for national elections. Instead, Diem began to consolidate his own power with the financial support of the United States.

Ho Chi Minh had agreed to the Geneva accords at least partly because he believed that national elections would assure re-unification under Communist Vietminh leadership. Ho was both a nationalist and a Communist. He saw the two ideologies as inseparable. He was a founding member of the French Communist party and an early Bolshevik supporter. Ho's writings are replete with examples of his view that only Communists supported with actions the aspirations of the peasantry and the colonized.

Ho spent much of his life abroad organizing various groups that were the forerunners of the Indochinese Communist party. He founded the Vietminh, a broad national front that united workers and peasants in the anti-French struggle. He was a ruthless organizer who tolerated no opposition to his nationalist policies. He followed Mao's maxim that power does indeed come from the mouth of a gun. Because he believed that organization was the key to a successful struggle against superior forces, he set up an intricate maze of cells manned by well-trained cadres. These cells became the foundation of the highly centralized and controlled North Vietnamese governmental system. Most importantly, he effectively elaborated on the nationalist ideology that united the bulk of the populace.

Ho's goal of a united Vietnam was scuttled when it became clear following the Geneva Agreements that Diem had no intention of merging with the north. Ngo Dinh Diem's nine-year rule began auspiciously as he rapidly moved South Vietnam toward economic recovery following decades of war. With the help of a massive United States AID program, Diem succeeded in generating rural and urban development. Although Diem's policies were initially supported by a large sector of the population, his regime became increasingly repressive and corrupt. He reversed a number of popular agrarian reforms begun by the Vietminh in the south in order to secure his popularity among the mandarin landowners. Diem, who was Catholic, appointed Catholic refugees from the north to high-level government positions and suppressed Buddhist organizations, thereby alienating large numbers of Buddhists. He uprooted the traditional systems of village autonomy by abolishing the elected village councils and replacing them with appointed officials. For many Vietnamese, Diem's regime appeared to be almost totally dependent upon United States support, causing his nationalist credentials to be suspect.

During Diem's rule in the late 1950s, South Vietnam became the site of guerrilla insurgency aimed against Diem's government. The political arm of the guerrilla activity was the National Liberation Front (NLF) which was initially an autonomous southern-based movement. A large number of northerners who had remained in the south following the Geneva Agreements joined these guerrillas. The strength of the insurgency movement resulted from the high degree of support afforded it by the peasantry (the peasantry was the willing "sea" in which the guerrillas could "swim" unmolested), from the repressive and increasingly unpopular Diem regime, and from the superb organization at all levels of the NLF.

In the early 1960s the North Vietnamese provided increasing military support to the NLF. The People's Revolutionary party, the Communist party of South Vietnam, which was itself controlled by North Vietnam, gradually dominated the NLF until ultimately the two were virtually indistinguishable.

To counteract the internal insurgency, Diem relied on United States advisors, weaponry, money, and soldiers. Between 1954 and 1956, fewer than 1,000 American advisors were stationed in Vietnam. By 1960 over 5,000 advisors and combatants had been sent to Vietnam. Despite the continued flow of weaponry and soldiers to Vietnam, Diem's position deteriorated and the guerrillas' area of control widened. Hence President Kennedy, who believed the United States was on the defensive internationally following the Bay of Pigs and the threats to Laos and Berlin, supported a coup against Diem by South Vietnamese military generals. The coup and Diem's subsequent death paved the way for a series of anti-Communist military governments too numerous to enumerate.

The clear anti-Communist thrust of these military juntas was congruent with United States policy. In August 1964, the Tonkin Gulf resolution was passed by the American Senate, ostensibly providing authority to the president to take all necessary measures to deal with North Vietnamese "aggression." In February 1965 the United States began the massive bombing of the north. The bombing policy was intended to interdict North Vietnamese supply lines, to erode morale in the north, and to provide time for the south to strengthen its forces. None of these three purposes, however, was achieved. The massive 1968 Tet offensive by the north showed the ineffectiveness of the American bombing policy. North Vietnamese supplies continued almost uninterrupted, and the South Vietnamese military regimes remained unable to effectively mobilize the population. The military continued to struggle among themselves for power;

corruption was rampant; and the government became more and more a client state of the United States. By 1965 the United States had taken over direction of the war and was subsidizing the bulk of the South Vietnamese budget.

The rationale for American intervention in Vietnam was based on several foundations. Of first concern was the perceived national interest of the United States itself. Most American policy-makers saw the fall of Vietnam to communism as one more stage of a spreading cancer that could eventually envelop America itself. South Vietnam became a testing ground for Communist wars of national liberation. It was believed that anything less than a committed effective stand against "Communist aggression" would be tantamount to an invitation for further aggression in other parts of the world. American credibility as a world power was also seen at stake. American policy-makers cited the commitment of four presidents, the terms of the SEATO treaty, and bilateral agreements with South Vietnam as proper sanctions for U. S. involvement.

Decisions regarding Vietnam were also a function of internal political pressure. Each president feared a political backlash if he were seen to be responsible for the defeat of South Vietnam. Vietnam became the test of presidential strength, especially for Presidents Johnson and Nixon, both of whom articulated the need for total victory.

American policy in Vietnam was also the product of a series of small steps, each insignificant in and of itself, but in sum a giant leap. In this sense American intervention was almost inadvertent, a policy of gradual escalatory moves that by themselves seem restrained but in sum committed the United States to a war in which over 50,000 American soldiers died, over 1,000,000 Vietnamese became casualties, and more bombs were exploded than in all past wars combined.

In the early 1970s the American government began a policy of "Vietnamization," that is, the gradual withdrawal of troops from Vietnam while escalating the bombing against the north. In January 1973 the Paris Peace Agreement was signed by North Vietnam, the Provisional Revolutionary government of South Vietnam, South Vietnam, and the United States. North Vietnam agreed to a cease-fire while the United States agreed not only to a cessation of bombing in the north but to the withdrawal of its troops.

The Paris Peace Accords were essentially a victory for the north, principally because the role of the United States was effectively ended. The fact that morale in South Vietnam plummeted following the signing of the agreement attests to the dependent relationship South Vietnam had with the United States. Without American bombing support and without financial aid (the United States spent over $112 billion in Vietnam after the early 1950s), South Vietnam could not withstand the pressure from the north.

In April 1975 North Vietnamese and provisional government troops moved swiftly through Vietnam, conquering province after province and eventually controlling Saigon. A war which had endured for three decades came to a startlingly swift close. The immediate causes of the Communist victory included the corruption of the South Vietnamese army, the decision of South Vietnamese President Nguyen Van Thieu to abandon strategic positions, and the refusal of the United States to provide any kind of aid. However, the long-range reasons for the Communist success provided the context for the more immediate causes.

> Ultimately, though, it was not a lack of military material that brought the government of Vietnam's collapse so much as the artificiality of the political system that had been shaped to respond primarily to the American interest in continuing the war and the use of a compliant but corrupt and ineffective military leadership for this purpose. Thus it was critically unresponsive to indigenous political interests and realities, including a vigorous native Communist movement oriented toward revolutionary change and capable of exploiting the corruption and incompetence in mobilizing its own mass support.[10]

The North Vietnamese moved swiftly and deliberately to consolidate their power. Ho Chi Minh's goal of a united Vietnam under Communist rule was reached, and in his honor Saigon was renamed Ho Chi Minh City. South Vietnam was temporarily ruled by a North Vietnamese military unit. In 1976 the Commu-

---

[10] John C. Donnell, "South Vietnam in 1975: The Year of Communist Victory," *Asian Survey*, 16 (January, 1976), 11.

nist leaders announced reunification, with Hanoi as the capital. The government set forth a policy to strengthen socialist construction in the north and to begin the process of building a socialist order in the south.

The Fourth Communist Party Congress, held in December 1976, established the north's political dominance over the south. The leaders of North Vietnam, many of whom were born in the south and went to the north during the first Indochina War, became the leaders of the united nation. Plans were outlined to transform the south to a socialist economy. Reeducation camps were established to indoctrinate former partisans of the South Vietnamese government with socialist values. The new administration attempted to mitigate the crowded conditions and high unemployment rate in Ho Chi Minh City by setting up New Economic Zones (NEZ) in remote areas where thousands of city dwellers were sent to engage in agricultural pursuits.

The end of the war and the unification of the nation did not lead to a desired era of progress and tranquility. On the contrary, the problems of bringing about a socialist utopia to Vietnam proved even more intractable than the problems of prosecuting the war.

The southerners did not take well to the economic programs of their new rulers. In particular, southern farmers resisted efforts to collectivize and redistribute the land. The peasantry deliberately sabotaged that part of their crops demanded by the central government. Vietnam, since 1975, has suffered a major food deficit every year until 1983. In addition to the resistance of the southern farmers, the deficit was exacerbated by three successive crop failures due to drought, the diversion of economic resources to the military stationed in Cambodia and along the Chinese border, and poor management and planning by central authorities.

As the Vietnamese government slowly but effectively ended the traditional free market system in the south, the indigenous Chinese, themselves the mainstay entrepreneurs in Ho Chi Minh City, fled the country. The government's reform of the monetary system virtually wiped out the savings of these shop owners. The result was that a second wave of refugees, this time some half a million ethnic Chinese, became "boat people" searching for a new home. The Vietnamese government made no attempts to end the exodus and indeed collected large bribes of gold to expedite the process. The economy of Ho Chi Minh City quickly deteriorated as the market system floundered. The result has been massive inflation, unemployment, and a black market economic system.

Vietnam's foreign relations also proved to be difficult in the postwar period. Although the Socialist Republic of Vietnam was accepted into the United Nations in September 1977, the United States and Vietnam have not yet reestablished diplomatic relations. Moreover, China ended economic aid to Vietnam in 1978 leaving the Soviet Union as the nation's only major ally and benefactor.

With the concurrence of the Soviet Union, on 25 December 1978, 100,000 Vietnamese troops invaded Cambodia and succeeded in establishing a puppet government led by an unknown Vietnamese-trained Cambodian refugee named Heng Samrin. Samrin headed the Cambodian National United Front for National Salvation, an army unit of about 20,000 troops who followed the Vietnamese into Cambodia. The Vietnamese claimed their invasion was launched to restore order and security to border areas by punishing Cambodia for a long series of border incursions and for intransigence regarding negotiations. The Vietnamese also insisted they were liberating Cambodians from the genocidal repression of Pol Pot's regime.

The results of the invasion were significant. Vietnam succeeded in enlarging its sphere of dominance to all of Indochina. Ho Chi Minh's dream of a Vietnamese-controlled Indochina federation was closer to fruition. The Soviet's role in Southeast Asia was enhanced while the Chinese, who had supported Pol Pot, correspondingly had their role lessened.

The invasion also acted as an impetus for the subsequent Chinese invasion of Vietnam on 17 February 1979. The Chinese hoped that their own offensive would force Vietnam to withdraw its occupation force of 200,000 troops from Cambodia. China desired to "teach Vietnam a lesson," to convince the Vietnamese that China was not a paper tiger, to punish the country for its harsh treatment of overseas Chinese, and to send a signal to the Soviet Union that China would not acquiesce to increased Soviet influence in Southeast Asia.

The results of the invasion were ambiguous. Neither nation

could claim a clear-cut military victory. The Chinese offensive was not carried out effectively. Both sides suffered extensive casualties and the economic infrastructure of the northern Vietnamese provinces where the fighting took place was devastated. The Vietnamese economy further suffered as the government was forced to pour more of its scarce resources into military affairs. The anti-Chinese feeling in Vietnam caused thousands more indigenous Chinese to leave the country.

In 1986 the Communist party of the SRV had ruled for over a decade. After the initial high expectations in the post-war era, the crushing reality of severe economic problems, a devastating legacy of physical and psychological destruction from the war, a protracted war in Cambodia, factionalism among the party leadership, and isolation from the world's great powers (except the Soviet Union), brought about a deep malaise and frustration among the populace. Reunification was far more difficult to achieve than first imagined.

Hanoi's 1978 policy of nationalizing industry and collectivizing the countryside in the south was disastrous as the economy declined and social unrest increased. Eventually, the government moderated its program and reintroduced some capitalist elements, but this reform divided the leadership between the "pragmatists" and the "ideologues." Secretary Le Duan and Prime Minister Pham Van Dong led the pragmatists while Troung Ching, state council chairman, was the leading hardliner. The Fifth Party Congress in March, 1982 reaffirmed the pragmatic policies but called for the eventual nationalization and collectivization of the entire country. The pragmatic path led to a rejuvenation of the economy and the rise of the black as well as the free market. This retreat from socialism galvanized hardliners who moved to erase the last vestiges of "bourgeois decadence," but in 1986 a mixed economy remained in the south.

One new innovation of the Fifth Party Congress was the contract system whereby farmers were able to sell their surplus on the open market or to the government at preferential prices. The system required that farmers first would meet a quota which was sold to the state at fixed rates. Once that obligation was met, farmers were relatively free to seek the best market conditions.

Vietnam continued its control over Cambodia and Laos although few of the world's nations recognized these Vietnamese sponsored governments. The Vietnamese government indicated its rule over Cambodia was irreversible, at least until China no longer posed a threat to the region. At the same time, Vietnamese leaders indicated they wanted closer relations with the United States and a diminished dependency on the Soviet Union. One example of this desire was Vietnamese overtures to resolve the missing-in-action issue which has been a major barrier to improved relations with the United States. Despite these overtures the non-Communist nations viewed Vietnam as the pariah of Southeast Asia and a major threat to the region's stability.

Traditionally the Vietnamese judged the legitimacy of their rulers in terms of the "mandate of heaven." If a ruler governed in a just manner, according to Confucian ideals, he was said to possess the mandate. If, on the other hand, a ruler lost power, it was assumed that he had lost the mandate of heaven because of unjust acts. The word "revolution" in Vietnamese means "changing of the mandate." The Communist takeover in 1975 surely is an example of such a change. But the new leaders' failure to be perceived as just by a large number of the citizenry suggests that the question of legitimacy is still in flux.

CAMBODIA

Present-day Cambodia traces its history back some 1,800 years to the kingdom of Funan. At the height of the great Khmer (Cambodian) civilization in the 12th century, the Khmers ruled over parts of modern-day Cambodia, Laos, Thailand, and Vietnam. The magnificent Khmer civilization, symbolized by the great temples at Angkor, lasted over 500 years and reached a level of military, technological, political, and philosophical achievement that was unmatched at the time in Southeast Asia. Angkor fell about 1432, when the Thais invaded the land. The Khmers had overreached themselves by building extravagant temples and irrigation systems which required extensive use of corvee labor. At the same time, major military campaigns into neighboring areas reduced the number of laborers available for the extensive water system, so that eventually both military and irrigation activities suffered. Large areas of Angkor were taken over by the Thai and Vietnamese. Dynastic struggles for power further weakened Cambodia until 1864, when the French took over Cambodia as a protectorate.

What remains of the Khmer Empire is a small nation about the size of Illinois, with slightly over five million persons. Cambodia's postwar search for identity and nationhood, free from French colonialism, was dominated by Prince Norodom Sihanouk, whom the French had placed on the throne in 1941 because he was considered "accommodating." During World War II the Japanese had taken over the colonial administration and had Sihanouk declare Cambodia's independence. Following the end of the war, however, the French returned and in 1946 made Cambodia an "autonomous" state within the French union.

Cambodia's independence was granted in 1954. One year later King Sihanouk abdicated the throne and organized his own political party, Sangkhum Reastr Niyum (People's Socialist Community), and henceforth was referred to as Prince Sihanouk. Sihanouk's party dominated all subsequent elections and the prince himself enjoyed unrivaled power. In 1961 he became chief of state, with full power over every aspect of political activity in Cambodia.

Prince Sihanouk's dominance of Cambodian political life from the end of World War II to 1970 was based on the plebiscite leadership he exhibited. He enjoyed the unsurpassed loyalty of the rural Cambodian people. He constantly strengthened his ties with the people. He was revered as a god-king in the tradition of the Angkor kings. He came to symbolize the glorious past, as well as the new, independent Cambodia. His authority, then, rested on charismatic, traditional, and legal foundations.

Moreover, Sihanouk controlled the important policy-making institutions. He dominated not only the major political party (which was essentially a public-relations organ for Sihanouk) but also the governmental bodies. When the legislative body questioned his policies, he established a national congress which was under his leadership and which was given power over other branches of the government.

Sihanouk's strength was also a function of a lack of unity among other elite groups, namely the military, intellectuals, bureaucrats, and the business community. Sihanouk exhibited a remarkable capacity to keep each major sector of society in check, never superior to any other group. His control over the distribution of resources encouraged the major interest groups to stay in his favor.

Thus, for much of Cambodia's postindependence history, the country was deemed a model of political stability, ruled by a popular leader. The overthrow of Prince Sihanouk on 17 March 1970, therefore, was a surprise to most analysts of Cambodian politics. On that date, while Sihanouk was in the Soviet Union, the Cambodian National Assembly, charging Sihanouk with a number of abuses of office, unanimously voted to oust him from his positions and to condemn him to death for treason and corruption. His position of power was assumed by General Lon Nol, the premier in Sihanouk's government.

The immediate cause of Sihanouk's downfall stemmed from the presence of North Vietnamese and Viet Cong forces in Cambodian sanctuaries. In 1968 these forces began to establish themselves in the eastern provinces of Cambodia, instead of passing through on the Ho Chi Minh trail. The Vietnamese bases in Cambodia became more permanent, hospitals were built, and weapon factories were constructed. By mid-1969 the Vietnamese had built a base of support in an area equal to almost one-fourth of Cambodia's territory.

Sihanouk's relations with the United States during this time were acrimonious. Cambodia had not received aid from the United States since 1963 and had broken relations in 1965. Sihanouk strongly supported the North Vietnamese and opposed American involvement in Vietnam. As the Vietnamese increasingly established themselves on Cambodian territory, however, Sihanouk changed the thrust of his speeches and began to argue the need for a United States force in Asia to provide a balance to the power of the Communist nations. In March 1970 Sihanouk had traveled to the Soviet Union and then to Peking to request aid in having Vietnamese troops withdrawn from Cambodia. During this trip, the military, under General Lon Nol, took over all power.

Sihanouk's short-term changes in policy direction were consistent with his overall objective of a neutral and sovereign nation. Cambodia's history has been characterized by constant attempts by more powerful neighbors and by Western imperialists to dominate Cambodian political life. Sihanouk's neutralism reflected an appreciation of historical precedents and a realization of the rising influence of China and a Communist Vietnam in Asia. The rising success of the Communist movement in Vietnam precipitated a reaction on the part of Sihanouk to ally once again with the West to assure a balance of power.

The Cambodian National Assembly deemed Sihanouk's "ambivalent and inconsistent" policies regarding Vietnamese intrusion as an act of treason. He was charged with having allowed the North Vietnamese and Viet Cong to operate in sanctuaries on their border, with having let the Vietnamese move supplies across Cambodia, and with having sold supplies for private gain in cooperation with his Vietnamese-born wife.

The assembly charged that the prince and his wife, Monique, had engaged in corruption, using various government agencies and gambling casinos. It was alleged that he organized costly festivities to distract attention from the nation's domestic problems. He was charged with wasting money by insisting on the nationalization of Cambodia's few industries and by building the port city of Sihanoukville, although only one ship per day docked there in 1969.

These announced reasons for the coup must be seen in a larger context. In the several years before his fall, Prince Sihanouk failed to retain the loyalty of the elite groups in Cambodia. The army, which had previously been factionalized, united around General Lon Nol and his view that Sihanouk was not moving strongly enough to remove the Vietnamese from Cambodian territory. The bureaucrats resented the total control Sihanouk wielded over policy-making and personnel decisions. Intellectuals opposed his policies of press and speech censorship, while university graduates became frustrated at the lack of job opportunities available to them.

Prince Sihanouk retained the loyalty of the rural masses, but in Cambodian politics that group wields little influence over the outcome of power struggles among the elites. Sihanouk's major failure was his inability to institutionalize the political system so that power relations were not exclusively a function of Sihanouk's desires and whims. The charismatic quality of Sihanouk's rule was the dominant political force in postwar Cambodia. Initially that quality was the primary integrating and stabilizing force; subsequently, his total dominance of Cambodian political life undermined the major institutions of the country and frustrated the elites who desired a larger share of power. Once these elite groups were provided with a cause around which they could unite, their common interest in gaining more power led to their coup d'etat against Sihanouk. The army became the dominant institution in Cambodian politics in March 1970. Immediately after the coup d'etat, Vietnamese Communist forces moved deeper into Cambodian territory. By mid-April, one-third of the nation was under Communist control. On 30 April President Richard Nixon, without first informing the Cambodian government, announced a troop invasion into Cambodia "to protect the lives of American solders," to ensure the success of the Vietnamization program, and to gain a "decent interval" for U.S. withdrawal from Vietnam. The president announced that the intervention would clean out major enemy sanctuaries, including the headquarters of the entire Communist military operation in South Vietnam. He stated, "If, when the chips are down the United States acts like a pitiful, helpless giant, the forces of totalitarianism and anarchy will threaten free nations and free institutions throughout the world."

The fall of Sihanouk precipitated a five-year period of total war on Cambodian soil. This nation that was often referred to as "an island of tranquility in a sea of chaos" was torn asunder by wars on two fronts, international and domestic.[11] The Lon Nol government proved to be incapable of coping with either front. The Vietnamese Communists eventually withdrew, after Cambodian Communist forces were prepared to continue the struggle.

The Lon Nol government declared martial law and abrogated civil liberties. The 1,168-year-old Khmer monarchy was abolished. Corruption remained rampant, there were food shortages for the first time, and inflation brought chaos to the economy. The war caused hundreds of thousands of Cambodians to leave their homes and seek refuge in Phnom Penh. Whereas in 1970 the capital city's population was 500,000, by 1975 it was

---

[11] Roger M. Smith, "Cambodia," in Roger M. Smith, ed., *Southeast Asia: Documents of Political Development and Change* (Ithaca, New York: Cornell University Press, 1974), p. 481.

2,500,000—five times the previous number. An estimated one-tenth of the Cambodian population was killed or injured in the war.

Initially, the power elite rallied around Lon Nol and his anti-Communist, anti-Sihanouk, and pro-American policies. However, Lon Nol's government was not popular with the rural people. His unpopularity pushed the radical rebels and Prince Sihanouk, who was in exile in Peking, China, into an alliance, whereas before the coup the radical groups had opposed Sihanouk.[12] The United States had given the Cambodians the means to fight each other, but had given them nothing to fight for.[13] The result was the inevitable deterioration of the Cambodian society into a civil war which did not end until April 1975, when the Communist forces took control of the countryside and strangled Phnom Penh into submission.

The Communist Royal Government of National Union of Kampuchea (GRUNK), led by Khieu Samphan, was established and immediately began the radical transformation of Cambodian life. Within a week of its victory, the new government ordered the forced exodus of Phnom Penh's population to the rural areas, including those who had lived in the cities their entire lives and had never farmed. Within a few days the capital was deserted except for a few soldiers stationed as guards. Thousands of persons were reported to have died in the evacuation. The new regime desired to weaken potential opposition by breaking up families, groups, and "spy networks."

It was not until 1977 that the Communist party of Cambodia was brought out in the open and it was revealed that Pol Pot (previously known as Saloth Sar) was the dominant force in the new Communist government. As premier and party secretary-general he was more powerful than Khieu Samphan, who occupied the ceremonial role of president. In the years following the Communist takeover information on political activities in Cambodia remained scarce. Officials and journalists were restricted. The borders were closed, so that only a trickle of ref-

---

[12] Ibid., p. 481.
[13] Peter A. Poole, "Cambodia 1975: The Grunk Regime," *Asian Survey*, 16(1) (January, 1976), 23.

ugees succeeded in escaping. These refugees, many of whom did not have political information beyond their village borders, were unanimously condemnatory of the repressive organization (*angka*) which they claimed ran the countryside.

On Christmas Day 1978, a Vietnamese-led invasion of Cambodia succeeded in overthrowing Pol Pot's regime and installing as president Heng Samrin, an unknown former Khmer Rouge division commander who had sought refuge in Vietnam. Pol Pot's Democratic Cambodia gave way to Heng Samrin's Peoples'Republic of Cambodia. With remarkable speed, the Vietnamese and Cambodian troops took Phnom Penh on 7 January and forced the Khmer Rouge to flee to the mountains in the West.

The new puppet government promised to undo the most onerous policies of the previous government. Heng Samrin announced that people could return to their native homes. Indeed, by 1980 Phnom Penh slowly began to be repopulated. A market system developed, and running water and electricity were made available. The draconian marriage and family restrictions were ended, the forced collectives abolished, and Buddhism was allowed to be practiced.

Despite these important reforms, the new government faced severe problems. The Cambodians disliked and distrusted the Vietnamese officials and troops (about 200,000 occupation soldiers). The historical enmity between these two societies remained intact. In addition, there was a total administrative vacuum caused by the decimation of virtually all highly trained and educated Cambodians.

The new government was also faced with a famine best described as a holocaust. At least one million Cambodians starved to death in 1978–1980 and the prospects for improvement during the next few years appeared poor. Rice seeds were in short supply, and the continued fighting between the Heng Samrin and Khmer Rouge forces and their "scorched earth" policies disrupted the harvest of what little rice was planted. Farmers were in such a weakened condition physically that they could not adequately care for the crops.

International refugee agencies were mobilized to bring food, and although thousands of people were saved from starvation, the effort was only partially successful. One major problem was that the Heng Samrin regime would not allow food to be distributed in areas controlled by the Khmer Rouge. Evidence of hoarding, favoritism, and corruption in Cambodia came to light, thus discouraging aid agencies. In general, there was too little food aid, too late.

The United Nations continued to confer international recognition on the Pol Pot regime despite the fact that the Khmer Rouge controlled about two percent of the population. The irony was especially pungent since the United States and other nations who voted with the majority, also branded Pol Pot as the world's worst violator of human rights. The Carter administration's vote for Pol Pot was based on the view that the Heng Samrin government had no "superior claim" to the seat and was an aggressor nation. The vote against the Vietnamese-backed Heng Samrin regime also reflected the desire to strengthen ties with China and to indicate displeasure with the increasing Soviet role in Southeast Asia.

If Cambodia had not been drawn into the Indochina War and not subsequently suffered from war devastation, genocide from a tyrannical regime, famine, and the fleeing of thousands seeking food and freedom, the 1980 population was estimated to have been almost ten million. Instead, the total population in 1980 was about five million. Few societies have sustained such tremendous losses.

By 1986 two governments were involved in running the nation's affairs. Heng Samrin's government (People's Republic of Kampuchea—PRK) controls the cities and the bulk of the countryside with the aid of about 150,000 Vietnamese soldiers and advisers. Other than the Soviet Union and its close allies, few nations recognize the Heng Samrin administration as the legitimate government despite its clear control over virtually all aspects of life in Cambodia.

The second "government" consists of a coalition of forces (Coalition Government of Democratic Kampuchea—CGDK) opposing the government of the PRK. The three factions within the coalition are disparate groups which in the past were enemies and are now "united" solely in their opposition to the Vietnamese sponsored regime in Phnom Penh. The Democratic Kampuchea (Khmer Rouge) faction is the largest and is headed by Khieu Sampan, the vice president of the coalition. The military arm of the Khmer Rouge comprises some 45,000 soldiers presumably led by Pol Pot, the person responsible for the policy of genocide when he was the leader of Cambodia from 1975 to 1979. Although information from within Cambodia has been scarce, it is believed that this faction has very little support, if any, among the Cambodians outside of a small controlled area in Western Cambodia.

The second faction is the Khmer People's National Liberation Front (KPNLF), an anti-Communist, right-wing group with about 15,000 troops under the leadership of Son Sann. Son Sann, who held numerous positions in former Cambodian administrations, is prime minister of the coalition. He is strongly supported by the non-Communist ASEAN states and has enjoyed the support of the largest group of refugees living in the border areas between Thailand and Cambodia.

Prince Norodom Sihanouk, the president of the coalition, leads the third and smallest faction. He was named president largely because of his international fame. His numerous "resignations" reflect the ambivalent feelings he has towards his coalition partners, especially the Khmer Rouge, who were responsible for the deaths of his family members as well as millions of Cambodians. His major goal to oust the Vietnamese from Cambodia by whatever means is necessary has brought him together with those he loathes. Sihanouk believes that the Vietnamese have systematically destroyed Cambodian culture and must be removed before the Cambodians cease to exist.

The presence of two non-Communist factions in the coalition has made it easier for foreign nations to recognize and grant diplomatic relations to the Coalition Government of Democratic Kampuchea. The major arguments in support of recognition of the coalition are that the People's Republic of Kampuchea came to power through aggression and the regime is a puppet of the Soviet Union and poses a threat to the security of Thailand. The Vietnamese, on the other hand, argue that only they can protect Cambodia from the return of the Khmer Rouge and the eventual hegemony of the Chinese in Southeast Asia. From the Vietnamese point of view, the Chinese have been the principal supporters of the Khmer Rouge because of China's desire to destabilize Vietnam, to offset rising Soviet influence in Southeast Asia, and to dominate the region.

By the mid 1980s Vietnamese control over Cambodia appeared irreversible. The major prospect was continuation of the status quo with the Cambodian people continuing to be the victims of both external and internal forces.

LAOS

The contemporary history of Laos is replete with crises and seemingly insoluble problems. Laos might best be described as a quasi-nation that emerged from the doodlings on maps by the European colonialists rather than from a sense of territoriality and nationhood among a united people. In the past 30 years, the Laotians have witnessed constant warfare among contending factions within the country as well as among external powers, namely the United States and Vietnam, both of whom have used Laos as a battlefield for their self-serving purposes. The Communist government which took power in 1975 faced extraordinary problems: relocating the fully one-third of the nation's populace that had become refugees during the war, uniting the various ethnic groups that had fought each other for decades, decreasing the huge gap between the urban rich and the rural poor, educating a citizenry that is overwhelmingly illiterate, and protecting the nation's sovereignty against the encroachments of its neighbors, Vietnam and Thailand, and the major powers, the United States, the Soviet Union, and China (which borders Laos on the north).

The present crises in Laos are partially a prolongation of centuries-old problems, when ancient Lan Xang, the "kingdom of a million elephants," was a battleground for the expansionism of neighboring states. It was not until the 14th century that a semblance of national unity emerged. However, dynastic quarrels in the 18th century undermined this unity and the area was divided into the kingdom of Luang Prabang in the north, Champassak in the south, and Vientiane in the central area.

Both Vietnam and Thailand periodically plundered Laos until the French colonized the area, from the late 1880s until the end of World War II. The French claim of suzerainty in 1899 brought Laos into a single political unit and forced the withdrawal of "Siam." French rule did little to modernize or integrate the nation. On the contrary, because a small group of elite Laotian families were allowed to consolidate their positions of power, the Laotians emerged from colonial rule more divided, isolated, and stagnated than ever.

From 1941 to 1945 the Japanese ruled Laos, although the Vichy French continued to administer many of the governmental affairs. At the end of the war in 1945, Prince Phetsarath, the premier of the Luang Prabang kingdom, proclaimed the reunification of Laos. However, the king of Luang Prabang negated the proclamation and the French recaptured Vientiane, the administrative capital, in 1946. Prince Phetsarath then formed the Lao-Issara (Free Lao), which was led by himself and his brother, Prince Souvanna Phouma, and his half-brother Prince Souphanouvong. The Lao-Issara, which established a government in Bangkok, Thailand, became the forerunner and nucleus of the pro-Communist, anti-French nationalist Neo Lao Hak Sat (NLHS) patriotic front.

Prince Souphanouvong broke with his brother and joined the NLHS in the Vietminh-held territories in Vietnam. By 1953 the front's military force, known as the Pathet Lao, seized control of the nation's northeastern provinces. At the same time, France accorded increasing self-government to Laos. The Geneva Conference in 1954 served to confer complete independence on Laos and to mediate between the left-wing NLHS and the rightists.

The aftermath of the Geneva Conference was a period of disarray as the competing sides vied for control of the populace and the countryside. In November 1957 the neutralists and Prince Souvanna Phouma, with backing from the United States, set up a government of national union with cabinet posts for the leftists and rightists. Special elections were held the following year, as called for in the Geneva Agreements. The NLHS candidates won a majority of the seats, an outcome deemed intolerable by Souvanna Phouma's government and United States diplomats. To overturn the results of the election and to reverse the apparent trend toward a Communist government, the United States, principally through the Central Intelligence Agency, began its massive support of right-wing military officials. For the next five years, Laos was governed by right-wing regimes that excluded NLHS representation. In 1960 Souphanouvong and other NLHS leaders were jailed. Numerous coups d'etat took place during this period as anti-Communist leaders jockeyed for power. The major beneficiary of the governmental chaos, however, was the NLHS movement, which continued to expand its sphere of control and which received increasing military supplies and support from the Soviet Union.

The Second Geneva Conference was called in 1961 with neutralist Souvanna Phouma, leftist Souphanouvong, and rightist Boun Oum agreeing on coalition rule. The United States reversed its previous support of right-wing rule and supported Souvanna Phouma's appointment as prime minister. Ministerial positions were divided among the left- and right-wing groups. However, the coalition succumbed almost immediately as factions maneuvered for power. The NLHS broke off from the coalition and Souvanna Phouma's government became a virtual client state of the United States.

The escalation of the Vietnam War changed the nature of the struggle between the NLHS and Royal Lao government forces. Hanoi's interest in Laos increased as the need for sanctuaries from United States bombing missions became paramount. Laos was swept up in the war as Hanoi, in violation of the Geneva Agreements, escalated its presence in the northeastern provinces, and as America, also in violation of the agreements, began its secret bombing missions in 1964. In the following years, the landlocked nation of 3,000,000 persons, representing dozens of ethnic groups, became one of the most heavily bombed countries in history, as some 2.5 million tons of bombs were dropped between 1964 and 1972. The U.S. Central Intelligence Agency trained and supplied hill peoples, clandestinely introduced military advisors, and used the Agency for International Development as a front for intelligence and training purposes. Laos became the battleground for a neighboring war fought by surrogate powers.

The 1973 Laos Peace Accords came about as the Vietnam War was brought to a close. The accords called for cessation of bombing, termination of foreign-supported forces, removal of all foreign troops, and establishment of a Provisional Government of National Unity (PGNU). At the time of the signing of the peace accords the NLHS controlled about three-fourths of the land area and one-half of the population. Both sides were allowed to preserve their own zones of temporary control until elections were arranged.

On 14 September 1973 a protocol was signed calling for Prince Souvanna Phouma to head the provisional government, with ministers representing all sides. The principle of unanimity was adopted for all governmental decisions. This third attempt at coalition rule was no more successful than its predecessors.

In December 1975 the Lao Communists dissolved the PGNU, abolished the 622-year-old monarchy, and established the Lao People's Democratic Republic. The change in government was preceded by the Communist victories in Vietnam and Cambodia and by pro-Communist demonstrations throughout Laos. The rightist ministers fled one by one, following threats to their lives by demonstrators. Their power bases were taken over by the pro-Communist forces, until eventually all power was in the hands of the Communists. Souvanna Phouma resigned and Kaysone Phomvihan, the Communist party secretary, became the new prime minister. Kaysone Phomvihan analyzed the Communist victory as follows:

> Under the clear-sighted leadership of the Lao People's Revolutionary Party and with great assistance from the people in the liberated areas, our people in the areas controlled by the United States and its lackeys, unable to tolerate living as slaves any longer, have resolutely mutinied and fought dauntlessly and vigorously and have successfully overthrown the dominating yoke of U.S. neocolonialism, compelling the reactionary chieftains to flee and causing their forces to collapse, and compelling the U.S. imperialists to dissolve the U.S. AID organization. . . [14]

A Supreme People's Council was set up, with Prince Souphanouvong as president. In that position he has functioned as chief of state, while Kaysone Phomvihan, virtually unknown to all but a handful of the Communist leadership before 1975, assumed political and administrative control of the republic.

The Communist victory foreshadows changes of great magnitude in Lao politics. For centuries the nation has been dominated by a small group of wealthy families who combined great political and economic influence. Those families have fled to Thailand, Europe, or the United States; or if they remain, have

---

[14] Quoted in MacAlister, Brown, and Joseph J. Zasloff, "Laos in 1975: People's Democratic Revolution Lao Style," *Asian Survey,* 16(2) (February, 1976), 193–194.

undergone "reeducation" programs to rid them of their "bourgeois mentality." The withdrawal of American forces from Indochina could also have far-reaching implications for the future of the area. Two leading scholars of contemporary Laos have stated:

> With United States power withdrawn from neighboring Indochina, the Pathet Lao has capitalized upon the repugnance felt by a small articulate Lao political public towards the self-serving and corrupt practices of entrenched, traditionally powerful right-wing families, and effectively played upon nationalist pride, especially among students, which resented U.S. manipulation and domination of Laos over the past two decades.[15]

To reach their goals of an independent and socialist state, the Laotian government launched a number of ambitious programs. Farms were collectivized and resource distribution taken over by the state. A serious drought in 1976 and 1977 undermined the regime's goal of self-sufficiency in food. In addition, the government's systematic expunging of civil servants and technocrats connected to the former administration left a leadership vacuum that seriously eroded the government's ability to administer and implement new programs. An estimated 300,000 persons, many among the most educated in the country, have fled to Thailand following the change in government.

In the two years following the Communist victory, pockets of resistance have harassed the new government. Hmong (Meo) hill tribesmen, who were former members of General Vang Pao's CIA-supported army, engaged in guerrilla insurgency. Some 20,000 former government civilian and military officials who remained incarcerated in "reeducation" centers as well as the refugees to Thailand constituted evidence of large-scale discontent.

In 1979 the leaders of Laos and Vietnam signed a joint revolutionary declaration, a Treaty of Friendship and Cooperation, granting approval to Vietnam to maintain an estimated 40,000 troops in Laos. China's role in Laos declined in rough correspondence to Vietnam's increased role. China accused Vietnam of creating an Indochinese federation dominated by the Vietnamese and withdrew its aid from numerous development pro-

---

[15] Ibid., p. 194.

jects. Laotian authorities responded by accusing China of supporting dissident Hmong as well as refugees for guerrilla operations against the Laotian Communist government. The future of Laos was not inextricably linked to the policies of the Soviet Union, Vietnam, China, and Thailand. The United States, formerly the dominant power in Laos, was relegated to a peripheral role. In 1985, after the United States and Laos met regarding American soldiers missing-in-action, several joint expeditions were planned to search for bodies.

The Soviet Union, with some 2,000 advisers and $50 million in annual aid, was the primary superpower in Laos, while Vietnam with 40,000 troops and 5,000 advisers became the dominant regional power. The problems of poverty, repression against ethnic minorities, shortage of trained manpower due to the refugee flow into Thailand, poor infrastructure, administrative inefficiency, the rigidity of the Soviet advisers, and the lack of port facilities all continued in the 1980s. Laos remained a quasi-nation with only partial control over its own destiny.

BURMA

Burma's postindependence search for *pyidawtha*, a peaceful, happy, and prosperous country, has not yet been achieved. Instead, postwar Burma has been characterized by ethnic disunity, economic stagnation, and political instability. The overriding purpose of the various governments of independent Burma has been to shape a national state, sovereign and unified, yet, from the earlier period of independence onwards, numerous factors have inhibited the attainment of this purpose.

The Burmese struggle for independence from the British culminated on 4 January 1948, following several years of demonstrations and often violent opposition to colonial rule. The struggle was led by the Thankin movement, a group of anti-British nationalists headed by Aung San, a fiery nationalist who received training in Japan. Initially, the Thankin movement received support from the Japanese during the occupation period, but subsequently the movement turned against the Japanese as their occupation became increasingly repressive.

The Thankin movement served as the core for the Anti-Fascist People's Freedom League (AFPFL), a united front group opposed to the Japanese. AFPFL forces cooperated with the British to oust the Japanese and then turned against the British in the struggle for independence. AFPFL negotiated independence and formed the first parliamentary government in 1948 under the leadership of U Nu.

The period 1948 to 1958 was known as the time of troubles. The well organized minority ethnic groups opposed the government's move toward a national state and, instead, supported the establishment of autonomous states for each group. The Shans and Karens, in particular, rose against the central authorities, precipitating a struggle that came close to becoming a full-scale civil war. The minority groups were supported by Communist insurgents or, in the case of the Shan rebels, by Chiang Kai-shek's Koumingtang army.

The second major postindependence problem concerned the poorly trained civil service which was not able to carry out government programs effectively. U Nu's government had proclaimed a socialist policy which required a high degree of centralized administration. The Burmese bureaucracy floundered, causing severe political and economic disturbances. For example, the price of rice constantly decreased, thereby undermining Burma's primary source of foreign capital. Moreover, administrative corruption had become rampant.

By 1958 the political condition of Burma was so chaotic that U Nu voluntarily turned over the functioning of the government to the military, led by General Ne Win. The caretaker government succeeded in stabilizing the cost of living and controlling the black market. Exports were increased and corruption was at least temporarily halted. Ne Win's government reorganized the bureaucracy to make it more efficient and restored a semblance of law and order.

> [General] Ne Win and his civilian and military officers did more than reestablish stability in a newly independent country; they provided a demonstration lesson in non-bureaucratic efficiency and puritanical incorruptability; they also provided a sufficiently different, if not unique, example of military and civilian support for nationalist ideals and a commitment to democratic processes and goals.[16]

[16] Frank Trager, *Burma: From Kingdom to Republic* (New York: Praeger, 1966), p. 189.

Despite the success of the caretaker government in a number of areas, the electorate in 1960 chose to return to U Nu for leadership. However, U Nu's government proved to be ineffective. Corruption returned and uprising increased among the ethnic minorities that opposed U Nu's plan to make Buddhism the state religion. The military believed that U Nu's federation plan, designed to provide the hill groups with more autonomy, would bring about increased disunity and potential for internal armed conflict. Indeed, secession of the Shans appeared imminent.

U Nu, although very popular with the Burmese people, was not able to control the economy. His concerns appeared to be other-worldly rather than pragmatic. He emphasized making Buddhism the state religion, and properly propitiating *nats* (animistic spirits) to improve the welfare of the people. The military perceived the civilian government of U Nu to be weak, lacking in unity, and dependent upon Western-style political institutions that were incompatible with Burmese culture. Finally, the military believed that their own power was being reduced under U Nu's leadership.

The outcome of these problems was a military coup d'etat on 2 March 1962, led by Ne Win. The seizure of power, which was rapid, nonviolent, and without major challenge, began an era of military rule which continues at the present time. Ne Win disbanded the Western-style parliament, banned political parties, and restricted civil liberties. He founded the Burmese Revolutionary Council, consisting of 17 military leaders dominated by the army, which set forth a program of radical economic and political policies called the Burmese Way to Socialism. The military program of socialism included the nationalization of major industries, schools, rice mills, small and large businesses, and financial institutions. The Burmese Way to Socialism became a political-ideological end justifying any governmental means. Parliamentary democracy was rejected as incompatible with the aims of the new state. Instead, the Revolutionary Council conferred all legislative, executive, and judicial powers on General Ne Win.

On balance, the objectives of Ne Win's Burmese Way to Socialism were more political than economic. He was determined to prevent the prospective breakup of the Union of Burma into separate and autonomous states. His program of centralized state monopoly of the means of production was at least partially designed to assure central control over a united Burma. The socialist program also included the goal of Burmanization of the economy; that is, the elimination of Indian and Chinese middlemen in the commercial sphere by substituting government agencies.

To mobilize support for the socialist program, Ne Win established the Burmese Socialist Program party (BSPP). The BSPP was intended to reach down to the village level along hierarchical lines, but with all power centered at the military-dominated top echelon of the party. The mass base of the party was to be the peasantry, working through peasants' and workers' councils that were established throughout the country but were subordinate to the military. The party's main function was to legitimize army rule and to act as a channel for communicating directives from the top down.

Ne Win's government moved toward a neutralist foreign policy that took the form of isolationism. The government refused foreign aid, abrogated treaties, and restricted the flow of tourists. Foreign capital was not welcomed. Burma's nonalignment was part of a program to Burmanize the economy and culture of the country. By rejecting all forms of Westernization, Burma, unique in Southeast Asia, has not accepted or encouraged the Western model of development.

In January 1974 Burma became the Socialist Republic of the Union of Burma, after the new socialist constitution had been passed by the electorate. The constitution conferred all power onto the Burmese Socialist Program party, thus assuring Ne Win continued power. Although Ne Win had discarded his military uniform in 1971 and hence became the "civilian" president of the new government, the military continued to be the dominant political force.

Theoretically, power was to be in the hands of the unicameral Pyithu Hluttaw (People's Assembly), but in practice power resides in the Council of State, a small group within the Hluttaw. The members of the former Revolutionary Council became members of the Council of State and elected U Ne Win as chairman. As chairman, Ne Win became the president of the Socialist Republic. The economic situation continued to deteriorate with a rise in inflation and unemployment and the increasing dominance of the black market as the major mechanism for the allocation of resources. Rice exports continued to drop. The abrupt imposition in 1965 of state control over virtually all aspects of the retail distribution of goods and services had a catastrophic effect on industrial and agricultural production. The economic disintegration resulted in an undercurrent of opposition to Ne Win's government. In December 1974, for example, Burmese university students protested against the government's decision not to bury former United Nations Secretary-General U Thant in a place of honor. The massive protest was used as a pretext for demonstration against "one-party dictatorship" and "disastrous economic policies."

During its first decade the Burma Socialist Program party (BSPP) ruled with little internal or external opposition. The monolithic unity was shattered in 1976, however, when factions emerged in the party. The principal problem was the country's serious economic decay. The Third Party Congress of the BSPP denounced the policies of the Second Congress by showing that production had fallen and corruption flourished. Moreover, the BSPP secretary general alleged that personality cults and authoritarianism had developed within the party. The prime minister, U Sein Win, was forced to resign, but U Ne Win continued his dictatorial rule. The Third Congress agreed to retain its doctrinaire socialist economic policies despite the fact that the decade between 1966 and 1976 averaged an annual growth rate of at best 2.5 percent as against a population growth of 2.2 percent.

Ne Win stepped down as president in 1981 but retained his more powerful position as head of the Burma Socialist Program party. In that position he was able to continue his dominance over political and economic policymaking. Although he claimed credit for a short lived period of economic rejuvenation in the late 1970s, the economy returned to stagnation in the 1980s.

In 1986 martial law continued. Universities and schools were closed for months at a time to discourage political demonstrations. Despite the government's highly publicized plan to end corruption and improve bureaucratic efficiency, the economy remained in disarray. Production continued below normal. Insurgency in the north and east of Burma forced the military government to place a large portion of its budget into counterinsurgency activities. The government faced problems stemming from the failures of its military past—corruption, the gap between the officials and the masses, lack of resources and goods, and intense dissatisfaction with the regime on the part of students, intellectuals and minority groups, an aging leadership, widespread insurgency, and the absence of a succession formula.

THE PHILIPPINES

The Philippines' search for identity in the postwar era differed from the other Southeast Asian nations' because of its unique relationship to Western colonialism. The Philippines is the only country in Southeast Asia that was colonized before widespread indigenous institutions had been established within the elite culture. Spanish culture was thrust upon the Filipinos in the 16th century and remains today an important force in the lives of the people. The American period, from 1900 to 1946, further intensified the impact of Westernization and the ambiguities Filipinos felt about their heritage.

Claro Recto, a former senator in the Philippines, described the unique character of the nation's search for identity:

> Our peculiar situation has been heightened by the unique circumstances in which we attained our independence. The other liberated Asian nations have been spared the ambiguities under which we labor; they faced issues that were clear cut; blood and tears, exploitation and subjugation, the centuries of enmity divided the Indonesians from the Dutch, the Indians and Burmese from the British, the Vietnamese from the French; and their nationalist victories were not diluted by sentiments of gratitude, or by regrets, doubts, and apprehensions.[17]

The Philippines is the most Westernized of all Southeast Asian nations. The fact that over 90 percent of the population is Christian reflects an important legacy of Spanish rule. The Spanish custom of *compadrazgo* (joint parenthood) has served as

----

[17] Quoted in David Wurfel, "The Philippines," in Roger Smith, ed., *Southeast Asia, Documents of Political Development and Change* (Ithaca, New York: Cornell University Press, 1974), p. 525.

a basis for Filipino political groupings and for the superior-subordinate relationships that pervade the entire society. Moreover, the Spanish established the basic political units at the rural level and set up a system of taxation and tributes known as the *encomianda*, which provided revenue to deserving Spaniards in return for protection. The *encomianda* system served as a model for the landlord system which eventually became an important element in the political and economic life of the Filipinos.

America took over Philippine colonization following the war with Spain. Initially, Filipinos supported the United States against the Spanish, but then fought bitterly against the United States when the latter invaded the country. The motivations for American intervention included the need for a base for the lucrative China trade; the desire for natural resources, especially sugar and tropical fruits; and establishment of a bulwark of Western civilization. President William Taft referred to "the responsibility to be a blessing to the people of these islands," while President McKinley spoke about the need to "uplift and civilize and Christianize" the Filipinos.

The Americanization of the Philippines came about quickly as missionaries, teachers, government officials, and businessmen arrived. The Philippine economy became integrated into the American economy. Massive programs to build infrastructure, education, and health facilities were established by the American administrators. Steps were taken to Filipinize the civil service. For elite groups in particular, the American presence was vital for the economic modernization of the country. The American policy was clearly predicated on the notion that if the United States could promote prosperity, social order, education, and civil liberties—and if all this could be linked to the continuation of American sovereignty—the Filipinos might themselves choose to retain a close association with the Americans. Such an association was cultivated by both sides. President Ferdinand Marcos has written:

> . . . America made an honest attempt to train the Filipinos for self-government, to raise the level of education, and to improve the health and physical well-being of our people. . . . During the American period in our history, we inherited the American ideals

of democracy. These ideals were not merely grafted but were assimilated by Philippine democracy.[18]

The American desire to retain sovereignty over the Philippines was not universally accepted by all American or all Filipino policy-makers. There was much ambivalence on both sides about the most effective relationship. Eventually the movement toward independence became inexorable as Filipinization of the civil service continued. The Japanese interregnum initially halted the movement but subsequently strengthened the nationalist sentiments of the Filipinos. The Huk movement (*Hukbo ng Bayan Laban Sa Hapon*: People's Army to Fight the Japanese), for example, which was formed shortly after the Japanese invaded, became a pronationalist, anti-American guerrilla resistance force that played an important political role after World War II.

Philippine independence was proclaimed 4 July 1946, with great fanfare and some discontent with American demands. The United States demanded that the Philippines change its constitution so as to give Americans equal opportunity with Filipinos in the exploitation of natural resources.[19]. The peso was tied to the dollar and free-trade agreements between the two countries were instituted. The Philippines could not then be considered truly independent since its economy was closely tied to that of the United States. Major political disputes arose between those who had collaborated with the Japanese and those who had not, although no punishment of enemy collaborators ever took place. The ruling elites who desired to retain their economic dominance cooperated with the Americans and were able to stay in power.

Postwar Philippines was characterized by rampant corruption largely stemming from the influx of huge amounts of American aid and the patron-client ties that pervaded the country. These ties are personal in nature and require the exchange of gifts and the mobilizing of subordinates by superiors. The major institutions of the political system were based on the American model with more freedom of speech and the press than in any other

[18] Ibid., p. 528.
[19] Ibid., p. 569.

Southeast Asian nation. A two-party system evolved and the presidency of the Philippines fluctuated from one party to another until 1969, when Ferdinand Marcos became the first president to be reelected. There were few if any ideological differences between the two parties. Instead, politics revolved around support of personalities rather than ideas.

The most famous of the postindependence presidents was Ramon Magsaysay, a former guerrilla leader, who had been appointed defense secretary in 1950. When Magsaysay became president in 1953, he put forth a number of reform programs designed to alleviate the poverty of the Filipino masses. His intentions were excellent, but the results were limited largely because of an ineffective bureaucracy and an obstructionist Senate, whose wealthy members opposed economic reform. Magsaysay's major achievement was to suppress the Huk rebellion, which threatened the nation's established order. His death in a 1957 air crash was a stunning blow to reform-minded Filipinos.

Ferdinand Marcos was elected president in 1965 and reelected in 1969. He had been a Liberal party member, but, like many political leaders, changed parties at the last minute when President Macapagal, a Liberal, chose to run again in 1965. Marcos' switch to the Nationalist party is indicative of the fluid, non-ideological nature of the two major parties. Marcos put forth a comprehensive development program with emphasis on road building and other public works. His goals were ambitious but the results were minimal because the Congress refused to vote the needed tax increases to finance his projects. Although Marcos could boast of an improved economic climate for both industry and agriculture, the political system was still beset by the problems of graft, corruption, and the dominance of a few fabulously wealthy families who controlled the Senate and much of the bureaucracy.

The inability (or refusal) of the government to enact agrarian reform programs brought about a revival of the Huks who proceeded to carry out selected acts of violence against landlords and certain officials. The Huks managed to attract a wide measure of public approval. Adding to the government's problems was the rapid rise in crime in Manila and the formation of private armies which protected wealthy elite families.

The economic and social instability during Marcos' first term did not bode well for his reelection chances. The vast disparity between the living conditions of the few rich and the many poor exacerbated the alienation and anger of the peasantry. The election campaign was devoid of substantive issues and revolved around which candidate was less corrupt. Shortly before the election Marcos provided $500 "for local development projects" to some 20,000 village chiefs. His election victory in 1969 was considered to have been "bought."

Marcos proclaimed martial law in September 1972, thereby ending the longest period of democratic rule in modern Southeast Asia. The proclamation abrogated the constitution and provided full powers to Marcos. He imprisoned numerous members of the political opposition, including several prominent senators such as Benigno Aquino, the leader of the Liberal party. The press was severely censored and civil liberties were curtailed.

The declaration of martial law came as a surprise to many who believed the democratic processes had been institutionalized. The Philippines was perceived to be relatively free of peasant revolutionary fervor, the military remained weak and incapable of mobilizing support, and the economic growth rate was considered satisfactory.

At the same time, however, the country was suffering from a severe law-and-order problem. Private armies clashed, guns were available to everyone, and crime was rampant. A large number of political leaders at every level of society were engaged in corrupt political behavior. Philippine society was characterized by a grossly unequal distribution of wealth and land. An ingrown elite group dominated the economic and political sectors of society. In addition, the country was plagued by an increasingly bitter and intense civil war in the southern islands between Muslim farmers and Christians who were settling in the area.

If these conditions were the general context for the declaration of martial law, the precipitant was the fact that Marcos was constitutionally barred from seeking a third term as president and desired to retain his power. Prior to the imposition of martial law, he called a constitutional convention in 1971 which would have changed the political order from a presidential to a parliamentary system. The new constitution allowed the president to impose martial law "in cases of invasion, insurrection or rebellion or imminent danger thereof."[20] Marcos claimed his declaration was justified on the basis of a growing revolutionary movement and the struggle for liberation among Muslims in the southern islands, which he said threatened the security of the country.

Marcos planned to become prime minister under a parliamentary system, thereby circumventing the constitutional provision prohibiting three terms of office as president. After martial law was proclaimed in September 1972, the constitutional convention ratified a provision giving Marcos complete power during the transitional period before parliamentary government was implemented. Moreover, he was given power to decide when the next election should be held. The declaration of martial law was supported by "people's assemblies" that had been established in every village. The lack of a secret ballot and the surveillance of the representatives to the assemblies by government officials raised questions about the validity of the overwhelming majority vote accorded Marcos. In a referendum in July 1973, 91 percent of the voters agreed to support indefinite continuation of martial law. Marcos was further supported when the Supreme Court declared that his proclamation of martial law had been legal, because of the necessity to resolve the national emergency caused by revolutionary activity in the country.

In October 1976, Marcos submitted a series of constitutional amendments to the voters, designed to enhance his authority. These amendments provided for an interim assembly with Marcos as president. He would continue to hold legislative and executive powers and was provided with "emergency" powers, valid even after martial law was lifted. The referendum which specifically asked voters if martial law should continue, received an 87.6 percent favorable vote.

Again, in April 1978, Filipinos were allowed to vote, this time for the Interim National Assembly. Marcos' New Society movement slate won overwhelmingly in the nation and captured every seat in Manila. The most famous opposition candidate, former Senator Benigno S. Aquino, campaigned from his jail cell where he had been sentenced to death by martial-law courts.

[20] Ibid., p. 580.

The elections for 165 seats in the 200-member Interim National Assembly were the first since martial law was proclaimed in 1972. The other 35 seats went to 20 cabinet officials appointed by Marcos and to representatives of youth, labor, and other sectors of the population.

Oppositionists were united in their view that election of an Interim National Assembly had not brought the nation closer to normalization. Because the elections were fraudulently carried out, critics questioned the very legitimacy of the assembly. Moreover, Marcos exerted complete control over the assembly. The assembly could not pass no-confidence votes against the government; could not repeal decrees promulgated earlier by the president; could not initiate bills unless recommended by the cabinet; and the president could veto the assembly's legislation.

Following the declaration of martial law Marcos declared a New Society designed to solve the major problems of the Philippines. Initially, many Filipinos had high hopes for the new regime. Marcos moved effectively to disband the private armies of the wealthy landlords and to confiscate guns in order to curtail the rapidly rising crime rate. He moved to create a more efficient government, free from the landlord-dominated Congress that heretofore had blocked legislation designed to aid the rural areas. After years of armed struggle, Marcos signed a ceasefire in 1975 with the Moro National Liberation Front (MNLF), bringing the war to a halt, at least temporarily.

However, the crime rate only temporarily declined and the government appeared unable to control the high inflationary rate and economic stagnation that afflicted not only the Philippines but most of Southeast Asia. Moreover, the ceasefire agreement was not honored. Instead, the war between government forces and the MNLF in the south became an international situation when Libya provided aid to the insurgents. Marcos attempted to set up an "autonomous region" in Muslim-controlled areas, but his plan was rejected by the MNLF. By 1980 the rebellion was no closer to settlement than in previous years.

The New Society leader proclaimed his desire to facilitate land reform programs. Marcos was no longer dependent upon the landlord-based political parties and Congress. He could take strong measures against bureaucrats and judges whose decisions had sabotaged land reform programs. Marcos declared that "the land reform program is the only gauge for the success or failure of the New Society. If land reform fails, there is no New Society." However, Marcos' verbal commitment to land reform entailed severe costs that thus far have kept the program from full implementation. The Philippines remains today a society with some of the highest tenancy and social inequality rates in the world. Marcos attempted to satisfy tenant farmers as well as landlords: to institute a consensus politics that tried to implement land reform without undermining the general power structure of the society. However, the peasantry was not able to organize themselves in order to articulate their interests. The result of his policies, then, was a continuation of the status quo which benefitted landlords and postponed the total restructuring of the nation's political and economic order.

President Marcos moved resolutely and with great agility to counter the forces against him. By using his powers over the media, his capacity to mobilize influential supporters and to coopt his opposition, and his skill in carrying out surprise moves, Marcos retained his enormous influence over every facet of Philippine political life.

At the end of 1980 Marcos announced that martial law would end in January 1981 and that elections for a new parliament would follow. In January 1981, he lifted several of the more onerous features of martial law including the use of military tribunals in civilian cases, but his decrees remained in force. Violations of human rights such as imprisonment of political dissidents, torture of detainees, "salvaging" (extra-judicial executions), and arbitrary terror against political opponents continued even after the lifting of martial law.

The assassination of Senator Aquino in August 1983, and the almost universal belief of Filipinos in the government's complicity, brought forth long suppressed grievances. The return of Aquino to the Philippines was thought to have the potential for reversing the misfortunes of the democratic opposition and uniting them. Intelligent and articulate, Aquino was one of the many opposition leaders the president had imprisoned for more than seven years. He had been sentenced to death by a military court for alleged murder, subversion, and illegal possession of firearms, but he denied these charges, as well as the legitimacy of his trial and conviction by a military tribunal. In 1980 he was allowed to go to the United States for a heart operation, and remained in exile as a research fellow at Harvard. He was shot as he stepped out of the airplane at Manila's airport, seconds after returning home from exile.

The millions of citizens who attended Aquino's funeral turned their grief into anger and protest aimed at President Marcos, his wife Imelda, and the military, whom they held responsible for Aquino's assassination. The view that the president himself had conspired in the murder meant their government had become abusive beyond tolerable limits and that their president was determined to stay in power by any means, including repression. Following the assassination of Aquino, a potential alternative leader for the country, all the economic and political problems of the country took on a new urgency, and Ferdinand and Imelda Marcos were seen as crisis perpetrators rather than problem solvers. Filipinos perceived a government that had lost its once unshakable grip on power, its credibility, and its moral authority.

Rarely in Third World nations have anti-government demonstrations been led by the privileged classes, but in the Philippines, the assassination precipitated mass demonstrations against the government by the educated class and business leaders. As the nation's economy deteriorated, domestic and international groups viewed Marcos, the supreme patron, as no longer able to cope with the crises and meet the needs of his own clientele. The vast majority of Filipinos found that they were not effectively covered in his patron-client system. In a society where patron-client ties predominate, that fact implied the unraveling of the regime's power.

Moreover, the assassination occurred simultaneously with the decline of the president's health, a particularly important variable in a clientelist society. Rumors throughout the Philippines focused on various ailments he was alleged to have, but specifically, systematic lupus erythematosus, a debilitating and fatal disease with periods of remission. In November 1984 the 67 year old president was not seen in public for two weeks. Some of his clientele, sensing his imminent demise, began to feel it necessary to disassociate themselves from him. In the absence of a clear succession mechanism, the uncertainty loosened the unity of the cabinet, resulting in turbulence and tension in the highest echelons of government and at all political and economic levels.

Despite the enormity of the nation's crisis following the assassination, President Marcos moved to defuse tensions and to assure the perpetuation of his rule. After a period of delay and an abortive attempt to appoint an investigation commission composed mostly of known supporters, Marcos established a five-person nonpartisan board, led by Judge Corazon Agrava. The board's majority found that Aquino was slain not by a Communist hireling, as alleged by Marcos and the military, but as a result of a "criminal conspiracy" led by the military, including General Fabian Ver, the armed forces chief of staff, the highest ranking general of the country, and a close friend and cousin of President Marcos. In the minds of many that finding indirectly implicated Marcos because from the beginning most Filipinos never believed that the indicted generals would order the execution of Aquino on their own initiative.

The Agrava Commission report documented what most Filipinos already believed. The case was then sent to the country's *Tanodbayan* (ombudsman), the government's designated prosecuter, who found sufficient cause; so the case went to a special court, appointed by President Marcos to try graft and corruption cases against government officials. General Ver and the other 25 indicted persons took a leave of absence from their positions until the court decided their fate, although Ver continued to live on the grounds of Malacanang, enjoy unlimited access to the president, serve as the president's bodyguard, and direct the National Intelligence and Security Authority. In late 1985 the court found all the defendants innocent, and supported Marcos' claim that the assassination was carried out by a Communist hireling. General Ver was once again named armed forces chief of staff.

Although President Marcos was suffering from severe bad health and political problems during this period, he moved adroitly to sustain his position. His renewed vigor, improved health, and increased presence, beginning in early 1985, revitalized his crumbling clientelist network. He established a constitutional mechanism for succession that would require a prompt election in the event of presidential death or incapacity, and agreement that the vice presidency would be restored in the next presidential election. He allowed the renewal of an opposition press that made the Philippines unique among Third World nations for tolerating criticism of the regime in power.

Most importantly, the 14 May 1984 elections proved to be a

somewhat more successful example of democratic vitality than almost anyone believed possible. In the preceding National Assembly, the opposition had held only 13 of some 200 seats. However, in the contested and relatively open 1984 election, 60 opposition candidates won seats. In spite of a major boycott by certain opposition groups and the memory of fraud in previous elections, 80 percent of the population voted. The results indicated that post-assassination disaffection with Marcos was not necessarily support for radicalism.

In metropolitan-Manila, the one area that was considered well controlled by Marcos forces, the opposition candidates won 15 of 21 seats. The landslide in Manila humiliated the president's wife, Imelda Marcos, the governor of Manila, who was the government party's campaign manager. The president boasted that the election showed the "free and democratic" character of the polity, in contrast to most Third World societies. Opposition candidates focused on the Aquino assassination, corruption and favoritism, the crippling of governmental, business, and judicial institutions, the impoverishment of millions of Filipinos, a growing Communist insurgency, and the government's moral bankruptcy. Although the National Assembly served as a forum for scrutiny of the government, the elected representatives soon found that it continued to be a rubber-stamp institution. President Marcos could still rule by decree, and no significant legislation was passed by the assembly after the election except for the national budget for 1985.

A momentous event in contemporary Philippine politics took place during three extraordinary months from December 1985 through February 1986. Bowing to intense pressure from the United States, wishing to take advantage of better health during a remission of his illness, desiring to end the unceasing attacks on him by the opposition, sensing the disarray of potential opposition candidates, and confident about his capacity to engineer a mandate, Marcos called for "snap elections" to be held on 7 February 1986.

The constitution provided for such a special election upon the resignation of the president, and constitutional experts interpreted that stipulation to mean immediate resignation. In order to be permitted to campaign as presidential incumbent from Malacanang Palace, however, the president submitted a letter of resignation to become effective *after* the election at the time the winner assumed a six-year term. Despite this violation of constitutional procedures, the Marcos appointed Supreme Court validated the elections.

From the moment Marcos announced the election, the key question was whether or not the opposition could unite around a single candidate. Until the final filing day, the answer was unclear. The president had long capitalized on the inability of the opposition to unite, to present a coherent alternative program, and to find a leader who had broad national appeal. The opposition had been able to unite only on its common disdain for Marcos. Because of the highly personalistic nature of Philippine politics, the competing ambitions of potential leaders, and Marcos' superb ability to manipulate and coopt rival forces, the opposition had had a difficult time presenting a serious alternative.

Factionalism among the moderate democratic oppositionists stemmed also from the fact that many of the groups' leaders were former pre-martial law government officials who themselves were distrusted by many Filipinos. There was a generation gap between those older politicians and members of new, more militant "cause-oriented" organizations who viewed the politicians as elitists and has-beens.

Structurally, the opposition suffered from the disintegration of the two-party system, where competition for leadership could more easily be resolved. Instead, many parties and organizations existed, each with ambitious leaders who desired to be the candidate to run against President Marcos. The abundance of parties—United Nationalist Democratic Organization (UNIDO); Liberal party; Nacionalista party; Filipino Democratic Party-Lakas ng Bayan (LDP-Laban); and cause oriented groups such as the New Patriotic Alliance (BAYAN)—meant that no leader stood out as a person behind whom the opposition could rally.

To bring unity to the opposition, the National Convenors' Group, led by Corzaon Aquino (the widow of Senator Benigno Aquino), and former Senator Lorenzo Tanada, the "grand old man" of the opposition, was established to draw up a list of presidential candidates. The list included former senators Jovito Salonga, Jose Diokno, Ramon Mitra, Salvador Laurel, and Eva Estrada Kalaw, Mayor Aquilino Pimental, and the brother of the

slain Aquino, Agapito Aquino. This attempt at bringing co-
herence to the opposition foundered when prominent oppositionists refused to support the group. In particular, Senator
Laurel, as leader of UNIDO, the largest and best organized of
the opposition groups, did not want his front-runner position to
be undermined by a group not under his control. Laurel, who
was proclaimed the presidential candidate of UNIDO, and who
had led the group that had managed to win assembly seats for
the opposition in the May 1984 elections, believed he deserved
the nomination.

Following Marcos' November announcement of snap elections, the once diffident "ordinary housewife" and then martyred widow, 53 year old Corazon "Cory" Aquino, emerged as
the one person all the oppositionists admired. Her genuine
reluctance to lead added to her attraction as a sincere, honest,
and incorruptible candidate, precisely the antithesis of the president, whom the opposition described as corrupt, dishonest, and
unscrupulous. A grassroots ground-swell of support culminated
in the presentation to Aquino of over one-million signatures
from Filipinos urging her to run for the presidency.

Although Aquino did not have direct administrative experience, she had lived politics all her life. Her wealthy grandfather,
father, and brother were congressmen and her other grandfather and an uncle were senators. She was the chief confidant of
her husband Senator Aquino and for the seven years he was
imprisoned by Marcos she acted on his behalf. During the 1984
National Assembly election campaign she proved to be an articulate, vigorous, and effective campaigner for the opposition.

On 3 December 1985 Corazon Aquino announced her can-
didacy. She then met with Senator Laurel, himself a declared
candidate, and fashioned an eleventh-hour agreement whereby
she and Laurel would be the presidential and vice presidential
candidates, respectively, under the banner of Laurel's UNIDO
party. Laurel was promised the position of prime minister in an
Aquino administration. For the first time since martial law was
proclaimed in 1972, the opposition achieved unity.

To preclude a threat to Marcos' one-man rule, the position of
vice president had been abolished when martial law was declared, but was restored in a 1984 constitutional amendment.
For his vice presidential running mate, President Marcos chose

the respected Arturo Tolentino, the former foreign minister, who months before had been fired by Marcos for insubordination. At age 75 Tolentino was not considered a threat to Marcos, and his reputation as an independent thinker balanced Marcos' predilection for sychophants.

President Marcos began the campaign with distinct advantages. His open access to government money during the campaign allowed him to raise officials' salaries, decrease taxes, and lower fuel and utility rates. By the end of the campaign some $500 million from the government treasury was spent to reelect the president. In contrast, the opposition spent $10 million from donations.

Marcos' KBL party organization, indistinguishable from the bureaucracy, was in place throughout the archipelago. Moreover, he mobilized the bureaucracy down to the barangay level, determined what news would be heard on the radio and seen on television, dominated the Commission on Elections (Comelec), the official vote counting organization, and held power over the military who were the guardians of the ballots. He set in motion plans for election fraud if the opposition appeared to gain strength and threaten his presidency.

Marcos' campaign focused on his experience, including his wartime record, in contrast to his opponent's "naivete." He stressed the need for strong male leadership rather than weak female leadership, suggesting that women's place was in the bedroom rather than in the political arena. He stated that Aquino was far from the ideal Filipina who is "gentle, who does not challenge a man, but who keeps her criticisms to herself and teaches her husband only in the bedroom." Marcos claimed that Communists had taken over Aquino's campaign, and that only he could handle the Communist insurgency. He accused Aquino of planning to abrogate the Military Base Agreement with the United States and to dismember the republic by giving away Mindanao. He promised to bring about reform, to revitalize the army, and to keep the United States as the nation's primary ally.

Imelda Marcos actively campaigned on behalf of her husband, stressing that she rather than Aquino was the proper woman to lead the country. The first lady noted that Filipinos would not vote for a woman who wore no lipstick and did not polish her nails. She noted that her party "would win the vote of homosexuals, most of them engaged in the beauty business, because the administration being offered by Aquino is less fashion-conscious."

Candidate Aquino, realizing that she could not match the president in financial or organizational strength, proclaimed a "people's campaign." In contrast to Marcos' well-planned rallies with entertainment from famous Philippine stars, Aquino's and Laurel's campaign rallies were last minute, underfunded, and unpublicized in the major newspapers. Despite these drawbacks the crowds at the rallies grew daily with the majority of supporters wearing yellow, the opposition color ever since the day Senator Aquino came home and was assassinated. Aquino and Laurel campaigned in almost every province, whereas Marcos concentrated on Luzon and Manila because of his poor health.

Aquino's campaign themes emphasized the country's economic chaos which she declared was directly attributable to Marcos. She pointed out that the Philippines was the only Asian economy with a negative growth rate. She pointed out that the nation suffered from double digit inflation, 20 percent unemployment, 40 percent underemployment, a $26 billion deficit, the stashing of huge amounts of wealth in overseas banks by Marcos and his family and friends, severe malnutrition, and the collapse of public health and educational institutions. She promised to end crony capitalism and to dismantle the monopolies.

Whereas her first campaign speeches stressed her "sincerity and honesty" and her empathetic qualities as a fellow "sufferer" under Marcos, her later speeches focused on issues and her program to reform the government. Aquino's speeches became more specific and hard hitting as the campaign progressed. She vilified the president for his corruption and immorality. Specifically, she noted evidence that the president had lied about his role as a hero in World World II and about his several billion dollar fortune in real estate around the world. The former issue arose after investigations of U.S. army documents disclosed that Marcos' claims that he headed a guerrilla resistance unit during the Japanese occupation of the Philippines were "fraudulent" and "absurd." U.S. congressional investigations also documented the president's wealth overseas.

Aquino and Laurel campaigned against the president's alleged human rights abuses and pledged to free political prisoners.

Noting that Marcos had used his decree power to consolidate his influence, Aquino promised to revoke that power. She agreed to comply with the Military Base Agreement until 1991 and then "keep her options open" regarding renegotiations. She promised to oust all the over-staying generals, to reform the army, and to make it once again a professional organization rather than a personal fiefdom of the president. In all her speeches she recounted the fate of her husband and named Marcos as the number one suspect for his murder. She offered the New People's Army a six-month cease fire to negotiate, and welcomed Communists back into the mainstream if they renounced violence.

In a major campaign speech she declared that the real issue was Marcos himself:

> How he and his cronies plundered the economy and mortgaged our future;
>
> How he and his wife have erected extravagant monuments to themselves that mock the painful poverty of our people;
>
> How he and his dummies have drained the National Treasury and stashed their hidden wealth abroad;
>
> How he and his goons have tortured and "salvaged" defenseless citizens;
>
> How he and his padrinos have turned the Batasan (National Assembly) into an expensive rubber stamp;
>
> How he and his misguided minions have prostituted professionalism in the military;
>
> And how he and his classmates have converted the Supreme Court into a compliant cabal of callous collaborators.

The major theme, then, of the Aquino campaign was that Marcos had brought economic ruin and political dictatorship to the nation and that she would restore integrity and reform. The campaign slogan *Enough! Stop! Change! (Sobra na! Tama na! Palitan na!)* was chanted at ever growing rallies ending with a million-person campaign rally in Manila.

The major concern on election day was the degree of cheating perpetrated by the ruling KBL party. Some 1,000 journalists from around the world and hundreds of official overseas observers investigated the proceedings. The National Citizens Movement for Free Elections (Namfrel) mobilized half a million persons to protect the sanctity of the ballot and to issue a "quick count" in order to preclude cheating.

Despite these safeguards, the voting process was marred by incontrovertible evidence of fraud. The unanimous opinion of journalists and official observers was that the KBL had committed illegal acts including vote buying, ballot box stuffing, intimidation, and deletion of names from voter lists (estimated at five million throughout the country). Vote counting was excruciatingly slow with the "official" count announced one week after the election. When that count gave Marcos 54 percent of the vote, the National Assembly, the final arbiter for voting controversies, proclaimed Marcos the winner.

The opposition immediately launched a peaceful crusade of civil disobedience designed to bring down Marcos and allow the actual winner, Aquino, to assume office. The campaign included the boycott of businesses, banks, and news media controlled by Marcos and his clients. The U.S. government, the official observers, journalists from dozens of nations, Namfrel, the Catholic church, and most Filipinos agreed that Aquino had actually won the election by a large margin but had been cheated out of her rightful victory. The Catholic Bishops Conference of the Philippines (CBCP) in a strong message read in Catholic churches throughout the nation called the election "unparalleled in fraudulence" and called for the Filipino people to take part in "a nonviolent struggle for justice to force the government to respect the clear mandate for change." The bishops, led by Cardinal Jaime Sin, stated that "a government that assumes or retains power through fraudulent means has no moral basis, for such an access to power is tantamount to a forcible seizure and cannot command the allegiance of the citizenry."

After receiving reports from the official delegation he sent to monitor the elections, President Reagan agreed that the election was "marred by widespread fraud perpetrated by the ruling party." He noted that so extreme was the misdoing that the election's credibility was called into question by all segments of Philippine society and the world community.

As Aquino's civil disobedience campaign took hold, two leading Marcos supporters, Defense Minister Juan Ponce Enrile and Lieutenant General Fidel Ramos, vice chief of the armed forces, defected from the Marcos camp and called for his resignation and the ascension to the presidency by Aquino, whom they agreed had been duly elected. This rebellion by former intimates of Marcos began a series of defections from the president leaving him with only a small hardcore group of supporters. The majority of army units, including a reform movement within the army called *We Belong*, supported the rebellion.

When Marcos threatened to retaliate by bombing the headquarters of Enrile and Ramos, thousands of Filipino citizens, urged on by Cardinal Sin, surrounded the building, some lying in the streets to keep the tanks from approaching. Eventually these tank commanders retreated and many defected to the opposition. The United States signalled its support of the rebellion, thereby undermining Marcos' claim that only he enjoyed the confidence of the superpowers.

On 25 February 1986 Aquino and Laurel proclaimed their people's victory and were "sworn in" as president and vice president by a supreme court justice. Because the National Assembly had the right to determine the election winner, the new president's swearing in was not constitutional. Two hours later, an isolated Marcos was "sworn in" by the supreme court chief justice. His taking of the oath was "constitutional" but because it was based on fraud, the ceremony was deemed illegitimate.

Marcos continued to issue orders to his military generals but they went unheeded. He attempted to persuade the U.S. government to support a "coalition government" to include the opposition, but this final plea was rejected. Instead, an emissary of President Reagan informed Marcos that the time had come for new leadership. Marcos no longer had the support of the United States, the army, the church, or the people. The next day he fled the country with his family to live in exile in the United States. President Aquino provided safe passage for him and his family and agreed not to seek extradition for his return to face charges of crimes against the nation.

With little bloodshed, "people's power" triumphed over a regime which had dominated the political, social, and economic life of the Philippines for 21 years. The end came remarkably quickly following the election and Marcos' victory claim. Just as rapidly, governments around the world recognized the new Aquino-Laurel administration. In her first day of office, she named her new cabinet including Laurel as prime minister and foreign minister, Enrile as defense minister, and Ramos as chief of staff. Leading oppositionists were appointed to key cabinet posts. Aquino also moved to restore confidence in the Philipines by announcing her plans to control corruption, end cronyism, revitalize the agricultural sector, disband monopolies, restore the writ of habeus corpus, end press censorship, restore professionalism to the army, appoint new supreme court justices, improve ties with ASEAN and the United States, support the Military Base Agreement, and provide amnesty to political prisoners and defectors from the Communist party and the NPA. She pledged to end the Philippine system of clientelism based on patronage ties forged by Marcos, his family, and close associates.

President Aquino faced overwhelming problems as she began ruling a nation that for four decades had been dominated by patronage relationships. She promised to appoint technocrats and politicians with public-regarding values, whose tenure and promotion were based on merit and fitness rather than on personal contacts. She began vigorous prosecution of corrupt officials and demanded full disclosure of government leaders' assets, an end to presidential decrees, and confiscation of illegally obtained wealth and privilege.

One month after assuming the presidency, Aquino abrogated Marcos' 1973 constitution, dissolved the KBL dominated National Assembly, and imposed a provisional "Freedom Constitution" that provided her with full powers until a new constitution was promulgated and accepted in a national plebiscite. Because the president now had full executive and legislative powers, the post of prime minister (filled by Laurel for one month) was abolished. The provisional constitution was to be replaced and a new national assembly elected within a year.

Few Third World nations have as much potential as the Philippines. Its natural resources, educated populace, experience with democratic rule, vast infrastructure, and freedom from outside threats are strengths that are shared by few developing nations. Yet, the nation has suffered from severe crises that the Marcos leadership could not solve, precisely because that leadership manipulated a clientelist system that was itself the problem. Under President Aquino, the executive, legislative, and judicial institutions have been revitalized, the military curtailed, political parties refurbished, electoral processes made honest and effective, the media freed, the cronies undercut, and the citizens given back their rights.

MALAYSIA

Malaysia, like the Philippines, gained its independence by generally peaceful means. And like the Philippines, the postindependence governmental institutions evolved from and reflected the impact of colonial rule. With minor changes appropriate to the Malaysian environment, Malaysia adopted the British parliamentary system, with a bicameral federal parliament and prime minister elected by the lower house. The distinctive Malayan contribution to the constitutional arrangements was creation of the position of Yang di-Pertuan Agong (paramount ruler), who was selected from the Council of Rulers, from each Malay state in a rotational system.

When Malaysia received its independence from British rule on 31 August 1957, the new country was called Malaya and consisted of the peninsular area south of Thailand to Singapore. The overriding characteristic of Malayan politics was its communal nature. Ethnic Malays comprised slightly less than 50 percent of the population; the Chinese comprised about one-third; whereas Indians, aborigines, and Europeans were smaller minority groups.

To cope with the severe tensions arising from the conflicting cultures and ambitions of the major ethnic groups, an alliance party system was devised in 1952 to meet the demands of all elements of society. The Malays were understood to have a privileged position in the political system, whereas the Chinese, and to a lesser extent the Indians, were to be predominant in economic activities. The leaders of the major groups were represented in the Alliance party, consisting of the United Malay Nationalist Organization (UMNO), the Malayan Chinese Association (MCA), and the Malayan Indian Congress (MIC). These leaders had the responsibility for explaining and justifying Alliance decisions to their respective constituencies and for securing their compliance.[21] The prime minister and head of UMNO was Tunku Abdul Rahman, the "father" of Malayan independence and leader of the nation from 1957 to 1970.

The Alliance idea worked well to bring about stability in a potentially explosive situation, mainly because the Alliance leaders were moderate ideologically and because each ethnic group perceived its best interests to be served by such a system. The alliance has continued, in somewhat modified form, up to the present as the primary institution of Malaysian politics.

When Malaysia became independent in 1957, Britain continued to exercise influence over its self-governing colony, Singapore, and over the dependencies of North Borneo (now Sabah), Sarawak, and Brunei, all situated on the island of Borneo. The leaders of Great Britain and Malaya agreed in 1963 to incorporate Sabah, Sarawak, and Singapore into a Federation of Malaysia. Singapore's urban and industrial economy was seen as a balance to the rural agricultural economy of Malaya. Singapore's unique situation as a city-state with no agricultural base raised questions about its viability as an independent state. The merger with Malaya was seen as a means to bring stability to both areas. To offset the increased number of Chinese in the new federation, Sabah and Sarawak were brought in to maintain a favorable proportion of Malays in the population. The new federation granted differing degrees of autonomy to the new states. Singapore, in particular, was granted wide-ranging autonomy over domestic matters.

The Federation of Malaysia lasted only two years in its original form. In August 1965, Prime Minister Tunku Abdul Rahman requested that Singapore leave the federation. The reasons for the ouster of Singapore are complex and inextricably bound up with communal problems. The prime minister of Singapore, Lee Kwan Yew, himself known as the father of Singapore independence, called for a "Malaysian Malaysia," that is, a Malaysia with equal participation from all areas and groups. His call contrasted with Tunku Abdul Rahman's design for a "Malayan

---

[21] Milton Esman, *Administration and Development in Malaysia* (Ithaca, New York: Cornell University Press, 1972), p. 24.

Malaysia" with special privileges reserved for the dominant ethnic group. Lee Kwan Yew, clearly, was attempting to strengthen his influence, and indirectly that of Singapore, in the national political arena of Malaysia by having his political party, the People's Action party (PAP), campaign for several seats outside Singapore in the 1964 election.[22] The PAP considered itself a national party. Tunku Abdul Rahman regarded this as a direct threat to the continued political dominance of the Malays and a threat to the political system as a whole.

The ouster of Singapore in 1965 did not resolve the communal character of Malaysian politics. Indeed, on 13 May 1969, following a national election, communal riots erupted in the capital city of Kuala Lumpur. These riots precipitated fundamental changes in Malaysian politics. The immediate cause of the riots was the erosion of support for the Alliance party in the 1969 elections. In the preceding two elections in 1959 and 1964, the Alliance held an overwhelming majority of the parliamentary seats. For the first time in the independence period the opposition parties won a majority (51.5 percent) of the votes, against the Alliance party's 48.5 percent. Although Alliance candidates still controlled a majority of the parliament despite losing 23 seats, the evidence from the 1969 election was that the Alliance party's capacity to govern effectively was seriously impaired.

To celebrate their "victory," anti-Alliance forces paraded in the streets of Kuala Lumpur. On 13 May UMNO supporters paraded. The demonstrations increased communal tensions to the point of provoking mob action which raged for four days. Scores of persons were killed and hundreds injured in the resulting violence.

To bring order to the country martial law was proclaimed, the parliament temporarily disbanded, civil liberties curtailed, and total authority was granted to a National Operations Council (NOC) under the leadership of Tun Abdul Razak, the deputy prime minister. Martial law lasted 21 months before parliamen-

---

[22] See Nancy Fletcher, "The Separation of Singapore from Malaysia," *Cornell Data Paper No. 73*, Southeast Asia Program (Ithaca, New York: Cornell University, 1969), p. 3.

tary rule was reestablished. Despite fear that the NOC would move vigorously against Chinese economic interests, most analysts found the NOC policies to be moderate. In 1970 Tun Abdul Razak became prime minister when Tunku Abdul Rahman resigned.

The rioting made clear to the NOC that a return to parliamentary rule would be disastrous unless significant changes were made in Malaysian politics. Tun Razak insisted that a series of Sedition Acts in the form of constitutional amendments be accepted by all parties before he would reconvene parliament. These acts extended the rights of Malays by setting aside for them a proportion of positions in higher education and certain businesses, and it prohibited discussion of "sensitive issues." Specifically, political debate was not allowed on the subjects of the prerogatives of the Malay rulers, special rights for the Malays, and the official status of the Malay language. The government reaffirmed that the chief of staff would be a Malay sultan, the official religion Islam, and that the national flag would feature the Islamic star and crescent. The political symbols of Malaysia were to remain thoroughly Malay.

In an additional effort to unite the nation, NOC put forth a new political ideology, or *rukenegara*. The ideology states five principles: belief in God, loyalty to king and country, upholding the constitution, rule of law, and good behavior and morality. All Malaysian citizens were to accept the commitment to achieve unity for Malaysia, to maintain the democratic form of life, to create a just society with the wealth of the nation equally shared, to ensure a liberal approach to rich and diverse traditions, and to build a progressive society oriented to modern technology.[23] The noble spirit of the *rukenegara* did not, however, mask the essentially contradictory nature of the five principles for a communal society.

The NOC believed that economic tensions were mainly responsible for the communal riots. To solve that problem a New Economic Policy was proposed to promote national unity and a just society. The policy called for an attack on poverty through

---

[23] Marvin Rogers, "Malaysia/Singapore: Problems and Challenges of the Seventies," *Asian Survey*, 11(2) (February, 1971), 123.

the provision of more job opportunities and the correction of the economic imbalance "so as to reduce and eventually eliminate the identity of race with economic function."[24] In essence, this meant that Malay participation in the economic sphere was to be increased by granting special privileges in terms of business ownership, tax breaks, investment incentives, and employment quotas.

A modified parliamentary government returned to Malaysia in 1971. By 1972 political stability was restored, and Tun Razak called for a new united front among the major political parties. He co-opted the potential opposition parties by his move toward socialism and neutralism in foreign affairs, and by his reliance on the Sedition Act to keep conflict under control. In the 1974 elections, Tun Razak's National Front won 90 percent of the parliamentary seats. The Front, an outgrowth of the Alliance party, continues to dominate Malaysian politics.

Tun Razak died of leukemia on 14 January 1976 and was succeeded by Datuk Hussein Onn, the deputy prime minister. Onn did not have a significant power base and it was generally thought he would serve temporarily. However, Onn proved to be an independent prime minister with considerable political skills. He moved to improve Malaysia's economic development by promulgating the Third Malaysia Plan which emphasized private investment and savings. He also filed formal charges of corruption against high-ranking officials including some in his own UMNO party.

Datuk Hussein Onn continued the policy of reducing opposition by co-opting as many parties as possible into the National Front. In 1978, the Front consisted of 11 parties and controlled all but ten seats in the parliament. However, within the Front itself, factions emerged that threatened the stability of the ruling group. Moreover, many Malays expressed dissatisfaction with the lack of progress toward economic equality for ethnic Malays. The New Economic Policy (put into effect by Tun Razak) had promised *bumiputeras* (sons of the soil, i.e., Malays) that their share of capital stock ownership would increase significantly. The actual rate of growth, however, was small compared to the

---

[24] Sevinc Carlson, *Malaysia: Search for National Unity and Economic Growth* (Beverly Hills, California: Sage, 1975), p. 6.

plan's projections. In May 1977 Onn launched a campaign of *Bersatu* (Unity) to mollify each of the three major ethnic groups, but tensions remained and communalism continued to dominate Malaysian politics.

Malaysia's communal problems were exacerbated in 1979—the year of the refugees—when Vietnamese boat people arrived on the nation's shores at the rate of some 20,000 per month. Because the overwhelming majority of the refugees were of Chinese descent, the Malay leaders feared communal upheavals unless the refugees were turned back or taken to other nations. The Malaysian government's alarm caused the United States and several other nations to increase the number of refugees admitted and Vietnam pledged to conduct a six-month moratorium on the refugee exodus.

Following a serious illness, Datuk Hussein Onn resigned in July 1981 and was succeeded by Deputy Prime Minister Sri Dr. Mahathir bin Mohamad. Mahathir, the first "commoner" prime minister with no roots in the traditional aristocracy, became a vigorous symbol of the modern Malaysian technocrat just as Kuala Lumpur, once a sleepy town and now an ultra-modern, heavily trafficked national capital, symbolized economically prosperous Malaysia.

Mahathir reaffirmed the New Economic Policy (NEP) with its goal of placing a larger share of control over the Malaysian economy in the hands of Malays. He set forth a "look East" economic policy arguing that the Western nations were not appropriate models for Malaysia to follow. Instead, he suggested that Malaysia look to Japan, South Korea, and Taiwan as more suitable nations to emulate.

Mahathir also introduced the idea of "Malaysia Incorporated" whereby business and government leaders were to work together as in a modern corporation. His policy of "privitization" of public utilities, communications, and transportation was an example of the attempt to bring the profit motive and increased efficiency to the Malaysian economy. His administration, however, was criticized for these programs on the grounds that the NEP goals of a larger economic role for Malays would be jeopardized. By the mid 1980s these goals were behind schedule.

Mahathir was often compared with President John F. Kennedy as a young, idealistic, articulate, and dynamic leader. The National Front's resounding election triumph in the 1982 election buttressed this perception and reaffirmed the National Front's dominant political position. The Front won 132 of the 154 contested parliamentary seats. The opposition Malaysia Islamic party (Parti Islam Sa-Malaysia—PAS), which called for a state governed by Islamic law, won only five seats. The only Chinese opposition party, DAP, won eight seats.

The central issue in Malaysia continued to be communalism, especially with the resurgence of Islamic fundamentalists who demanded an Islamic state. Mahathir attempted to defuse the issue by launching an "absorption of Islamic values" program. However, the non-Malay population remained fearful of any attempt to force them to accept alien religious ideas. The issue kept tensions high among all groups within Malaysia.

Mahathir's emphasis on "clean, efficient, trustworthy" government suffered in 1983 following reports of maladministration and corruption in Malaysia's largest government sponsored bank. The resignation of the deputy prime minister in 1986 further undermined Mahathir's initial reputation as an effective leader. However, Mahathir's call for elections on 4 August 1986, eleven months before the end of his five-year term of office, led to a landslide victory for the National Front Coalition. The 13 party coalition won 148 of the 177 parliamentary seats, despite criticism of his government by Islamic fundamentalists. The Islamic PAS party won only one seat.

The excellent economic growth among most sectors in the past decade provided a cushion for the Malaysian government. Communal tensions remained beneath the surface as the people perceived that their needs were being met. An economic decline could bring to the surface and exacerbate these tensions.

SINGAPORE

Singapore and Malaysia have long had important political, economic, and social ties. Both nations had been ruled by the British and were separated as recently as 1946, when Singapore became a distinct crown colony. Under its new status as a crown colony, Singapore continually moved in the direction of merger with Malaya. Merger was supported as a means to assure economic stability by providing an agricultural balance to its city-state trade economy. Moreover, Singapore desired merger as a defense against Communist advances, thereby providing stability and confidence for foreign investors. Finally, Singapore saw merger as a means to assure the continued viability of the city-state. Prime Minister Lee Kwan Yew noted:

> It would be utterly ludicrous for us—with our 1.6 million people—to try to chart our own way in this world . . . . This is an age when man and his efforts must coordinate. Any country that has not got sufficient ballast, sufficient depth of economic strength, would fall by the wayside.[25]

Lee Kwan Yew, the Cambridge-educated prime minister of Singapore and leader of the People's Action party (PAP), saw Singapore as the center of a Malaysia with its identity intact. Malayan Prime Minister Tunku Abdul Rahman agreed to the merger when he was convinced that, otherwise, Singapore could become Malaysia's "Cuba" and that the economic viability of the island was questionable under the status quo of separation.

Following the establishment of Malaysia in September 1963, Lee Kwan Yew reiterated his view of a Malaysian Malaysia with the clear implication of a more significant role for Singapore. He moved aggressively, especially in the political sphere, to win a place for his ideas in the peninsula and to enhance the political position of the Chinese. The Malaysian prime minister perceived Lee Kwan Yew's behavior as a threat to the continued Malay control of the political sphere. Accordingly, on 9 August 1965, Rahman ousted Singapore from the federation.

Singapore suddenly became an independent city-state. The PAP emerged as the sole effective political party and its leader, Lee Kwan Yew, has dominated Singapore's politics up to the present. The nation embarked on an intensive economic development program that raised the standard of living to the point where Singapore citizens enjoy the second highest per capita income in Southeast Asia. Until 1985 the economy grew at an annual growth rate of 9.1 percent in per capita income. That remarkable growth rate ended in 1985 when Singapore posted a negative growth rate for the first time in its modern history.

[25] *Straits Times*, September 29, 1962, quoted in Nancy McHenry Fletcher, *The Separation of Singapore from Malaysia*, Cornell Data Paper No. 73 (1969), p. 6.

In the 1968 elections, Lee Kwan Yew's party won all 58 seats in the legislative assembly. PAP in 1972 and December 1976 again obtained all 69 seats in the assembly, winning 69.1 and 72.4 percent of the votes respectively. In December 1980 PAP increased its winning percent of the votes cast to 75 and won all 75 seats, the fourth consecutive election Lee Kwan Yew's government returned to power without losing a single seat. The success of PAP comes from the tight political hold the party has on the bureaucracy, as well as from the demonstrated ability of the ruling party in the areas of economic development, social welfare, and national security against insurgents. PAP succeeded, during its two decades of continued rule, in transforming itself from a mere political party into a national political institution.

One opposition member was elected to the assembly in a 1981 bi-election and two were victorious in the 1984 general election. Although the PAP won 47 of 49 seats, their share of the popular vote declined from 75 to 63 percent. The election was interpreted by many commentators as a "defeat" for Lee Kwan Yew's PAP as well as a small indication of democratic vitality in a one-party authoritarian state. The nation's leadership was also concerned about the fact that the country's gross national product dropped from an 8.2 percent growth rate in 1984 to minus 1.7 percent in 1985. an unprecedented reversal of steady growth in the past several decades.

Lee Kwan Yew pledged to resign in 1988 at the age of 65. He appointed a "new generation" cabinet and groomed potential successors (including his son who is a military general as well as cabinet minister). The new cabinet promised to continue Singapore's unique mixture of capitalism and centralized planning, and parliamentary democracy and personalistic rule.

BRUNEI

The newest independent nation of Southeast Asia is Brunei, which became sovereign on 1 January 1984. Ironically, the sultan of Brunei worked against British desires to grant independence on the grounds that the new nation would be vulnerable to attack from its larger neighbors, namely Indonesia and Malaysia. Both of these nations had experienced tense relations with Brunei and the Malaysian state of Sarawak actually surrounds

Brunei. Although the 1984 agreement granted Brunei full sovereignty including responsibility for defense and foreign relations, internal self-government had been in force since 1959. In many respects Brunei is an anomaly in Southeast Asia. With a population of only 200,000, a per capita income of about $22,000, and tremendous oil revenues (oil and gas exports comprise 80 percent of Brunei's gross national product), the absolute monarchy is not comparable with any of its neighbors.

The income from oil exports has been used by the government to establish one of the most complete welfare states in the world. All citizens are provided with free education and medical care. There is no income tax. Roads, schools, temples, hotels, dams, and other large construction projects are ubiquitous and still the nation has huge fund reserves.

Brunei's government is also unique in Southeast Asia. The absolute monarchy is headed by the sultan, Sir Muda Hassanal Bolkiah, the 29th ruler in a dynasty which originated in the 13th century. As head of state he has ceremonial responsibilities. As prime minister, minister of internal affairs, and minister of finance, he also has total control over the day-to-day affairs of state. There is no elected parliament, all bureaucratic positions are appointed by the sultan, the media is controlled, and there is little if any significant opposition.

Brunei joined the Association of Southeast Asian Nations (ASEAN) just one week after receiving independence. The nation's foreign policy has been characterized by its pro-West and anti-Communist stance and by increasingly close ties with ASEAN.

4
Political Culture

The political systems of Southeast Asia are made up of individuals who perform politically related tasks. These individuals embody a unique configuration of values, beliefs, and attitudes that affect the way the systems function. The collective values, beliefs, and attitudes of a society—that is, the particular patterns of orientations that are shared by a citizenry—constitute the political culture of the society. The constellation of political orientations of the citizenry provides the context in which politics occurs.

Every facet of politics is affected by a society's pattern of values, beliefs, and attitudes about political objects. Political culture can help us understand the problems and prospects of political stability, integration, and conflict. Research on the degree of perceived self-efficacy and trust relationships among the populace can provide information on the kinds of demands made on the political system, as well as on the kinds of authority relationships between rules and the ruled. Moreover, the study of political culture seeks to understand the factors that facilitate or impede development and modernization.

In this chapter no attempt is made to posit a cause-effect relationship between cultural orientations and actual behavior. Instead, this chapter seeks only to present a general context of political orientations to give insight into Southeast Asian politics. The study of the political culture of each Southeast Asian society will provide some order and meaning to the political processes of these societies and will provide additional material which accentuates the general theme of the richness and diversity in Southeast Asia.

The particular constellation of religious beliefs constitutes the most salient and long-held value orientation of the Southeast

Asian and it is important to present an overview of the predominant religions. Although each of the major world religions is represented in Southeast Asia, this chapter emphasizes Buddhism, Islam, and animism.

BUDDHISM

The Buddhist religion is predominant in mainland Southeast Asia. The great majority of the people of Burma, Thailand, Loas, and Cambodia adhere to the tradition of Theravada Buddhism and have arrived at their beliefs through many centuries of interaction of ideas.* Hence the religious belief system of the people in each of these lands is strikingly similar. The Buddhist values in each of these four nations inform and inspire basic social, political, economic, and cultural patterns of life for the individual, family, village, and nation. Indeed, there is a profound sense in which to be Burmese, Thai, Laotian, or Cambodian is to be Buddhist.

Buddhism, as practiced in mainland Southeast Asia, is syncretic. Buddhism combines elements of animism and Brahmanism. Over the centuries pure Buddhism has melded with and been molded by indigenous beliefs in omnipresent spirits and by the elaborate rituals and hierarchicalization of Hindu-Brahman worship. The Thai versions of Buddhism and spirit worship are important elements of the cultural framework vis-á-vis political activity. Buddhism is not a God-oriented system of faith and worship. In Buddhism, no belief must be taken on faith, such as belief in a supreme being; rather, all faith must be believable in light of one's experience and reason. Buddha guides his followers by pointing out the path on which they can proceed, but each person must tread the path himself.

The most distinctive doctrine of Buddhism is *karma,* which pertains to the sum of one's good and bad actions. Moreover, all

---

*In Vietnam, Mahayana Buddhism is the major religion. Mahayana, like Theravada Buddhism, originated in India, but came to Vietnam via a northern route through China rather than via a more southern route through Burma and across the Indian Ocean. The two branches of Buddhism are similar in most respects although the Mahayana stream emphasizes the compassion of Buddha and potential Buddhas (Bodisatva) for salvation.

change is determined by karma. Good actions in this life will lead to a better spiritual and material existence in the next life. The operating principle in the karmic process is merit, which can be accumulated by performing meritorious deeds. Good and bad actions affect one's next existence but not the state of one's present life—just as the present is the consequence of the sum of actions in previous existences.

To achieve *nirvana,* the absence of suffering, one must be freed from the cycle of karmic rebirth and must live by the Four Noble Truths. The first Noble Truth holds that all existence is suffering; the second teaches that suffering results from desire; the third teaches that suffering will cease when desire and greed cease; and the fourth indicates the Noble (eightfold) Path that one must follow to bring suffering to an end. The Noble Path connotes right understanding, right thought, right speech, right action, right livelihood, right effort, rightmindfulness, and right concentration. But following the eightfold path is impossible for the layman, who must cope with the daily vicissitudes of life. Thus Buddhism emphasizes the need to withdraw from society in order to meditate and perfect the discipline that is necessary for achieving nirvana. Buddhist monks have chosen to follow this path.

There is a widespread tendency to explain Thai political behavior in terms of the religious beliefs of the people, on the assumption that their religious norms are an internalized part of the motivational system. The Thais' deference to authority, for example, is sometimes explained by noting that people of high status (superiors) are those who in their previous existences performed virtuous deeds. Subordinates, on the other hand—by the same rationale— have less virtuous backgrounds and hence are duty bound to respect their superiors. Similarly, the Thais' political passivity, the low level of economic development, and the lack of materialistic values have been explained in terms of the Buddhist idea that desire and greed cause suffering. Finally, the Thais' spontaneity and individualism have been seen as the product of the Buddhist stress on the individual's responsibility for attaining nirvana.

The Buddhist interpretation of Thai politics has also focused on the concept of merit to explain superior-subordinate relationships. Lucien Hanks transposes these cosmic concepts of hierarchy and merit to the sociopolitical processes of Thai society.

David Wilson concurs with Hanks in his cosmological view of the Thai. Wilson is quoted at length because his statement best represents the view that Thai politics reflects Buddhist values.

> According to this view, the world is a moral continuum. All elements of the cosmos are related to each other in terms of power determined by virtue and moral value. It is the moral value of things which is their true nature and which determines their place in the universe. . . . In the human universe one's place is a result of one's will and one is therefore ultimately responsible for one's own position in society.
>
> The position of being, human or otherwise, in this universe may be measured by the degree to which he is subject to the will of and has power over others. This conception is the one which must be kept in mind in any discussion of Thai politics, that is, the necessary and just unity of virtue and power. Those who have power are good and deserve power. Those who gain power are good and deserve their good fortune. Power justifies itself. This is not to be understood in a cynical sense which would lead to the view that might is right. It is rather a magico-religious view that right is might.[1]

Such explanations, however, are at best tenuous because religious beliefs are not usually an important element of one's motivational system and because these beliefs contain contradictions. Deference to authority may be congruent with Buddhism's notion of merit, but deferential behavior was an operative force in Thailand even before Buddhism was firmly established. Non-Buddhist Thais, as well as non-Buddhists in most of Asia behave deferentially. Nor is deference necessarily consistent with the Buddhist idea of personal accountability for moral perfection— an idea that could conceivably promote egalitarianism rather than elitism. Most importantly, there is little evidence that the Buddhist idea of karma affects behavior patterns. Deference to superiors, for example, can be explained by the instrumental

---

[1] David A. Wilson, *Politics in Thailand* (Ithaca, New York: Cornell University Press, 1962), p. 332.

rationality of the Thais. Superiors have resources that subordinate need—money, land, jobs, shelter—for which the latter offer deference in return.

The relationship between the Buddhist norms of desire and the low level of economic development is also tenuous. Although, normatively, Buddhism eschews desire, it teaches that a more comfortable existence awaits the person who does good deeds. The desire for a more comfortable existence, for a higher standard of living, is therefore an important determinant of behavior. Furthermore, the Buddhist who builds a temple in order to gain merit may be more "materialistic" than the person who spends his money on material goods, as the former seeks to guarantee a more comfortable life for himself in his next existence. To stress the point again, it is the desire for a better life, rather than belief in karmic rebirth, that motivates behavior.

Many studies have indicated that the villagers' religious beliefs do not limit their level of production or consumption, nor do they lessen the Thais' strong interest in money, security, and comfort. Herbert Phillips, in his study of the peasant personality in central Thailand, found an overriding concern with such practical matters as money, earning a living, achieving status, and having sufficient food. These Thais gave some attention (but relatively little) to religious concerns and to satisfactions of an interpersonal nature, including those of one's family. The overwhelming majority of informants in Phillip's study expressed desire for only one thing: money.[2]

The foregoing should not lead one to the conclusion that Buddhism and spirit worship have no impact on political activity. On the contrary, Buddhism's inherent tolerance, flexibility, and lack of dogma have encouraged the principle of compromise in Thai politics and discouraged narrow ideological dogmatism. Moreover, the Buddhist emphasis on serenity and virtue has mitigated the violence of the rulers toward the ruled. Also, Buddhism provides a sense of national unity and identification that is partially responsible for the high level of social stability. The Thai king, as the spiritual leader of Buddhism, symbolizes

[2] See Herbert Phillips, *Thai Peasant Personality* (Berkeley: University of California Press, 1965).

the Thai nation, and rarely is any political activity undertaken without the blessings of the Buddhist monks.

Moreover, there is a ritual rhythm to the life of the Theravada Buddhist.

> The yearly round of festivals is a ritual cycle coordinated with the agricultural cycle. All of the rituals of the Buddhist way, taken together, promote and express a symphony of life in which all of the various themes—the monk, the layman, the old, the young, the living, the dead, and spirit power are constantly interacting in reciprocity.[3]

Theravada patterns of belief and practice are fundamentally attuned to a village environment, an agrarian society with relatively simple patterns of social, economic, and political interaction. Modernization has placed considerable strain on these traditional patterns. Urbanization, industrialization, and the like have upset the ritual rhythm of the Buddhist. In addition, the Communist Loatian and especially the Communist Cambodian governments have systematically attempted to destroy the Buddhist teachings. The monks have been harassed and the temples turned into rice storage centers. As modernization and oppressive regimes continue to be thrust upon the Theravada Buddhist peoples, the future of Buddhism is problematical. The irony is that Buddhism, with its emphasis on individualism, moderation, ethical values, and serenity, is especially relevant and promising for human welfare in the fast-changing Southeast Asian world.

ISLAM

Islam is the predominant religion of the Indonesian people, the Malays in Malaysia, and the Filipinos in the southernmost islands of the Philippines. Like Buddhism in mainland Southeast Asia, Islam has changed over centuries, adapting elements of Hinduism, Buddhism, and animism to meet the needs of its adherents. As with Buddhism, there is no one Muslim religion. Indeed, Islamic variants, diverse in rituals, beliefs, and values,

---

[3] Robert C. Lester, *Theravada Buddhism in Southeast Asia* (Ann Arbor, Michigan: University of Michigan Press, 1973), p. 146.

can be found throughout Southeast Asia. One village may differ greatly from its neighboring village. The rituals of urban Muslims differ from those of rural Muslims.

Islam is an ethical religion based on the teachings of the Koran, the words of Allah as spoken by the prophet Muhammed during the years 610–622 A.D. The word "Islam," which means surrender, suggests the rather austere tone of the religion, with its emphasis on submission to Allah. Islam does not have a complex or formal church organization. Instead, the focus is on the individual and his relationship to the almighty and judgmental Allah. The bedrock act which all Muslims share in common is the confession of faith: "There is no God but Allah and Muhammed is his Prophet." By repeating that phrase, and believing it, a person is a Muslim, equal in faith to all other believers.

The ethical nature of the religion is shown in the Islamic laws which have been developed over many centuries. These laws establish rules concerning how and what to eat, when to wash, how to pray, and what to wear. There are Islamic laws relating to marriage, business operations, and to almost all aspects of life. Because Islam has no formal eccleiastical hierarchy, these laws are an especially important institution of the religion.

Islam in Indonesia

Islam's emphasis on an austere ritual, the emphasis on ethical teachings in every aspect of life, and the universal nature of the teachings, as well as the equality and individuality of the believers, were foundations appropriate and attractive to Southeast Asians who prior to the coming of Islam worshipped many gods or spirits with elaborate rituals within a hierarchical ecclesiastical organization. Indonesian Islam initially was adopted in the commercial and coastal cities. The principles of equality and simplicity seemed more suited to the world of trade than to the agricultural society. A faith which did not discriminate on the basis of socioeconomic or ethnic origins helped to unite the diverse peoples who had arrived in Indonesia as traders.[4]

---

[4] J. D. Legge, *Indonesia* (Englewood Cliffs, New Jersey: Prentice-Hall, Inc., 1964), p. 47.

During the Dutch colonial period in Indonesia, Islam gained strength as it increasingly became the symbol of common resistance to foreign domination. The first formal anticolonialist and nationalist organizations were outgrowths of Islamic groups. In the early 1900s, for example, Islam formed the basis of the first mass nationalist organization, Sarekat Islam.[5]

The Western scholar who has written most extensively and authoritatively on the role of Islam Indonesia is the American anthropologist Clifford Geertz. In his classic book *The Religion of Java,* Geertz sets forth three subtraditions of the Indonesian religion.[6] These three categories, he is careful to point out, are not pure types. Instead, they represent general patterns of Javanese syncretism that differ in terms of their emphasis on animistic or Islamic factors.

The Santri variant stresses the Islamic aspects of the syncretism and is found principally among merchants. Santris are particularly concerned with the five ritual acts which they see as the heart of the religion and obligatory for salvation. The first act is the confession of faith, which is said in the ear of the newborn baby and which is repeated many times each day throughout one's life. Prayers constitute the second act. Their recitation, five times each day, helps resign the worshipper to Allah and provides comfort.

Fasting, the third act, is prescribed for Ramadan, the ninth lunar month. The fasting ritual calls for total abstinence from food and drink during the hours of daylight. The pilgrimage to Mecca once in a lifetime is the hope of all Muslims and is the fourth ritual act of the Santris. The fifth act is the payment of a religious tax, the *zakah,* for the purpose of aiding the poor, supporting religious teachers, or carrying out religious wars.

The Abangan variant, in contrast to the Santri variant, stresses the animistic aspects of the Indonesian syncretism and is principally practiced by the peasant element of the population. For the Abangan, attention to the details of doctrine are less important than certain ritualistic aspects of Islam, such as the *slametan* festival. A slametan is a ritual communal feast to celebrate im-

[5] Ibid., p. 52.
[6] Clifford Geertz, *The Religion of Java* (Glencoe, Illinois: The Free Press, 1959).

portant passages in life, such as birth, circumcision, house moving, illness, and marriage. The slametan protects one from spirits and brings about unity. For the Abangan, the basic unit is the family household, whereas, for the Santri, the religious community, the *unmat,* is the basic unit of identity. The last variant is Prijaji, which stresses the Hinduist aspects of religion and is related to the bureaucratic element of society. The Prijaji category appears to be more of a socioeconomic group than a religious group. A Prijaji may be more predisposed to the Santri or Abangan variants. Prijaji are the "aristocratic" class in Indonesian society and they emphasize hierarchy and status in social relationships.

The fact that Indonesian society is divided into these three religious groups is important for understanding the political processes prevalent since the end of World War II. For example, the broad outlines of the political party configurations are a function of these religious divisions. The Santris, who can be divided into traditional and modernist groupings, have been loyal to Muslim organizations such as the Nahdatul Ulama and Masjumi parties. Both of these parties have played an important role since Indonesian independence.

The Abangan, on the other hand, are typically opposed to Muslim organizations. They believe that politically victorious Santris would discriminate against them. This Abangan fear of Santri power has been a dominant theme of Indonesian politics. Abangans have been associated with the Indonesian Communist party (PKI) and the Indonesian Nationalist party (PNI) under President Sukarno's leadership.

At the beginning of the 20th century the social structure of Java was fairly clearly divided between the Prijaji, Santri, and Abangan groupings. More recently, however, as modernizing and reformist trends became more salient, Javanese society could better be divided into four groups: on the one hand reformist and orthodox Santri, on the other hand the administrative and peasant Abangan, corresponding respectively to the four major parties, Masjumi-Nahdatul Ulama and PNI-PKI.[7] These loose affiliations of religious variants into political

[7] Bernhard Dahm, *History of Indonesia in the Twentieth Century* (New York: Frederick Praeger, 1971), p. 172.

party configurations represent an important element of Indonesian politics. They indicate that party affiliation is not simply a function of ideological or personal predisposition but is a function of deep-rooted religious and socioeconomic affinity.

Malaysia and Islam

Indonesian Islam is different from Islam in other areas of the world because of its particular blend of Hindu, Buddhist, and animistic traditions. In Malaysia too, prior to the great wave of Islamic conversions in the 13th century, the people of the area were animists or combined elements of animism with Hindu-Buddhism. The particular blend was achieved with little tension as Islam was adapted to meet the existing social structures. As in Indonesia, Islam became a symbol to help unify the nation and was used as a means to legitimate authority. In addition, Islam played a central role in providing social integration within the Malay village. Gordon Means writes:

> Social solidarity was promoted by the common prayers, rituals, rites and festival. The cycles of life—planting, harvesting, marriage, birth, puberty, death—were all cloaked in religious mystery. Special rites and ceremonies were celebrated to mark each of these events. Most peasant Malays were quite conscientious in performing daily prayers and worshiped regularly at the local mosque, prayer house, and shrines. They also observed the fasting month of Ramadan and the major Islamic holy days. Most of the rites and ceremonies were public in nature, thus strengthening social integration and a sense of identity with the community. The same is true of the quasireligious kenduri (in Indonesia: slamentan) communal feasts, which each adult male villager gave for his friends and village notables at the time of rites of passage, on religious holidays, and when he was seeking to influence the inhabitants of the spirit world. These feasts were important agents of social integration helping to alleviate conflicts within the kampong.[8]

[8] Gordon Means, "The Role of Islam in the Political Development of Malaysia," *Comparative Politics*, 1(2) (January, 1969), 270.

In Malaysia, all Malays are by legal definition Muslim. Islam provides both legal and political privileges to Malays that to lose would be tantamount to a renunciation of the Malay way of life. The communal nature of Malaysian politics with its emphasis on ethnic differences between the Chinese and Malay peoples has strengthened the bond of Malayans to their religion. The idea that to be part of the Malayan community is to be Muslim effectively excludes the non-Muslim Chinese from important areas of community life. Communally oriented politicians often exploit the Malays' religious devotion when attempting to mobilize them for political action.[9]

The Malaysian constitution defines a Malay as one who professes the Muslim religion, who speaks the Malay language, and conforms to Malay customs.[10] Hence, the religious qualification is crucial for understanding political and legal rights and obligations. For example, Malays, constitutionally, are provided with special privileges in the areas of government service, education, trade and business, and property. Thus, adherence to Islam provides opportunities not available to non-Muslims.

The religious element is also central to the political-party orientations of Malayans. In the independence period parties were formed that were defined almost exclusively in terms of their degree of Islamic orthodoxy. Although, thus far, moderate Islamic parties have been dominant in the ruling alliance, the principal opposition parties are Islamic and they use their religious doctrines for political objectives. The ruling United Malay Nationalist Organization, the Malay party in the Alliance and National Front Coalition, was pressured to be more sensitive to Muslim demands as the Islamic parties grew in strength.

Of course, the increasing use of religion in politics, while gaining support from Muslims, alienates non-Muslims. The Chinese minority in Malaysia, in particular, is threatened by the religious emphasis. The violent 1969 communal riots between Malays and Chinese in Kuala Lumpur were largely the result of

---

[9] Gordon P. Means, *Malaysian Politics* (London: University of London Press, 1970), p. 17.
[10] Ibid., p. 280.

bitterness stemming from religious and ethnic issues. To a great extent, religious and ethnic issues are one and the same thing.

ANIMISM IN SOUTHEAST ASIA

Throughout the history of Southeast Asia the life of the peasant has been one of great risk, with constant threats to the maintenance of life itself. The peasantry has been at the mercy of the environment, suffering from periodic droughts and floods, malnutrition, and devastating epidemics. The inability to manipulate and dominate environmental conditions has nurtured a fatalism among Southeast Asians that is manifested in a belief in spirits, ghosts, and the like, that are felt to have control over life. The rice fields, homes, forest, and communities are all believed to be inhabited by spirits that determine the quality and quantity of the harvest, the health of oneself and loved ones, the safety of travel, and the general well-being of the populace.

Southeast Asians of every class propitiate spirits, practice magic and divination, and live in fear of ghosts and sorcerers. In Thailand, for example, the first name given to a baby is often an ugly one (e.g., Little Rat), so that the evil spirits will be fooled into thinking the newborn is unloved and therefore will not covet the baby and take him away. Astrologers are consulted for auspicious times from when to begin feeding rice to a baby to when to promulgate new constitutions. Miniature spirit houses are found next to people's homes and are used to propitiate the house spirits. Thais also wear amulets for protection against malicious and evil spirits. In the rural areas, spirit doctors are utilized to exorcise disease and evil.

Spirit worship offers an important alternative to the Buddhist explanation for suffering. In contrast to the Buddhist teaching of individual responsibility, spirit worship provides a more satisfying explanation by placing the blame for suffering on malicious spirits rather than on the sufferer himself. Buddhists, who also propitiate spirits, observe that while spirits do not harm those with good karma, they can cause mischief to those whose karma is bad. Melford Spiro presents the dilemma of the Buddhist:

> Should he repudiate the doctrine of kharma, he not only repudiates Buddhism, but since the doctrine of kharma provides him

with the means for acquiring a better future, he also repudiates his only hope for avoiding future suffering. Should he, on the other hand, repudiate his belief in the causal agency of nats (spirits) and in the efficacy of nat propitiation as a means of avoiding suffering, he repudiates his only hope for resolving present suffering.[11]

Spiro also points out the striking doctrinal conflict between Buddhism and animism. He notes that Buddhism is an essentially ethical religion whereas animism is amoral, in the sense that individuals are rewarded or punished, not in terms of their merit or good acts, but solely in terms of their having propitiated the spirits. Furthermore, where Buddhism stresses a path to enlightenment based on reason, meditation, and serenity, animism stresses fear, emotion, and violence as the basis of the spirits' control over believers.[12]

In Java, animism remains an important element of the culture and politics. The Sukarno regime was the archetype of the political system immersed in mystical symbols. President Sukarno consciously surrounded himself with the trappings of the mystical world in order to endear himself to his followers through the suggestion of supernatural powers. His successor, President Suharto, while adhering to Muslim beliefs, also follows the word of traditional gurus and mystical leaders before making important decisions, and he cloaks himself in the symbols of the mystical world. Following the overthrow of Sukarno in 1965, for example, the decree naming Suharto president was titled Supersemar, an ingenious acronym referring to Semar, an important mystical character in the Mahabharta epic. Suharto has attempted to identify with Semar, who regularly flouts aristocratic rule.

In Malaysia, too, spirit worship and belief in magical powers are interwoven with the agricultural cycle. Ceremonies are held before the harvest to find the most propitious time to begin the planting and to drive the evil from the fields. A person's entire life cycle is thought to be affected by magic. Rituals are per-

---

[11] Melford Spiro, *Burmese Supernaturalism* (Englewood Cliffs, New Jersey: Prentice-Hall, Inc., 1967), p. 256.
[12] Ibid., pp. 258–263.

formed to assure safe births and the correct naming of a baby. Also important are the celebration of rites of puberty and marriage, and proper funeral arrangements. Malay medicine is largely magical. The causes of diseases are said to stem from supernatural forces, and cures are carried out by magical practices.

In Southeast Asian society, belief in spirits pervades every level and has been integrated with the formal religions of Buddhism, Islam, and Christianity. The elaborate animistic rituals have been an integrating factor throughout Southeast Asia as otherwise diverse people share a common belief in and fear of mystical phenomena.

AUTHORITY RELATIONSHIPS

The composite attitudes, values, and beliefs of the Southeast Asian peoples determine the kinds of sociopolitical interaction among the citizenry that form the foundation of political behavior and organization. In Southeast Asia, "exchange processes" are at the heart of power and authority relationships. These exchanges comprise certain rewards and values, which one person provides for another in exchange for like benefits. A person who has command over resources attains power over others who need those resources but have only limited access to them. Imbalances in control over resources in exchange relationships bring about differences in power, as power is relational and results from the mutual need of persons to maximize rewards and to minimize costs. "Mutual need" emphasizes the notion of reciprocity in exchange relationships, and "interaction" occurs when both persons in a relationship perceive that some desired benefit is forthcoming.

In Southeast Asia the principal pattern of interaction is superior-subordinate exchange relationships, characterized by personal, reciprocal ties between persons or groups of persons who command unequal resources and by mutually beneficial transactions that have broad political ramifications. These sociopolitical systems, in short, are based on hierarchical, face-to-face, superior-inferior relationships of reciprocity. These relationships, often referred to as patron-client ties, form the basis of the political and social structure of the Southeast Asian nations, and they continue to exist primarily because they are perceived by persons at various levels of the hierarchies as structures that maximize rewards and minimize undesirable ends.

Patron-client ties are not exclusive to Southeast Asia. Indeed, such bonds are found in most societies that have only a few institutionalized and differentiated structures that carry out specified functions and that act as linkages between the state and the citizenry. In societies where new institutions—such as bureaucracies, political parties, pressure groups, legislatures, and the like—are not available or are highly restricted, patron-client bonds become the primary intermediaries between officials and citizens and are the most important organizational unit for resource allocation. In undifferentiated societies, personal alliances do what impersonal structures are supposed to do in more institutionalized societies.

Similarly, patron-client bonds flourish in societies where there are marked inequalities in wealth, status, and control.[13] For the peasant of Southeast Asia and other regions of resource scarcity, where basic needs of subsistence and security are paramount concerns, personal alliances are formed to ensure survival. As the sources for goods and services expand, a client or patron is less dependent on a single, personal bond. In Southeast Asia, where resources have traditionally been insufficient, those with limited access to the resources form alliances with individuals at higher socioeconomic levels. The latter retain power over their clientele and extract labor, protection, deference, or some other reward in return for dispensing benefits to the subordinates.

Patron-client ties do not exist autonomously but are linked with other dyads into a network that pervades society at all levels.[14] This network plays an integrating role, as client is linked to patron, for the patron of one group is a client of a group higher in the hierarchy. Theoretically, it is possible to graph a hierarchical chain of patron-client bonds from the peas-

[13] James C. Scott, "Patron-Client Politics and Political Change in Southeast Asia," *American Political Science Review,* 66 (March, 1972), 101.

[14] See Carl H. Landé, "Networks and Groups in Southeast Asia: Some Observations on the Group Theory of Politics," *American Political Science Review,* 68(1) (March, 1973), 103–127.

ant farmer to the highest reaches of the power elite in the capital city. Information flows through this network of overlapping and interrelated groups from patron A to client B and from patron B (the same person as client B) to his client C, and so forth.

Each of the general themes presented above will be explored more fully by using the Philippines, Indonesia, Thailand, and Vietnam as case studies—four nations that are distinguished more by their differences than by their similarities. The Philippines was colonized by Spain before an indigenous culture had become widespread, and the Catholic religion was so effectively thrust upon the indigenous population that little of the animistic tradition of the pre-Spanish Philippines exists today. The Hispanization of the Philippines was followed by the equally powerful impact, at least in the political sphere, of American culture. In contrast, Thailand was never formally colonized, although the Thai society adapted important features of many cultures (especially those of India and China), and Buddhism has been integrated into traditional animistic and Hindu beliefs to form a distinctly Thai religion.

Indonesia's background differs greatly from that of the Philippines and Thailand. Although Indonesia was colonized by the Dutch for more than 300 years, it has retained much of its traditional way of life. The island nature of Indonesia, however, has bred linguistic, ethnic, and religious heterogeneity. Although Indonesia is not formally an Islamic state, the overwhelming majority of Indonesians practice some form of Islam.

The Confucianist philosophy, with its emphasis on hierarchy and a mandarin bureaucracy of learned persons, is unique to Vietnam. The dramatic influence of China on Vietnam resulted from almost a thousand years of subjugation.

The Philippines

Politics in the Philippines is characterized by patron-client relationships that pervade all levels from the *barrio* to the central government, and personalism is at the heart of these patron-client bonds between superiors and subordinates. These relationships are formed when individuals believe that each has something to gain thereby. In the Philippines, the key element of the relationship is reciprocity.

There are three basic forms of reciprocity in exchange relationships in the Philippines.[15] The first is contractual reciprocity, for a specified situation, and is not necessarily related to vertical ties. Such a relationship might be found among a group of farmers who agree to take turns plowing one another's fields.[16] In this case the reciprocation is equivalent, and once the work is finished there is no continuing sense of obligation.

The second type of reciprocity is quasi-contractual, where the terms of repayment are not as specific. Hollnsteiner suggests that reciprocity in this quasi-contractual relationship is automatic without prior arrangement, and that repayment is made in a circumscribed, nonaffective manner. For example, when a person dies it is customary for members of the community to contribute a sum of money, or an equivalent *abuloy*, to the deceased's family. This contribution is carefully calculated and recorded, so that when the abuloy giver suffers a death in the family, he will be given an equivalent sum. This kind of reciprocity may obtain among peers as well as between superiors and subordinates. Even in this quasi-contractual relationship, failure to reciprocate brings censure.[17]

In neither of the first two types of reciprocal obligation is there a sense of gratitude or affective feeling of obligation; the essence of the third type, however, is precisely the feeling of indebtedness of one person to another.

The first principle in the system of rules for reciprocal obligation is that an act of giving establishes a unilateral obligation or state of indebtedness between the giver and receiver, which is called *utang na loob* (debt of gratitude).[18] Because the utang na loob system pervades so much of the interaction among Filipinos, it is crucial to understand this concept in order to under-

[15] Much of the following discussion is based on Mary R. Hollnsteiner's numerous publications, and especially *The Dynamics of Power in a Philippine Municipality* (Manila: Community Development Research Council, 1963).

[16] Mary R. Hollnsteiner, "Reciprocity in the Lowland Philippines," in Socorro C. Espiritu and Chester L. Hunt, eds., *Social Foundations of Community Development* (Manila: R. M. Garcia Publishing House, 1964), p. 336.

[17] Ibid., p. 338.

[18] Charles Kaut, "*Utang na Loob:* A System of Contractual Obligation among Tagalogs," *Southwestern Journal of Anthropology,* 17(3) (1961), p. 259.

stand the structural base of sociopolitical life in the Philippines, for the degree and kind of utang na loob also defines one's position vis-á-vis others. The repayment of an utang na loob may be with interest or it may be a partial payment, depending on the desires and relative statuses of the persons involved. Mary Hollnsteiner notes:

> In the case of status equals, one tries to repay with interest, which means that the creditor position is held now by one, now by the other. Where a clearly superordinate-subordinate relationship of some permanence occurs, as in the case of landlord and tenant, the subordinate party is not even expected to repay with interest. In fact, partial payments suffice because they indicate recognition of the indebtedness, and therefore the appropriate sense of gratitude on the *utang na loob* debtor's side.[19]

Literally, utang na loob means "a debt inside oneself." The motivation for repayment and the reluctance to remain indebted encourage full payment with interest (but not necessarily an identical payment) at the first opportunity. Failure to repay an utang na loob debt causes shame and embarrassment, or *hiya*. Hiya is incurred when there is no utang na loob between persons, with the result that each person is not sure how to respond to the other, and it is also incurred when one person feels he has not lived up to the utang na loob expectations of the other.

Failure to reciprocate brings shame and an eventual break in relationship between the two individuals. This extreme action usually occurs when one has a conflicting obligation to more than one person and must choose to repay only one of them.

Utang na loob is so strongly felt that a Filipino bystander may be unwilling to "interfere" when a stranger is in distress, as he may be unwilling to place the afflicted person under obligation in return for his help. The distressed person, in turn, may not desire to be helped because he does not want to incur utang na loob if he can manage without it.

> The Filipino bystander, sharing these social values [of *utang no loob*], can appreciate the victim's feelings. Unconsciously, or perhaps out of conscious kindness, he gives no help unless it is asked

---

[19] Hollnsteiner, *The Dynamics of Power*, p. 66.

for; he will not force anyone to contract *utang no loob,* to be obliged in honor to a misguided benefactor giving unwanted service.[20]

The notion of reciprocity extends through the basic structural relationships in Filipino society. Traditionally, however, the Filipino feels a closer alliance and a stronger sense of reciprocity to his family than to those more distant. David Steinberg writes that:

> The individual ideally should be more loyal to the close family than to the extended family, to close friends than to acquaintances, to the local community than to the distant province, to the personal political leader than to the distant impersonal governmental agency. . . . The pattern of concentric circles of allegiance has always placed great emphasis on the personal character of loyalty in relationships.[21]

Thus the Filipino's primary loyalty is to the nuclear family and close kinfolk, and there must be extraordinary reasons for rejecting these ties, for the family is the strongest unit of society, demanding the deepest loyalties of the individual and coloring all social and economic activity.

Instead of rejecting his family, when a non-kin alliance appears to be in his best interest the Filipino brings the non-kin individual into the family structure through a ritual kinship (*compadrazgo*) in the form of godparents (*compadre*). This institutionalized means of formalizing a friendship or alliance is generally employed between persons of higher status (the compadre) and lower status. The compadre system, originally intended by the Catholic church to provide for a child's spiritual upbringing, has evolved into a reciprocity pattern in which the higher-status compadre renders material benefits and prestige and the lower-status family provides loyalty, deference, and support.[22] The

---

[20] Honesto Ch. Pacana, "Notes on a Filipino Rule of Conduct: Non-Interference," in Espiritu and Hunt, eds., *Social Foundations of Community Development*, p. 333.

[21] David Joel Steinberg, "The Web of Filipino Allegiance," *Solidarity,* 2(6) (March–April, 1967), p. 25.

[22] Hollnsteiner, *The Dynamics of Power*, p. 74.

family retains an especially high degree of utang na loob toward the compadre.

The compadrazgo system has become an important element of Filipino political life, and may be exploited by both the compadres and the families. A candidate for public office, for example, may be asked to sponsor a marriage or newborn baby in return for election support, and the family then has the right to seek political patronage from its new compadre.[23] Politicians are equally desirous of becoming sponsors to ensure a wide base of electoral support.

Politicians are especially eager to become compadres for *liders*, or "precinct captains," who themselves have a following and who promise support for a candidate in return for favors. The relationship between a politician and his lider is based on the idea of reciprocity and utang na loob, and candidates constantly attempt to add to their power by being compadres to their liders. Being a compadre for the child of one's lider strengthens the bond between the candidate and the lider, making them quasi-relatives with correspondingly intense feelings of utang na loob. The lider thereby gets the patronage he seeks, and the candidate gets much-needed support.[24]

Mary Hollnsteiner provides another aspect of reciprocity in the sociopolitical system of the Philippines in her discussion of intermediaries:

> The widespread use in Philippines society of intermediaries to approach a person on behalf of another person also hinges very greatly on the concepts of *utang na loob* and *hiya*. In Hulo, when a person (A) goes to visit another person (C) with the intention of asking a favor, he rarely goes alone unless he is closely related or on very familiar terms with the person being visited. Person A will hesitate to approach any person not in his alliance system unless he has with him someone (B) who is allied to that individual. Without B, A will be too *hiya* or embarrassed to talk to C as their relationship is not such as to provide a basis for the opening of delicate negotiations. Moreover, A realizes that C owes him

---

[23] Ibid., p. 75.

[24] Mary R. Hollnsteiner, "Lowland Philippine Alliance System in Municipal Politics," *Philippine Sociological Review*, Nos 3 & 4 (July–October, 1962), 169.

nothing, that is, has no *utang na loob* to him and, therefore, will not feel compelled to help A.

Because C has a special relationship with B, he will listen to the request and decide accordingly. If his *utang na loob* is strong, then he will feel a strong moral compulsion to grant the favor if he can. . . . In granting the favor, C does so primarily because B asked him and only secondarily because A needs it. B is now the one who owes a debt of gratitude to C even though he may not directly reap the material benefits that go with the favor, as A will. But A in turn now has *utang na loob* to B for his intercession in the matter. A also has *utang na loob* [to C], although not as much as he does for B since C did the favor mostly for B rather than for A.[25]

Utang na loob, then, has both affective and instrumental characteristics. The debt of obligation is strongly felt and internalized, but exists only as long as there is mutual expectation that the reciprocal obligation is in the best interests of both parties. There is a conscious and unsubtle manipulation of persons with the purpose of maximizing desired ends, and the manipulation continues as long as the particular relationship provides rewards and as long as alternative relationships do not appear to offer more.

Networks of dyadic interactions, based on reciprocal obligations between superiors and subordinates, have also emerged in the Philippines. Each person in such a network knows his particular role in the network, thereby bringing a high degree of practicality, efficiency, and predictability to sociopolitical patterns. Despite the emphasis on personal relations, the Philippines sociopolitical system is highly structured according to degrees of reciprocity among individuals. Indeed, the ability of these personal relationships to fulfill the needs of the Filipino has caused many citizens to ignore the more institutionalized structures. Structures larger than face-to-face groups, such as labor unions, cooperatives, and the like, that tend to impose impersonal obligations do not have the same psychological reality for the individual, nor do they provide him with the same security as the personal alliances he forms by himself.[26]

---

[25] Hollnsteiner, *The Dynamics of Power,* p. 80.

[26] John J. Carroll, "Philippine Social Organization and National Development," *Philippine Studies,* 14(4) (October, 1966), p. 580.

One result of the system of patron-client bonds in the Philippines is a lack of class-consciousness and horizontal identity. John Carroll tells of a group of businessmen who served a lavish dinner and then played blackjack for huge stakes while the men's chauffeurs watched. He noted that the drivers identified vertically with their bosses rather than horizontally with their socioeconomic peers—the other drivers.[27] This supports the findings of Carl Landé and others who see Philippine society as consisting essentially of networks of vertical mutual-aid relationships between prosperous patrons and their poor and dependent clients.[28]

Landé also shows how even the rational political parties consist of vertical chains of dyadic patron-client relationships extending from the "big people" down the hierarchy and eventually to the ordinary peasants—the "little people."[29] It seems possible that the vertical identity of the "little people" with their "big" patrons helps explain the relative absence of class-consciousness in the Philippines.[30] What in other societies is a major cause of class antagonism and tension—the gap between the few rich and the many poor—has become, in the Philippines, an integrating factor based on the notion of reciprocity.

Indonesia

Indonesia, like the Philippines, is a society where vertical alignments predominate and where there is a high degree of social stratification between aristocrats (playing the role of patrons) and the peasantry (playing the role of clients). Patronage relationships have been observed in the Javanese social system as well as in the traditional *wayang* shadow plays. The patron-client social structure is referred to as *bapakisme,* or "fatherism."

The Javanese place much value on deference to those of

---

[27] Ibid., p. 583.
[28] Carl H. Landé, *Leaders, Factions, and Parties,* Monograph Series No. 6 (New Haven, Connecticut: Yale University Press, Southeast Asia Studies, 1964), p. 1.
[29] Ibid., p. 2.
[30] John J. Carroll, "The Filipino Dilemma," *Solidarity,* 3(11) (November, 1968), p. 67.

superior status, such as the village headman, members of the aristocracy, and persons of high education or socioeconomic class. This value can be summarized in the statement that every encounter between two Javanese "involves a mutual recognition in language, gesture, and attitude of [one's] relative place in an elaborately and subtly stratified social order."[31]

The relations between persons of higher and lower status are motivated by as complex a set of factors as those in the Philippines. Reciprocity is the foundation of the relationships and, as in the Philippines, is based on both hard-headed calculations of how best to enhance one's position and on traditional values of deference to authority.

The notion of reciprocity is seen most clearly in the Javanese tradition of *gotong rojong,* a generic term that can be translated as "mutual aid" or "mutual coordination." President Sukarno adopted gotong rojong as the cornerstone of his ideology for Indonesia. He announced that his political and economic policies were based on Indonesian gotong rojong traditions that were hundreds of years old and had survived the Dutch colonization. Gotong rojong has traditionally referred to a social institution in which a group of persons collectively accomplishes something that touches their common interests.[32] The term has been used in the sense of "mutual cooperation" in building a community house or public dam, and is distinguished from "reciprocal assistance," which is concerned with private matters, such as aid to an individual farmer in his fields.

At present, gotong rojong refers to a wide variety of public and private relationships that require cooperation and coordination, some of which are spontaneous and voluntary, while others demand close calculation of every service performed.[33] Volun-

[31] Ann Ruth Wilner, "The Neotraditional Accommodation to Political Independence: The Case of Indonesia," in Lucian W. Pye, ed., *Asia: Cases in Comparative Politics* (Boston: Little, Brown, 1970), p. 259.

[32] Modestus Widojoko Notoatmodjo, "Gotong Rojong in Indonesian Administration" (unpublished Ph.D. dissertation, Indiana University, 1962), p. 11.

[33] The following discussion relies heavily on Koentjaraningrat, *Some Social-Anthropological Observations on Gotong Rojong Practices in Two Villages of Central Java* (Ithaca, New York: Cornell University, Modern Indonesia Project, Southeast Asia Program, 1961).

tary gotong rojong practices, in which there is no expectation of reciprocation, pertain to a death or some other family tragedy within a particular village community; in such cases the community rallies to support the bereaved or beset family. Work projects for the whole village also are spontaneous, but in this case there is a strong sense of interdependence among the community's citizens. For example, when a village member institutes a feast, it is considered proper for the guests to make a contribution in keeping with their wealth and status. According to Koentjaraningrat,

> If there is a guest who does not make a contribution, this soon becomes a subject of general talk in the village. And those who erred in the amount of their "tariff" will even not fail to hear, a few days after feast, some critical remarks from secondary sources. A person who thus "errs" frequently is certain to suffer dire consequences . . . very few persons, to his great shame, will attend his own celebration.[34]

Gotong rojong activities that include help in work that needs to be done around the house or in the fields are not voluntary, and strict calculations are made of the kind and amount of work and services so performed. This kind of labor debt must be repaid in full, not because of fear of critical gossip but because the notion of reciprocity has now become the major motivation. The rules of gotong rojong are so internalized that everyone follows them automatically.

In almost every case, gotong rojong expresses a spirit of mutual cooperation, unity, and community—a feeling of belonging together. It is true that one requirement for gotong rojong is the preexisting unity among community members, but it is precisely the gotong rojong concept itself, as manifested in previous experiences of the community members, that has created the collective feeling. Like utang na loob in the Philippines, gotong rojong is a very important integrative concept for the Indonesian social system and one that has done much to maintain the existence of the village community.

As in the Philippines, the dyadic relationships among the rural

---

[34] Ibid., p. 32.

Indonesians form the web of national integration, as Indonesian villagers are organized into chains of enduring superior-subordinate relationships. Karl Jackson notes that in the lower layer of the social structure in rural Indonesia "the chief act of participation for an individual is in his selection of his superiors, his patrons. . . . Political decision-making is . . . placed onto those with whom he has formed a dyadic, personal, and initially nonpolitical connection."[35]

The notion of reciprocal obligations at the heart of superior-subordinate relationships is found throughout the literature on Javanese culture. The power dynamic in these relationships, however, is characterized by a subordinate's automatic acceptance of his superiors' decrees. Traditional authority in Java is a form of power that does not require persuasion, rewards, sanctions, or other consciously calculated gains and losses. Karl Jackson reports that once the claim of traditional authority is established, the leader need not threaten, offer material or symbolic rewards, attempt to persuade, or refer to rules regulating roles; his commands are accepted solely on the basis of who he is and the kind of relationship he has with each of his followers.[36] The pattern of power is not simply one of quid pro quo reciprocity, although at times this is an important element of the relationships. Rather, the bonds are affective as well as instrumental. In fact, the optimal strategy for establishing traditional authority is "to transform the followers' perception of a transaction from one involving a debt of money into one involving a debt of moral obligation (*hutang budi*)."[37]

The hutang budi concept, which is felt by the patron toward his client and vice versa, is a major factor in explaining the long periods for which these relationships endure. The affective quality of the relationship differentiates it from the more mechanistic and calculated superior-subordinate bonds in Thailand, where there is more emphasis on the material qualities of the exchange process.

[35] Karl D. Jackson, "Traditional Authority and National Integration: The Dar'ul Islam Rebellion in West Java" (unpublished Ph.D. dissertation, M.I.T., 1971), p. 146.
[36] Ibid., p. 148.
[37] Ibid., p. 155.

Gotong rojong and bapakisme are important integrating factors in Indonesian society. The former is the basis of reciprocal ties and the latter is the basis of vertical relationships. Both concepts are highly instrumental for maximizing resources in the noninstitutionalized and economically underdeveloped Indonesian social-political system.

The emphasis on status in interpersonal relationships plays a crucial role in the performance of the Indonesian bureaucracy. In a fascinating study of the Indonesian civil service, Ann Ruth Wilner shows that the cause of poor administrative services is due less to an absence of skills and more to traditional values.[38] She explains that upper-echelon officials might postpone consideration of important issues for weeks because the relevant documents were not available. The file clerks in charge of these documents might be absent from work and it was not deemed appropriate to the status of those higher in the hierarchy to obtain the documents themselves. Nor could subordinates be guilty of disrespect for a superior's status by initiating action for obtaining the documents. Standards of propriety, etiquette, rank, and ritual intervened to thwart smooth administrative processes.[39]

Moreover, persons in authority find it difficult to "rationalize" the operations of the bureaucracy. Wilner cites a case study of an administrative head who was advised by an American expert to improve the productivity of the official's department by asserting his authority over subordinates through detailed job descriptions, on-the-job training, and threats of dismissal. The American expert was ignorant of the Indonesian system of authority, called by Wilner "nonauthoritarian paternalism," wherein status is legitimized by ascriptive criteria and those in authority are seen as benevolent. She points out that:

> In the traditional context, authority figures rarely find it necessary to exert overt force to exact compliance, attempt to avoid

[38] Ann Ruth Wilner, "The Neotraditional Accommodation to Political Independence: The Case of Indonesia," in Lucian W. Pye, ed., *Asia: Cases in Comparative Politics* (Boston: Little, Brown, 1970).

[39] Ibid., p. 268.

doing so, and do so only as a final and drastic measure. Paradoxically, exerting overt force tends to diminish presumptive authority in constituting a tacit admission that it can no longer be taken for granted.[40]

Power, then, is not manifested simply by holding formal power. Instead, power derives from status rather than action. Indonesians tend to distrust persons engaged in frenetic activity and implementation of programs. More respect is paid to *halus* persons (refined, passive) whose slightest desires are obeyed by their subordinates and followers.

Traditional authority differs from the exchange of relationships in the Philippines and Thailand because support isn't based so much on careful calculation of rewards versus costs. Traditional authority relations are not based on immediate calculations but depend upon the passage of time across generations. Moreover, patron-client ties are based on the resources available to the two parties. The bases of control are generally material, whereas in traditional authority relationships there may be no material benefits to exchange. However, traditional authority relationships in Indonesia are similar to patron-client ties in the Philippines and Thailand in that they are vertical, personal relationships between superiors and subordinates.

Thailand

The key element in the structure of Thai society is superior-subordinate relationships.[41] When two or more persons interact there is an automatic "feeling out" of relative status to ascertain who is superior and who is subordinate. In most cases there is

---

[40] Ibid., p. 272.

[41] The standard literature on superior-subordinate relationships in Thailand includes L. M. Hanks, "Merit and Power in the Thai Social Order," *American Anthropologist* (1962); David A. Wilson, *Politics in Thailand* (Ithaca, New York: Cornell University Press, 1962); Fred Riggs, *Thailand: The Modernization of a Bureaucratic Polity* (Honolulu: East-West Center Press, 1966); Herbert J. Rubin, "Will and Awe: Illustrations of Thai Villager Dependency upon Officials," *Journal of Asian Studies*, No. 3 (May, 1973), pp. 425–444; and James C. Scott, "Patron-Client Politics and Change in Southeast Asia," *American Political Science Review*, 66 (March, 1972).

little if any ambiguity, as one person will clearly be older, wealthier, better-educated, and/or the holder of a higher position of power.

In Thailand, status differences are based primarily on power. Power breeds status and decides whether a person is high or low in the eyes of others. A doctor prefers being a hospital director and the university professor prefers to become a dean or rector in order to have power over subordinates.[42]

> Power, be it small or absolute, enables one to take a man's life or to change a man's fate, is respected and desired by most Thai. The one who had neither power nor a powerful position is abused and not respected or honored by the general public, but when he gains power and position, those who used to abuse him will change immediately showing deference, paying respect, and serving him energetically.[43]

The superior is expected to be compassionate and kind and is expected to manifest these qualities by protecting, aiding, complimenting, and giving generously to those whose status is inferior. In return, the subordinate, or client, is expected to act deferentially to the superior, who is his patron. He is expected to perform his tasks efficiently and with the least amount of trouble for the superior.

Not wanting to trouble or embarrass another person— a traditional virtue in Thailand—is known as *kreng*. Rather than ask a favor of a superior that might in any way inconvenience or bother him, the subordinate will find an alternative way to meet his particular need and thereby preclude embarrassing confrontations with his superior. Indeed, kreng can hinder communication between superiors and subordinates by inhibiting the latter so that they dare not speak. It also serves the function of protecting the superior from endless demands by subordinates.

The patron-client relationship is not one of perfect balance,

[42] Kamol Somvichian, "The Thai Political Culture and Political Environment," *Social Science Review,* 1 (1977), 111.

[43] Phaitoon Kruegao, *Characteristics of the Thai Social Organization and Principles of Community Development* (Bangkok: Kuakul Press, 1967), p. 13. Quoted in Somvichian, ibid., pp. 111–112.

despite the reciprocal nature of the tie, because the superior (patron) has power over the subordinate (client). Power, as we have indicated, stems from imbalances of obligations—so that if an individual has few resources at his command but has great needs, a person who can supply the needed resources attains power over the recipients. However, there are limitations on the power a superior has over his subordinates. For example, excessive demands by the patron will cause his clients to seek a new patron.

In contrast to Indonesia, where traditional authority patterns are highly stable, and to the Philippines, where the sense of shame (*hiya*) keeps such ties relatively stable, the Thais exhibit high mobility from one set of bonds to another, and hence little sense of commitment to any particular patron-client grouping. Both the patron and his clientele continually assess the advantages and disadvantages of the relationship to determine whether it offers the greatest possible rewards. In many cases, subordinates who ascertain that a particular patron-client relationship would be disadvantageous must avoid contact with the potential patron so that they will not have to meet the obligations of such a bond. Similarly, potential patrons often must avoid contact with certain groups and projects so as not to overextend their resources.

Initially, patron-client bonds stem from personal relationships such as kinship groupings, official ties within the bureaucracy, school ties, or common village origins, and are based largely on personal loyalty. However, the personal element declines in significance as the tie becomes instrumental over time.

In rural Thailand the patron-client tie appears to be undifferentiated; that is, a patron meets the varied needs of his clientele. One's job, housing, and educational needs, for example, will be met or supplied in return for labor, deference, and protection. It is not necessary to reciprocate in kind, but reciprocation is expected to be equivalent. In the urban areas patron-client ties are more specialized and impersonal, and hence a client will arrange to have more than one patron so as to meet his multiple needs.

The notion of reciprocity in Thai social relationships is especially clear in the mutual labor patterns in the rural areas, as in the village of Ban Ping in northern Thailand, whose three forms of farm labor exchange—*lo, termkan,* and *aw haeng*—have been described by Moerman:

> The first, *lo,* is cooperative farming. It occurs when two or more households agree to work together until all have completed the tasks stipulated in their agreement. If households agree to *lo,* they keep no account of the number of days spent at each task and plot. *Termkan* and *aw haeng,* the other two forms of what I call exchange, are often merged in casual speech. "But in *termkan,*" says an articulate former headman, "there is no compulsion to return the same service that one has been given, nor need the return be immediate. . . . *Aw haeng,* on the other hand, is like a formal contract in which [for example] one must return a day of male reaping labor for a day of male reaping labor." If A comes to *term* (literally, "to add to") B, then B is expected to go to *term* A on some job fairly soon. This is called *termkan,* "adding to one another." Alternatively, B may return a "gift" (*pan*) instead of labor. For such an exchange, the reciprocal (*kan*) is not used. One is told, instead, that "A did such-and-such to *term* B, so B *pan'd* such an amount to A." Labor contributions that villages call *term* can thus be reciprocated by any of the rewards.[44]

Howard Kaufman reports that in the central plains area the two main systems of obtaining help are *awraeng* and *khawraeng.* The latter (which means "requesting strength") usually emanantes from a wealthy landowner who requests help from his tenants or debtors; but reciprocity is not expected. *Awraeng* ("a borrowing of strength"), on the other hand, entails a reciprocal and equivalent exchange of labor. In both cases, Kaufman points out, aid in the form of labor is first rendered in the neighborhood of the rice farm, irrespective of family ties. Thus, family obligations are no more salient than neighborhood ties.[45] In neither case, however, are the reciprocal obligations as effective or all-consuming as those in the Philippines and Indonesia.

In Thai politics, patrons become patrons largely because of the official position they hold in the government hierarchy. At

---

[44] Michael Moerman, *Peasant Choice and Agricultural Change in Thailand* (Los Angeles: University of California Press, 1968), p. 117.

[45] Howard Kaufman, "Bangkhuad: A Community Study in Thailand" (unpublished Ph.D. dissertation, Indiana University, 1955), pp. 59–60.

the national level, the highest-level patrons are persons who command positions of power in the cabinet, and the patron-client network descends through every level of the hierarchy. The superior-subordinate role expectations strongly influence the manner in which political decisions are made. Within the context of his position, a subordinate will comply with a superior's decision because it is natural and proper for him to do so. Moreover, the former will rarely initiate action.

The overlapping nature of the patron-client bond, on the other hand, allows intrusion into the hierarchy at times, so that clientele input can be significant. In addition, a patron feels compelled to take care of his clients' needs in the most benevolent manner in order to retain their loyalty. Thus, subordinates play a significant role in the manner in which the patron-client relationship is carried out.

A striking aspect of the patron-client relationship is the leeway it allows for individual action; for it does not enforce a rigid identity with group action. Yet the Thai is aware of his own role (and that of others) in the social hierarchy. He recognizes the social inequalities that stem from wealth, power, position, and knowledge, and he conforms his behavior to what is expected of him.[46] Such superior-subordinate relationships, which are at the heart of Thai society, are manifested in the language, customary greetings, deferential behavioral patterns, and the expectations and attitudes of both the superiors and the subordinates. Outside the hierarchical relationships, however, role constraints are not found, and the Thais do very much what they as individuals wish to do. But while he interacts with a superior, a Thai's most proper and acceptable form of role behavior is that of deference.

This tension between Thai "spontaneity" on the one hand and "deference to authority" on the other stems from the dual socialization process Thais experience in their formative years. In the Thai society, the family socialization process emphasizes freedom and individualism whereas the bureaucratic socialization process as found in schools and in the political system emphasizes dependence and authoritarianism.

---

[46] See Jacques Amyot, *Changing Patterns of Social Structure in Thailand, 1851–1965* (Delhi: UNESCO Research Center, 1965).

In the thoughts and mind of the Thai there are always two conflicting forces, the desire to live without restrictions on the one hand and the necessity of living under the control of superior power on the other.[47]

The perception of patron-client relationships and their importance to the political process in northern Thailand was shown in a study by the present author.[48] The responses of provincial leaders to a series of statements confirm the view that patron-client ties are an integral part of Thai politics. For example, 84 percent of the fifty leaders interviewed agreed with the statement that personal ties are more important than formal administrative ties for accomplishing important tasks. Seventy-eight percent agreed that if a subordinate does a favor for his superior it is necessary for the superior to reciprocate in some way. Similarly, 72 percent concurred that paying respect to your immediate superior is more important than being an effective administrator in determining career mobility.

At every level, patron-client entourages perform the functions of disseminating information, allocating resources, and organizing people. These groupings, therefore, play a key role in the integration of Thai society; indeed, they are the web of the society, or—to change the image—an infinite number of dyadic groupings, each of which is a link in a network of reciprocities that extends throughout Thai society and cuts across bureaucracies and extrabureaucratic structures. In some cases a patron-client grouping will be complete in itself, whereas in other cases such ties or groupings will run through the entire governmental hierarchy. The constant flux in superior-subordinate arrangements assists the integrative function of the relationships by bringing those who are lower in the hierarchy into contact with a diverse and continually expanding group of higher-status individuals.

The exchange relationships among individuals in the Philippines, Indonesia, and Thailand may be viewed as highly rational

---

[47] Kamol Somvichian, op. cit., p. 105.

[48] Clark D. Neher, "Political Corruption in a Thai Province," *Journal of Developing Areas,* July, 1977.

bonds of reciprocity that enable each participant to maximize his desires and values. In Indonesia and the Philippines these bonds are long lasting and affective, whereas in Thailand they seem to be primarily instrumental. In the Philippines the family and kin groupings are the focus of patron-client relationships, whereas in Thailand, extrafamily ties, such as those of business or school, are paramount. The "debt of obligation" between superiors and subordinates is greater in the Philippines than in Thailand, where patron-client bonds are looser.

In all three nations—the Philippines, Indonesia, and Thailand—the superior-subordinate bonds are the major integrating element of society, and they form the basis for the social and political structures of all three societies. Inasmuch as all social relationships are embodied in social exchanges, a description of these relationships also provides insight into the central questions of organization in any society—in Southeast Asia and elsewhere.

Vietnam

As in the Philippines, Indonesia, and Thailand, patron-client relationships flourish in Vietnam in those areas where institutions have not yet taken over the traditional functions of these ties. In North Vietnam, where the Communist government has carried out fundamental changes in the relations between landlord and peasant (for example), patron-client ties have been weakened. Nevertheless, the traditional notion of deference to authority remains an important part of the Vietnamese political culture.

Historically, Vietnamese attitudes and beliefs were determined by the Confucianist philosophy which pervaded Vietnam for centuries. Confucianism stressed principles of government under which political authority was centralized, with the emperor at the top and a mandarin bureaucracy administering the state according to his whims.

The centralized mandarin state was crucial for building an extensive network of dikes for irrigation, for preserving national independence, especially against the constant intervention of the Chinese, and for guarding against peasant revolts. To carry out these goals, the state had the capacity to mobilize fully the entire society.

Two important values emerged from the traditional Confucianist state. First, traditional Vietnamese culture rested on the notion of duties of the lower to the higher: the ruled to the ruler, the son to the father, and the pupil to the teacher. Second, the individual did not view himself as an independent and isolated person, for he did not distinguish himself from his position in the society. Obligations to superiors were the cement of the Confucian order. These obligations were translated into deferential and unquestioning behavior toward those in authority.

According to traditional Vietnamese ideas, there is a universal moral order which remains in harmony as long as each person carries out his duty by fulfilling the obligations of subordinate to superior and vice versa. The emperor is as obliged to rule according to moral principles as the peasant is to follow his commands. When harmony does not exist, or when, for example, there are wars, pestilence, or natural calamities, the ruled may perceive that the emperor has lost the "mandate of heaven." The personal virtue of the emperor is lacking, for otherwise the cosmos would not be out of harmony.

The concept of the mandate of heaven is important for illuminating authority relationships in Vietnam. On the one hand, one can interpret the cosmological beliefs of the Vietnamese as essentially conservative, since the mandate of heaven is lost or gained largely for fortuitous means that are beyond the control of individuals. On the other hand, the cosmological view can provide a rationale for rebellion, for if the emperor is lacking in virtue, with a consequent disharmonious effect on the cosmos and society, his mandate is perceived as lost and his rule is called into question. Proof that the new revolutionary regime has taken over the mandate of heaven is the rise of a new government, totally in control, replacing the previous regime's doctrines, policy, and leadership. The ruled transfer their allegiance to the new government with a renewed sense of community that takes form through a harmonious arrangement between the cosmos and society.

The change to a Communist government in April 1975 was the most recent example of such a total change. Clearly, a large sector of the Vietnamese population had sensed the changing of the mandate during the post-World War II struggle, first against the French and then during the second Indochinese War. Ho Chi Minh inherited the mandate when he declared the independence of Vietnam in 1945. For many in the southern section of Vietnam, that mandate was temporarily lost as Ngo Dinh Diem and his anti-Communist government rose to power. But the inexorable movement of the North Vietnamese and the insurgent South Vietnamese convinced more and more people that the mandate was Ho Chi Minh's.

The Communist triumph caused authority relationships to shift rapidly, and traumatically, to the new Communist rulers. The Marxist view of collective discipline is congruent with the Confucianist concept of societal mobilization. Marxists also share with Confucianism the principle of political morality whereby leaders should exemplify high moral standards.[49] The centralized, hierarchical nature of the command structure under a vanguard class is similar to that of the Confucianist mandarin state. For these reasons, and because the Communist government has total control of society, the Vietnamese are likely to carry out their duty to obey the sovereign leaders, like a son to his father.

POLITICAL CORRUPTION IN THAILAND

The following study of Thailand points out the relationship between political corruption and authority relationships. Political corruption is a pervasive phenomenon in Southeast Asian politics. Graft, conflict of interest, kickbacks, and other forms of unsanctioned use or manipulation of public office for private, self-interested ends has become (or remains) an important aspect of the political culture.

The term "political corruption" has been defined variously by numerous authors. Indeed, a major problem for those who write on political corruption is that the norms or specifics of one society do not agree or correspond with those of another society. Corruption is culturally conditioned.[50] Generally, political cor-

[49] Nguen Khac Vien, *Tradition and Revolution in Vietnam* (n.p.: Indochina Resource Center, 1974), p. 47.

[50] David A. Bailey, "The Effect of Corruption in a Developing Nation," in Arnold J. Heidenheimer, ed., *Political Corruption: Readings in Comparative Analysis* (New York: Holt, Rinehart and Winston, 1970), p. 522.

ruption refers to the unsanctioned use or manipulation of public office for self-interested ends. In Thailand, officials are familiar with the Western label "corruption" and have even borrowed the term to describe unsanctioned official behavior. "Corruption" is one of several Thai words that are used to describe such behavior. *Tucharit to rachakan* (fraud against the government), *kin sinbon* (bribery), *cho rat bang luang* (to cheat the public), and *kong luang* (to cheat the government) are terms which refer to officials' corrupt behavior and which are used interchangeably.

In Thailand, financial considerations have been paramount in determining political participation. Throughout Thai history, politicans have been bought and sold by the regimes in power to perpetuate political dominance. Rulers who were not able or willing to satisfy financial demands, or who were not willing to countenance corruption, quickly lost their positions. For example, Prime Minister Khuang Aphaiwong (in 1947) did not accede to the financial demands of certain military officers and was promptly overthrown. Similarly, when Prime Minister Phibun Songkram blocked Marshal Sarit Thanarat's access to the huge fund from the State Lottery Bureau (which Sarit used illicitly to enrich his friends and himself), Sarit promptly led a successful coup against Philbun.

The practice of using state funds for private purposes was perfected by Sarit during his rule, and by his successors, especially Generals Thanom and Prapat. The ruling bureaucrats and military established links with the leaders of the business world, sharing the profits of major corporations in return for favors. For example, in 1974 it was disclosed that the exiled "three tyrants," Thanom Kittikachorn, Prapat Charustien, and Narong Kittikachorn, had assets worth $70 million. The fear of losing access to these sources of corruption was one of the principal reasons why Thanom and Prapat groomed Narong, who was Thanom's son and Prapat's son-in-law, to take power after their retirement.

Not only the top leadership is influenced by financial considerations. Every election in Thailand has been characterized by the buying and selling of votes. Following the 1969 election, the United Thai People's party (UTPP), which was controlled by the military, spent millions of *baht* to persuade national assemblymen who had won election as independents to join the party. The UTPP was thereby able to run its plurality into a solid majority and to prolong the dominance of the ruling elite.

The traditional practice has continued to the present time, as politicians forge reciprocal links with wealthy businessmen. Party programs and principles are secondary to financial considerations in determining who will join which party. Competition for office revolves around the struggle for the perquisites that top political positions provide, so that the public's interest is thoroughly subordinated to private self-interest. Accountability is directed toward those who have financial resources rather than to the general public. Corruption, then, is one activity that officials engage in to maximize their desired goals of financial and status rewards. In many respects, corruption is an outgrowth of the traditional Thai offering of gifts to those in office. In Thai history, there has never been an administrative structure in which private and public affairs have been strictly separated. Officials were given an administrative post much as if it were a fiefdom, with the expectation that these officials would make their living off the people in the administrated area. They would *kin muang*, "eat the realm," by collecting fees, taxes, and gifts from the citizenry for private advantage.

Political corruption in Thailand has been documented in several major works.[51] The basic thrust of this literature is that Thai bureaucrats, at all levels, engage in unsanctioned use or manipulation of public office to assure financial, or other resource benefits, for themselves or for persons within their entourage. The authors emphasize the personal benefits derived from corruption and focus on the lack of extrabureaucratic controls as a principal reason for the widespread incidence of corrupt be-

[51] See Fred Riggs, *Thailand: The Modernization of a Bureaucratic Polity* (Honolulu: East-West Center Press, 1966); Edward Van Roy, "On the Theory of Corruption," *Economic Development and Cultural Change* (October, 1970); Uthai Hiranto, "Bureaucratic Corruption in Thailand," *Thai Journal of Development Administration* [in Thai] (January, 1969); James C. Scott, "Corruption in Thailand," in James C. Scott, *Comparative Political Corruption* (Englewood Cliffs, New Jersey: Prentice-Hall, Inc., 1972); David Morrell, "Legislatures and Political Development: The Problem of Corruption," unpublished paper presented to the Conference on Legislatures in Contemporary Societies, Albany, 1975. In addition, numerous articles in the Thai press have focused on corruption.

havior. Furthermore, these authors contend that the personal nature (as opposed to institutional nature) of the political system, with emphasis on patron-client relationships as the heart of the political process, explains the prevalence of corruption. They argue that those in superior positions (patrons) require resources to protect, aid, and provide generously for those whose status is inferior (clients) to retain the subordinates' loyalty. The superiors' position is enhanced in the struggle for power among factions by retaining a sizable following.

Fred Riggs notes that high-level officials and individual businessmen, often ethnically Chinese, have developed a reciprocal relationship he refers to as "pariah entrepreneurship," whereby bureaucrats pass laws favorable to businessmen in return for financial favors.[52] James Scott concludes that political competition in Thailand concerns personal cliques organized according to a patron-client model which are motivated around a "more or less amoral quest for power and spoils."[53] Scott suggests that clique relationships are cemented or held together mainly by the material incentives available to officials. Patrons must offer tangible inducements to attract and retain followers:

> Here is where corruption centers, since these inducements may take the form of political promotions, opportunities for profits, or the promise of such benefits. Although many rewards (e.g., promotions, assignments, etc.) can be granted within the law, others violate even the relatively permissive Thai legal order. Thus the diversion of public funds, mismanagement of state enterprises, and kickbacks from government contracts are a natural part of clique building.[54]

Corrupt activity in Thailand exists among legislators as well as executive branch officers.[55] Morrell, for example, discusses nine categories of corruption and indicates the impact of each type on the political system.[56] He concludes that perhaps as many as 75 percent of the elected representatives were involved to some

---

[52] Riggs, *Thailand*, p. 251.

[53] Scott, *Comparative Political Corruption*, p. 59.

[54] Ibid., p. 63.

[55] Morrell, "Legislatures and Political Development," p. 13.

[56] The nine categories: expediting, bidding, "honest graft," bribes, stealing, kickbacks, discriminatory law enforcement, buying jobs, and buying policy.

extent in the kickbacks on development projects, payoffs from party leaders for supporting specific legislation, and "squeezes" of local businessmen.[57] Corruption on the part of the representatives, however, was small compared to the corruption of senior bureaucrats and military leaders. Bureaucratic corruption is estimated at some $800 million—about 50 percent of the government's national budget.[58]

The ubiquity of political corruption was substantiated in the answers of 50 leading figures in northern Thailand to a series of questions related to corruption.[59] A significant percentage of the Thai elite clearly perceives a relationship between patron-client relationships and corruption. Over 70 percent of the provincial leaders agreed with each of the following statements: to understand corruption in Thailand, you have to understand superior-subordinate relationships; to provide gifts to their subordinates, some officials engage in corruption; once a person becomes a superior over others, he is likely to use his status to benefit himself; it is important to give gifts to your subordinates if you want them to remain loyal. Over 80 percent of the Thai leaders agreed with the statements: political corruption has be-

[57] Morrell, "Legislatures and Political Development," p. 33.

[58] Ibid., p. 34.

[59] Data for this paper were derived from in-depth interviews with fifty leading figures in Chiang Mai Province, northern Thailand, in 1974. The local leaders were chosen through a complex procedure that included elements of the three major methods of research in elite studies: the positional, reputational, and decision-making approaches. The latter two approaches were used initially and then compared with a list of occupants of formal governmental, social, and business positions. Fifty is an arbitrary number and does not imply a closed group of like-minded persons or a "power elite."

Originally, 55 leaders were chosen but five declined to be interviewed. Of the 50 leaders, 22 were top-ranking bureaucrats, 18 were businessmen, and ten were social and religious-educational leaders. Eighteen of the 50 were born in Chiang Mai and had spent most of their lives in that town. The other 32 leaders, including all the bureaucrats, were born outside Chiang Mai.

The data on role expectations and orientations were derived from a combination of open-ended and forced-choice interviews with the 50 leaders. The questionnaires were formulated by myself; my research associate was responsible for transcribing the questions into Thai, for assuring that the questions made sense in the Thai cultural context, and for carrying out a substantial number of the interviews.

come so integral a part of the Thai government that it is the expected norm; subordinates who give gifts to superiors are likely to be treated better by the superiors than subordinates who don't give gifts; I have the duty to follow the orders of my superior even if he requests or encourages corrupt actions on my part.

The study showed that immediate superiors or subordinates, as well as informal clientele, play the dominant role in determining the role behavior of officials. Superiors often placed their subordinates in positions where they could collect fees and taxes, or decide contracts, with the understanding that the subordinate was allowed "discretion" in his assessments. Furthermore, there was the understanding that the subordinate was beholden to the superior for being placed in that position and for continuing in the position, and hence reciprocation was expected.

Thai officials seek to maximize their personal interests in terms of financial rewards and sociopolitical status. On all accounts, political corruption can be seen as a rational means to reach goals rather than an aberration, and as compatible with a personalistic network of interactions.

POLITICAL CULTURE IN INDONESIA: THE IDEOLOGY OF "GUIDED DEMOCRACY"

Although all persons maintain certain attitudes, values, and beliefs about political activities, only a small minority of a people articulate systematic and explicit ideologies. Political ideologies are belief systems that explain and justify a preferred political order for a society and that present guidelines for its attainment. The minority who have well-developed ideological beliefs tend to be highly influential in a society. Political ideologies, then, although a part of the political culture, are most systematic and more often articulated by those in command.

Political ideologies have a number of important functions. First, commonly held ideologies provide the foundation of a stable political order by integrating the ruled with the rulers. To serve as a legitimizing and stabilizing force, a political ideology must be reasonably compatible with the more general political culture of a society. Second, political ideologies provide simple and coherent explanations for a complicated world. Ideologies reduce ambiguity and provide a "lens" through which the world is seen as congruent with established cultural beliefs, attitudes, and values. Finally, political ideologies provide a sense of purpose and commitment to action.

One of the most striking political ideologies of modern Southeast Asian politics was that enunciated by President Sukarno during the period of guided democracy from 1958 to 1965. His view of guided democracy consisted of a number of slogans as well as the consistently argued beliefs that functioned as the basis for the Indonesian state for some seven years. The strength of Sukarno's political ideology rested in large part on its congruency with perceived Indonesian attitudes, beliefs, and values.

Sukarno's ideology consisted of two basic themes: revolution and the *Pantja Sila* (Five Principles). His view of revolution called for fundamental change in every facet of Indonesian life. A new Indonesian man was to be created, free of the fetters of the colonialist legacy. He called for the complete restructuring of the political, economic, and social institutions of Indonesia by any means needed to accomplish the task. The purpose of the revolution was a "just and prosperous society." Sukarno spoke of a revolution of the deepest possible kind that "penetrates into the bones, into the marrow, into the mind, into the feeling, into the soul, and into the spirit . . ."[60]

Sukarno's revolutionary rhetoric was matched by the transformation he ordered of the political institutions. He issued a decree of 5 July 1959, dissolving the Constituent Assembly that had been established during the Liberal Democratic period and substituting a People's Consultative Assembly. In the same decree he abolished the constitution and reintroduced the 1945 revolutionary constitution with its emphasis on presidential rather than parliamentary government. He "retooled" the executive body, the armed forces, and the political party system. He decreed that the government would henceforth take over and supervise the vital instruments of production. He called for the total restructuring of decision-making processes to make them compatible with indigenous means and to assure his own dominance. The president became the state.

---

[60] Herbert Feith and Lance Castles, *Indonesian Political Thinking* (Ithaca, New York: Cornell University Press, 1970), p. 101.

However, the revolution involved more than fundamental change in government structures. The revolution itself was the highest order of power to which everyone owed allegiance. For Sukarno the revolution enveloped every aspect of his life.

> Frankly, I tell you: I belong to the group of people who are bound in spiritual longing by the Romanticism of Revolution. I am inspired by it, I am fascinated by it, I am completely absorbed by it, I am crazed, I am obsessed by the Romanticism of Revolution.[61]

The Pantja Sila represents the second principal theme of the ideology of guided democracy. Sukarno saw the Five Principles as the embodiment of the character and identity of the Indonesian nation. Nationalism, the first principle of the Panja Sila, merged with the second principle of internationalism. These two principles were characterized by solidarity among the newly emerging forces (NEFOS) against the old established forces (OLDEFOS). The NEFOS were the "progressive" Third World and Communist nations undergoing revolution. The OLDEFOS, on the other hand, represented the neoimperialist nations and their allies. The United States was the leader of this group. Sukarno's confrontation policy against Malaysia which began in 1962 and ended in 1965 was described as a classic example of NEFOS struggle against an OLDEFOS lackey.

The Pantja Sila, in its third principle, democracy, spelled out the dimensions of guided democracy. Sukarno had only disdain for what he referred to as "majoritarian" or "50 percent plus one" democracy. This Western concept of democracy he viewed as causing division among the populace. Sukarno eschewed Western democracy and instead called for a true democracy based on traditional village procedures of making decisions by means of deliberation and consultation (*musjawarah*) and the search for unanimous agreement (*mufakat*). Under this principle of democracy, all decisions are to be made by a process of consultation with all sides of questions deliberated openly. Once the leader makes a decision based on an objective and thorough

---

[61] Sukarno, "The Dynamism of Revolution" (1960), in ibid., p. 114.

analysis of the deliberations, all parties to the decision will unanimously support it, since it results from prolonged discussion and the emergence of a group consensus.

The spirit in which the deliberations take place is that of gotong rojong, or mutual aid, in which there is a unified feeling for the consideration of everyone's views, a spirit of tolerance and generosity, an objective view of all sides, and a willingness to put one's own views aside for the best interests of all. Gotong rojong became the central theme of the democratic concept of guided democracy.

The musjawarah-mufakat processes were ostensibly incorporated into the political system of Indonesia by appointing advisory councils with broad representation given to diverse interests. Even the legislature (called the Gotong Rojong Parliament) which was established in 1960 consisted primarily of functional groups representing various interests such as farmers, laborers, educators, the military, Communists and Muslims.

The attempt to apply village-level procedures to national-level decision-making bodies did not work well and became more a cloak for power struggles and personalized rule than an augmentation of the number of people involved in decision-making. The councils mainly performed a rubber-stamp function for decisions made by Sukarno himself.

The fourth principle of the Pantja Sila is social justice for all Indonesians. Sukarno argued that social justice could come about once all forms of colonialism and imperalism ended. Sukarno blamed the Dutch colonialists for the widespread conditions of poverty in his nation. To overcome poverty, there must be a revolution to throw off every vestige of colonial exploitation, so that no person can oppress another. Sukarno used the name Marhaen to describe the destitute people of Indonesia. Marhaen is the name of a pauper with his own land and hoe but who is nevertheless barely able to subsist.

> And of poor Indonesians there are not one million, not two million, or three, but almost all of the Indonesian People. Almost all of the People of Indonesia are Marhaen! They are the poor, common people; yes, the poor workers; yes the poor peasant; yes, the poor fisherman; yes, the poor clerk; yes, the poor stall

vendor; yes, the poor cart driver; yes, the poor chauffeur—all of these are embraced by the one term Marhaen.[62]

To bring about social justice, Sukarno spoke of the need to promote economic democracy with people's cooperatives, to stand up against capitalist enterprises, of the need for compulsory and free education for every child from elementary school to university, and for a massive fight against illiteracy. Workers should be paid sufficient to live as civilized human beings.

These goals remained elusive during Sukarno's rule. Although the rhetoric of that guided democracy era supported socialist principles, the economy was organized more along corporate or state capitalist lines. The Marhaen remained desperately poor, and when Sukarno was overthrown in 1965 the Indonesian economy was in shambles.

The last principle is belief in one Supreme God. Sukarno stressed that this principle guaranteed a tolerance for all persons who believe in God whether Muslim, Buddhist, Christian, or members of any other religious group. Although extremist Muslims would have have preferred Indonesia to be proclaimed an Islamic state, Sukarno opted for a state with no set religious orthodoxy.

According to Sukarno, if all five principles of the Pantja Sila were compressed into one, that one would be gotong rojong.

> The state of Indonesia which we are to establish must be a gotong rojong state. Is that not something marvelous a Gotong Rojong state! . . . Gotong Rojong means toiling hard together, a joint struggle to help one another.[63]

In retrospect it is clear that guided democracy was instigated by Sukarno at least partly to enhance and perpetuate his own personal dictatorship. Sukarno systematically dismantled the governmental institutions of the Liberal Democratic period and replaced them with consultative structures that he was assured of controlling. During the period of guided democracy, he dis-

---

[62] Sukarno, "Marhaen, A Symbol of the Power of the Indonesian People" (1957) in ibid., p. 157.

[63] Sukarno, "The Pantja Sila" (1945) in ibid., p. 49.

solved the elected parliament, curbed political party activity, censored the press, and encouraged a personality cult around himself.

On the other hand, Sukarno did make an effort to create a uniquely Indonesian political system based on traditional indigenous values of consultation. From a Western point of view such a procedure might well be seen as a disguise for dictatorial rule. From an Indonesian point of view, however, Sukarno might be perceived as sincerely drawing upon the collective wisdom of the people. It is much too simplistic to see Sukarno as a dictator in control of every aspect of political life. On the contrary, Sukarno was forced to balance the diverse demands of powerful interest groups including the military, the Communists, the extremist Muslims, Javanese leaders, and outer-island representatives.

Sukarno was a poor day-by-day administrator. He had little interest in and ability to cope with the bureaucratic procedures necessary for effective administration. His legacy, then, was in his ability to fashion a uniquely Indonesian political ideology which provided an ideal toward which the Indonesian populace could identify and aspire. His achievement was providing Indonesians with a new sense of self-confidence following several centuries of oppression and exploitation by a foreign power.

POLITICAL CULTURE AND THE PROSPECTS FOR DEMOCRACY IN SOUTHEAST ASIA

Few Southeast Asian nations have sustained governments in which the general public plays a leading role in determining governmental policies and in which the political leaders accept the public's role as legitimate. Such democratic governments depend on democratic-oriented attitudes, beliefs, and values deeply enough ingrained in the consciousness of elite and ordinary citizens that the citizens don't readily abandon democracy because it is difficult or inefficient. The emergency and maintenance of a democratic political system depend at least partly on the existence of a political culture that supports the basic principles of democracy.

Following are three case studies of Southeast Asian nations whose political culture has been analyzed by three different authors. They found similar patterns of political attitudes, beliefs, and values that appear to diminish democracy's chances.

Political Ideology in Malaysia

James C. Scott has analyzed the political views of Malaysian bureaucrats and found that democratic beliefs have not penetrated deeply into the minds of his sample of elite respondents.[64] Indeed, their basic value-orientations have not provided a hospitable climate for democratic political systems.

Scott found that the elites in Malaysia hold a formalized view of democracy which tends to crumble when encountered by more deeply held values. The overwhelming majority of bureaucrats were willing to endorse a "crisis dictatorship," for example, when stability was threatened. This might account for the almost total absence of opposition to the suspension of parliament and of the democratic process following the 1969 communal riots in Malaysia. Clearly, the value of stability and security took precedence over democratic values.

Scott also notes that a substantial majority of those bureaucrats he interviewed were pessimistic about the durability of democracy in their nation. Their pessimism focuses on the willingness to forsake democracy when it threatens the values of unity and economic development or when communism threatens.

Malaysians are cynical about democratic norms in organizations. They tend to see individuals exploiting organizations for social recognition, power, and material rewards. This stress on man's selfishness and untrustworthiness stems from deep-seated negative evaluations of human nature in which all human actions are believed to be prompted by self-interest. Scott shows that the orientation of Malaysian civil servants toward nature conforms closely with what one would expect of a society with limited resources. Malaysia has a "constant-pie" orientation that assumes a fixed scarcity of desired material goods. In a situation of scarcity there is not enough power, wealth, status, or security to go around. One person's benefit is another's loss. He argues that the quality of politics in a community where the pie is assumed to be constant is fundamentally different from politics in a society where the pie is thought to be expanding. Where the

[64] James C. Scott, *Political Ideology in Malaysia* (New Haven, Connecticut: Yale University Press, 1968).

pie is constant, distrust prevails. Where the pie is expanding, cooperation and generosity are possible.

According to Scott, Malaysian cynicism about human nature results from early socialization processes experienced by young Malaysians. He argues that child rearing in Malaysia is marred by seemingly unpredictable alternations between shows of affection and its withdrawal. The consequence is a learned distrust of those in authority and a lack of confidence in managing the environment.[65] Malaysian socialization processes are also said to emphasize punishment for bad behavior rather than rewards for accomplishment. The result is a lack of ego strength and a belief that passive obedience is in one's best interest. Scott suggests that the habits of automatic obedience and of submission to the wishes of authority figures are hardly characteristic of the democratic personality.

> The emphasis on dependence, non-participation, uncritical compliance with authority, and fear and the absence of dependable parental responses are at variance with the growth of interpersonal trust, with mastery of the environment, with an independent spirit, and with norms of participation—all of which are related to the "democratic style."[66]

School and group socialization experiences strengthen the patterns learned earlier. Teachers are typically authoritarian, demanding rote learning and obedience. Voluntary organizations are viewed as facades behind which individuals pursue their own selfish interests.[67]

It is only through the manifest socialization processes that the citizenry learns to support democracy. In the family and in the schools, the young are taught that democracy is the best form of government. That democracy has fared as well as it has in Malaysia is due in large part to explicit learning about democracy, as well as to the generally adequate level of governmental effectiveness. Its future would be cast in grave doubt if the level of satisfaction with the system's output were to decline for any

[65] Ibid., p. 155.
[66] Ibid., p. 157.
[67] Ibid., p. 159.

reason.[68] That kind of support for democracy is more tenuous than support based on deeply rooted values.

Scott sums up his analysis of Malaysian elite beliefs:

> If primary socialization does not contribute to the growth of democratic personalities, neither do the basic value orientations that have been described. The orientation toward man is one that stresses his narrow selfishness and lack of internal restraint. The heavy burden of misanthropy and suspicion generated by this orientation leaves little room for the trust and cooperativeness implied by a democratic system. . . . Finally, the belief that most desired values are scarce and their quantity fixed by nature leads these civil servants to conceive of political and economic life as a zero-sum contest. Each of these orientations nurtures political beliefs and values that are scarcely hospitable to a democratic style.[69]

Nation-Building in Burma

Lucian W. Pye, like James Scott, was concerned with why a Southeast Asian nation, in this case Burma, has had such great difficulties in creating an effective, modern, democratic state.[70] Pye introduced his argument by observing that many of the problems of transitional societies are obvious: shortage of capital, absence of trained personnel, inadequate social and educational facillities, excessive population in relation to land, and grossly imperfect means for mobilizing both human and material resources.[71] However, beneath this manifest level there are psychological problems, involving attitudes, beliefs, and values, which tend to inhibit effective action and which restrain the entire process of nation-building.

Pye believes that the core explanation for the problem of nation-building in Burma stems from the particular political culture that has evolved over many centuries. The root problem is the lack of trust exhibited by Burmese in human relations.

---

[68] Ibid., p. 167.

[69] Ibid., p. 158.

[70] Lucian W. Pye, *Politics, Personality, and Nation Building: Burma's Search for Identity* (New Haven, Connecticut: Yale University Press, 1962).

[71] Ibid., p. xv.

From his interviews with a sample of Burmese politicians and administrators Pye developed a view of the Burmese as so calculating and distrustful of others that they are lacking in the capacity or desire to form associational groups. Only individuals who have developed associational sentiments, he argues, can effectively participate in organizations. Because such sentiments do not exist amoung Burmese politicians, organizations and groups are not formed. Pye then suggests that such groups are an integral and necessary part of modern democratic government.

Pye found that impossible barriers are established between persons interacting in a bureaucratic setting. Status considerations and formal rules tend to close off the flow of communication. These barriers are erected out of a pervasive sense of insecurity which causes everyone to fall back on the safest course of action. Burmese insecurity is said to be a product of the family socialization experiences.

Pye's analysis of the family socialization process in Burma bears striking resemblance to that described by Scott in Malaysia. Mothers vacillate between extremes of warmth and indulgence and of disinterest.[72] The child is thus brought up to feel that he or she has no control over the ways in which he is treated by others. The child sees himself in a world in which there is no rational relationship, no recognizable cause-and-effect connection between his desires and the fulfillment of those desires.

Pye argues that Burmese children are not rewarded for their achievement and that obedience is the primary virtue. The child thus tends to expect security from being subservient and yielding to his superiors.[73] Behavior is controlled by threats (malicious spirits will carry the child off) or by shame, so that few internalized standards of behavior are instilled in a child.

The Burmese child, then, exhibits traits of distrust, passive obedience, the fear of making mistakes, and restraint on creativity and innovation. This Burmese child, a product of traditional socialization patterns, is later exposed to the Western

[72] Ibid., p. 182.
[73] Ibid., p. 183.

beliefs and standards imported during the colonial period and its aftermath. The result is a sense of discontinuity and identity ambiguity for the Burmese elites who are thrust into the Western administrative system set up by the British. The fear of failure immobilizes the civil servant. His sense of self-confidence and trust in others decreases as his own identity becomes problematical. Burmese civil servants learn to rely on authoritarian rulers and to defer in an exaggerated manner to rituals and rigid procedures.

Political Culture and Democracy in Thailand

This third case study of Thailand rests on data derived from in-depth interviews with 90 Thai villagers and 50 leading figures in northern Thailand. As with the studies by Scott and Pye, the author argued that a capacity to cooperate with others for mutual benefit, to trust the responses of others, to relate on the basis of equality, and to have a feeling of self-competency are important cultural preconditions of a flourishing democracy.

In Thailand, a sample of the general public and local leaders were asked to respond to a series of statements on "faith in people."[74] The responses of the general Thai public show a high degree of distrust and a belief in the necessity of caution in dealing with others. Ninety-two percent of the sample of the general public and 72 percent of the provincial elites agreed that "if you don't watch yourself, people will take advantage of you." Only 18 and 28 percent of the same group agreed that "most people can be trusted." The Thais' view of human nature was revealed in the responses to the statement that "human nature is fundamentally cooperative." Thirty-eight percent of the general public and 52 percent of the leaders agreed with that sentiment. Only ten and 14 percent of the two groups agreed that "most people are more inclined to help others than to think of themselves first."

The responses show the sample of Thais to have low levels of trust and to be negative and suspicious about their interpersonal relationships. Confidence and trust in relationships increases,

[74] The questions were adapted from Gabriel Almond and Sidney Verba, *The Civic Culture* (Princeton, New Jersey: Princeton University Press, 1963).

however, among those of higher political and socioeconomic status. The relatively influential and wealthy Thai local leaders, who average 12 years of schooling, consistently show less distrust than the general public, who average six years and whose economic status is far lower.

These findings are significant for the political system because they directly relate to group activity and the relationship between government officials and the citizenry. In Thailand, those few who expressed high degrees of trust also opted for group cooperation to realize their goals. There appears to be a relationship between the degree of trust among people and the possibility for democratic rule. The degree of political cooperation and group formation among the citizenry is at least partially related to one's sense of trust or distrust of other persons' actions. People will interact formally and informally more effectively and enthusiastically if they are not constantly on the defensive and suspicious of others' motives.

The involvement of the citizenry in governmental decision-making necessitates some degree of cooperation if the individual is to have any impact at all on government decisions. Given the high degree of distrust most Thais feel toward each other, one would surmise that such cooperative activity is rare. When asked what they would do to try to influence their local government officials only eight and 16 percent of the general public and leaders respectively said they would enlist the aid of others by forming informal groups, mobilizing friends and neighbors, or working through a political party. Twenty-two and 42 percent respectively said they would act alone by means of direct contact: write a letter, visit a local leader, or vote against offending officials. Fully 70 percent of the public and 44 percent of the leaders said they would take no action at all.

The data show that those respondents indicating high degrees of distrust in interpersonal relations were least likely to engage in cooperative group activity. The eight percent of the general-public sample who indicated they would participate in group activity to realize desired ends were precisely those few respondents with high levels of interpersonal trust. The Thais' lack of trust in their relationships is correlated with the almost complete absence of group activity on the part of the ordinary citizens. Only six of the 90 citizen respondents perceived themselves as belonging to a social-political organization. Among the local leaders, half belonged to some organization (the most prominent being the Rotary Club, golf club, and various alumni organizations).

The belief that cooperative activity is possible and an effective political action is at the heart of the participant orientation. To measure the influence a person believes he can exert on government officials, the sample of Thai citizens was asked what they could do about an unjust local law. Twenty-four percent of the Thai public and 60 percent of the leadership said they could do something about an unjust law.* Among those few Thais who felt competent to do something about an unjust law, only a small number were willing to enlist the aid of others in their endeavor. As shown above, fully 70 percent of the general public indicated they could do nothing to influence local government, either through formal groups, informal relationships, or alone. The finding supports the prevalent view that Thais are reluctant to take a leading role in the determination of government policies.

The lack of social trust, the low regard for cooperative group activity, and the low level of perceived self-competency results partially from the fact that, for centuries, Thai interpersonal relationships have been based on superior-subordinate (patron-client) interaction. Once the patron-client relationship is established, certain behavior patterns emerge. While interacting with a superior, for example, the Thais' most acceptable and proper role behavior is one of deference. The salience of personal ties that are highly instrumental and status-oriented, and in constant flux and jeopardy, leads to a lack of interpersonal trust among Thais. Furthermore, the prevalence of hierarchical relationships inhibits the ability to relate on the basis of equality.

Also, the lack of group activity in Thailand should not be surprising, given the pervasive network of superior-subordinate relationships throughout the society. These ties take the place of formal groups by providing the citizenry with an alternative way of meeting their needs. The relationship depends on the maximization of reciprocal benefits without submission to enduring

*In the United States, United Kingdom, Germany, Italy, and Mexico, Almond and Verba found the percentages to be, respectively, 77, 78, 62, 51, and 52.

or oppressive group bonds. Personal ties substitute for the multitude of formal groups (voluntary associations, political parties, etc.) found in Western democracies.

The above discussion suggests several propositions. Democracy entails citizen involvement. Ordinary individuals acting alone, by definition, can have only slight impact. For involvement to occur an individual must feel competent to exert influence. If a person is to have some political influence, he must cooperate with his fellow citizens in common cause. Cooperation requires a degree of trust. On all accounts, perception of self-competence, willingness to work in concert, and degree of interpersonal trust, the prospects for democracy in Thailand are problematical at best. The absence of the "democratic character" presents to the nation's leaders an open invitation to authoritarian rule since they are free from accountability. Notwithstanding the absence of democratic structures, the absence of potential demands and involvement from the citizenry alone encourages arbitrary rule.

To further measure how democratic the values of the Thai citizens were, each respondent was asked to answer four questions and to comment in detail.[75] The first measured the degree of scorn or faith the respondents had for the mass electorate. Each person was asked whether or not everyone should have an equal vote no matter how ignorant or careless. Eighty of the 90 ordinary citizens and all of the leaders opted for the democratic variant that all should have an equal vote. This stunning rejection of elitism by itself bodes well for democracy's chances in Thailand. However, some perspective is needed before attempting to interpret precisely the meaning of the unanimity.

The second question measured the respondents' tolerance of the inefficiency of democracy. Each person was asked whether or not he thought that sometimes democracy created confusion and prevented important things from getting done. Almost 80 percent of the general public and 50 percent of the local leaders indicated that the liabilities of democracy were so great that the Thai society might not be able to cope and that change to a more efficient kind of government might be preferable.

---

[75] The criteria were used in James C. Scott, *Political Ideology in Malaysia* (New Haven, Connecticut: Yale University Press, 1968).

In particular, the Thais expressed intolerance for the wave of strikes and demonstrations throughout the nation. The question was asked at a time when there was a large number of labor strikes, student demonstrations, farmers' marches and the like, and the responses may reflect a temporary disdain for the turbulence. A number of the general public reminisced fondly about the days of General Sarit Thanarat, who ruled Thailand with a heavy hand from 1958 to 1963. During those days, "people knew their place," "the price of rice remained stable," and "the Chinese were not allowed to exploit the people." The first general question about voting equality indicated a firm commitment toward demoractic ways, but the response to the second, more specific, question showed an intolerance of democracy's delays.

The third question asked was about the willingness or reluctance of respondents to grant temporary authority to a dictator in times of crisis. Whereas the previous question about delays in the democratic process concerned normal situations, this third question asked the respondent about democracy's ability to cope in times of stress. As expected, an even greater number of respondents, 90 percent of the general public and 60 percent of the leaders, believed that democracy could not cope in times of crisis and that a temporary dictatorship would be preferable. American working-class responses to the same question showed an almost unanimous reluctance to endorse a temporary dictatorship even in wartime. Clearly, the Thais' commitment to democratic procedures is weak when threatened by political insecurity and instability.

Among the local leaders the comments on the need for temporary dictatorship stressed the need for "decisive action in times of crisis," the need to "protect the society from domestic and foreign agitators," and the need for stability. Among the general public, ten of the 90 indicated they opposed temporary dictatorship, and, of these, only five mentioned that demoractic governments had the capacity to cope effectively with any situation.

In the abstract, the Thais favor democracy. The respondents almost unanimously named democracy as the form of government they prefer most. Yet when queried about specific situations, most respondents were willing to move away from a commitment to democracy. Other values such as security, development, deference, economic stability, and the like took precedence over those values more directly related to citizen participation in governmental affairs. The democratic orientations of the Thais are formalistic in the sense that they have little depth and are secondary to other values.

Given the political background of Thailand, the formalistic nature of democratic norms is not surprising. The respondents have lived all their lives (except for a few brief periods) under centralized authoritarian rule. Moreover, the primary socialization agents such as the family, schools, and religion have fostered, maintained, and reinforced the traditional cultural patterns. Respect for elders and authority, obedience, compliance, and distrust are traits which are fostered from birth to death. Even in the universities, the school curriculum teaches government in terms of duty to family, school, society, constitution, and king. With their emphasis on authority and obedience, the school systems are microcosms of the larger society.

Each of the three case studies suggests that focus on the society's political culture can provide a useful perspective for the understanding of political activity. In these three cases, certain attitudes, values, and beliefs of the citizenry were found to be incompatible with a functioning democratic system. Clearly, culture is not a static concept and is as much affected by changes in the system of government as the system of government is affected by the public's political orientations.

5
Rural Politics

The vast majority of people in Southeast Asia live in rural villages. These villagers consist of a wide array of persons of different ethnicity, traditions, and economic standing. Hence, one should be careful about attempting broad generalizations. Even within a given society there are fundamental differences in culture and behavior among the rural villagers.

Notwithstanding their diversity, certain characteristics of the Southeast Asian villager can be enumerated. Agriculture is the center of life. Villagers are most likely poor, although increasingly in Southeast Asia, wealthier farmers who control large amounts of land can be found. But more typically, the villager is, economically, at the mercy of the elements. Droughts, floods, and typhoons can bring disaster to a subsistence-level peasant with a small farm.

Villagers are also at the mercy of people more powerful than they. For example, the typical farmer has connections with urbanites, landlords, moneylenders, and officials, all of whom can and do exploit him. Their superior power vis-á-vis the villager has been a part of the Southeast Asian societal pattern for centuries.

For most rural people in Southeast Asia, the family is the basic unit of social organization, and rice farming is the main means of livelihood. Rural families live in village societies, typically made up of some one to three hundred households. Southeast Asian villagers are generally caught in a vicious cycle of poverty: their labor productivity is low and therefore barely sufficient for family subsistence; the dearth of surplus crops keeps them from earning capital; and the lack of capital precludes savings and/or investment. Furthermore, conditions are worsened by the in-

167

creasing numbers of mouths that must be fed, the decline in arable land as the family plot is divided among the heirs, the debilitating diseases which sap the farmer's energy thereby exacerbating the problem of low levels of productivity, and enervating weather conditions.

Because rural Southeast Asians are part of the larger society, they must constantly interact with people who, for the most part, have more resources and clout. The farming community is the poorest element of society and the most exploited. They are at the mercy of others because they cannot afford to take any risk that might jeopardize their very survival. Even in their relations with peers, rural people are likely to exhibit feelings of distrust. They are often individualists, withdrawn and self-reliant. Because they perceive their world as having only a constant quantity of available resources, the village Southeast Asians are competitive in their attempts to maximize their interests.

Social relations in Southeast Asian villages are characterized by strong primordial attachments to the family, extended family, kin group, and fellow villagers. The villagers' major units of identity are those with whom they interact on a face-to-face, daily basis. The scarcity of mass media in Southeast Asian villages and the severe problems preventing travel outside the villages mean that the horizons of the average villager are narrow. The more distant the relationship to the family, the more distrust is felt.

An important element of rural life in Southeast Asia is the prevalence of hierarchical relationships that act as the major integrating force of society. The relationships, referred to previously as patron-client ties, provide an important stability and security in an otherwise unstable life. These ties, based on the reciprocal needs of both patron and client, are related to the very livelihood of the farmer. The villagers painstakingly establish links with landowners, officials, entrepreneurs, and others to assure the family's basic needs and security. In return, they provide their patrons with labor, protection, or deference.

Most villagers in Southeast Asia are conservative in the sense that they accept the status quo and traditional methods. This trait stems from the "safety-first" principle by which subsistence-oriented peasants typically prefer to avoid economic disaster rather than to take risks to maximize their average income.[1] For many Southeast Asian villagers, the need for subsistence is the basic motivation for economic and political decisions. Any decision which endangers subsistence is unthinkable, even if that risk could, in the long run, mean a sharp increase in the family's standard of living.

The conservative nature of Southeast Asian villagers is also explained by a high degree of fatalism stemming from the major religious traditions, especially animism. The pervasive presence of malicious spirits, or a karmic situation over which one has no present control, are belief systems which are not conducive to strict planning or attempts at controlling the environment.

Because Southeast Asian villagers have been dominated by others throughout history, they have been kept at arms' length from the economic, political, and social sources of power. In particular, the owners of land and capital have set up an elaborate system to keep the bulk of the peasantry in poverty conditions. A large part of the cultivated land area of Southeast Asia has traditionally been under the control of a landed elite, and remains so today.

> Virtually everywhere in lowland Southeast Asia the colonial introduction of capitalist forms of landownership, coupled with population growth, fostered the development of a large class of tenants and sharecroppers whose livelihood was contingent on their arrangements with a landholder. Village sharing and casual wage labor were not unimportant for members of this class, but their subsistence security or insecurity derived largely from the system of land tenure under which they cultivated.[2]

The tenant-farmers, who now comprise a majority of the Southeast Asian rural people, have relatively few means to improve their lot. The landlord fixes the quantity of crops the tenant-farmer may keep from his labor. The landlord, in his capacity as a patron, provides favors for the tenant-farmers,

---

[1] James C. Scott, *The Moral Economy of the Peasant, Rebellion and Subsistence in Southeast Asia* (New Haven, Connecticut: Yale University Press, 1976), p. vii.
[2] Ibid., p. 44.

who, in return, find themselves in steep debt to their benefactor. The essence of the relationship between landlord and tenant is the extraction of agricultural surplus from the peasantry. About one-half of the entire Southeast Asian population is dependent on elite landowners for their lives and livelihood.[3] Given this kind of relationship, it is easy to understand that resistance to change, rather than being simply a symptom of traditional values, can be explained as a result of a prolonged period of exploitation and repression.

Notwithstanding the powerful forces against change, Southeast Asia has witnessed a great transformation in recent times. Contrary to conventional wisdom, peasant life has not been altogether static. Despite the conservative nature of many rural villagers, certain events have occurred within rural society that are beyond the control of any one class of people.

One such event is the rapid population increase throughout the area. At the present time, most of the Southeast Asian nations are growing at such a rapid rate that the population is doubling about every 20 to 30 years. This extraordinary growth has caused millions of rural peasants to leave their overpopulated farms and to seek work in urban areas. The urban environment, in turn, has undermined the traditional attitudes, beliefs, and values of the peasant.[4]

The introduction of cash economies into the rural areas has destroyed some of the village self-sufficiency. Interpersonal relationships have changed drastically as market needs have begun to predominate over societal needs. The customary bonds of peasant society have broken down as traditional patrons have given way to new entrepreneurs. As the economy of the rural areas has become more specialized, the scope and style of the exchange between patrons and clients has narrowed. The ties have become more instrumental than those of the more traditional, comprehensive, and personal patron-client relationships.

---

[3] It is too early to assess the changes in land ownership resulting from the 1975 changes in the governments of Laos, Cambodia, and Vietnam. Prior to the Communist takeover 5.4 percent of the South Vietnamese population controlled 50 percent of the land.

[4] Many rural villagers go to the city, yet retain their traditional ways as they settle into neighborhoods inhabited by persons from their same birthplace.

The entire configuration of power relationships in the rural villages of Southeast Asia has changed, as rice entrepreneurs, rice-mill owners, moneylenders, teachers, officials, and absentee landlords have gained control over village resources. The composition of the elite has changed as its members are drawn from a wider set of socioeconomic backgrounds.

Change results also from the assertion of the primacy of the central political authorities over a widening group of constituents. National political leaders have increased their capacity to mobilize and exploit the major means of communication throughout the nation. They have built roads and radio stations, with the result that few areas of Southeast Asia are entirely isolated from the central authorities. As the nation's leaders control these means of communication, they are able to control the kind of information heard by rural peoples. In turn, villagers have easier access to market towns, provincial capitals, and the capital city where they learn new values. Central authorities, too, have easier access to rural villages. The rural areas have witnessed the development of increasingly complex political structures that have taken over many of the functions formerly carried out by the traditional rural elites.

As the central government becomes more involved in the daily affairs of the rural people, new groups have arisen, based on kinship groupings, ethnic organizations, or farmers' associations, to facilitate the articulation of demands. These groups differ from patron-client relationships in that the latter are based more on individual needs than group needs. The result is that groups based on horizontal identities have formed along class lines as villagers band together to express their interests. This new class identity contrasts with the vertical cross-class linkages of patron-client ties. However, the patron-client grouping remains the primary societal structure for Southeast Asians, as they attempt to satisfy their basic needs.

In recent decades the central government authorities have initiated a number of programs in the rural areas. In Thailand, the Philippines, Malaysia, and Indonesia, especially, the governments have established projects with the purpose of promoting economic development and countering insurgency. The implementation procedures have more than ever brought officials and villagers into contact with each other. At times these contacts have exacerbated the problems of distrust between villagers and officials when arrogant officials have thrust unwanted projects on a village, coerced peasants into labor gangs, or otherwise exploited the villagers. On other occasions, meaningful programs have been established resulting in positive relationships between villagers and officials, and in constructive village change.

Throughout rural Southeast Asia, increasingly complex political structures have developed, and existing institutions have taken on different and more specific functions. Political parties have formed as villagers are drawn into the political process. For the most part, party organization at the village level revolves around personalities rather than party ideologies. In most of Southeast Asia, however, political party organization is not a salient aspect of political activity. The exception, of course, is in the Indochina nations, where the Communist party apparatus extends to every village. The breakdown of traditional patterns and the introduction of new groups and personalities undermine primordial sentiments, as local attachments are replaced by wider identifications that go beyond the village. These changes, in conjunction with the move away from the rural villages to urban areas, have brought about wrenching changes and instability in Southeast Asian society. To meet the rising demands of the increasingly "modernized" masses, the central authorities must fundamentally transform their institutions and procedures or risk the opposition of a radicalized peasantry.

Following are overviews of the dynamics of two rural societies in Thailand and the Philippines. Thailand is a nation that has rarely witnessed active rural involvement in its national-level political system. In contrast, in the Philippines a significant peasant rebellion took place following World War II.

THAI VILLAGE-POLITICS[5]

Rural Thailand often gives the impression of a somnolent community, irrelevant, or at least peripheral, to events in

[5] The section on Thai Village Politics is taken from the author's previously published monograph, *The Dynamics of Politics and Administration in Rural Thailand* (Athens, Ohio: Ohio University Center for International Studies, Southeast Asia Program, 1974).

Bangkok. However, behind the facade of an isolated, traditional, static, rural community is a vibrant political life every bit as fascinating as the political life of the capital.

The Thais generally identify with their village communities, although the relationship is sometimes tenuous and depends on the particular region and village structure. However, Thai villages conform to central patterns; they are distinguished more by their similarities than by their differences. A self-sufficient subsistence economy, irrigated rice-farming, a central Buddhist village temple, several influential kinship groupings, and common religious ceremonies (including the worship of spirits) are the most important characteristics of almost every Thai village. Yet Thai villages also exhibit individuality. In addition to regional differences, the principal factors influencing village structure and behavior are a village's resources, its proximity to main roads and urban centers, kinship patterns, internal cohesion, government programs, and local leadership. As these factors combine into various patterns, a village takes on its own identity.

Only a few village groups require the involvement of the villager. The Buddhist temple and the school are symbols of the community, but they do not necessary symbolize, or demand a special *esprit*. This is not to say that there is no "community;" there is much evidence of group activity based on a loose, quid pro quo relationship. For example, the farmer rarely works alone in his fields. In addition to his children, who work along with him, neighbors and kin work together on an informal basis of mutual aid. Although no formal record is kept of who worked for whom and for how long, each farmer is expected to return all services rendered to him by others.

The key element in the structure of rural Thai society has been patron-client relationships. In rural Thailand a patron meets the varied needs of his clientele. The client's job, housing, and educational needs, for example, will be met in return for labor, deference, and protection. In urban areas, patron-client ties are more specialized and impersonal; hence a client will arrange for more than one patron to meet his multiple needs.

Thailand is divided administratively into 72 provinces, or *changwat*, which are the primary units of territorial administration. Each province is administered by a governor (*phuwarachakan*) appointed by the Minister of Interior. The provinces are subdivided into districts (*amphur*), which are administered by district officers (*nai amphur*) also appointed by the Ministry of Interior. Thailand has 618 districts, or about eight districts in each province.

Although the district office is the lowest administrative unit of the central government, it is one of the most important instruments of Bangkok's control. Programs planned in the capital ultimately are tested by the districts' ability to put them into effect. With administrative and supervisory responsibility for the district, the officers must manage the activities of 20 to 50 staff members and look after the welfare of 5,000 to 150,000 inhabitants living in villages in their district. The average district contains approximately 100 villages.

Any study of village politics must begin with the reminder that village leadership patterns vary greatly. Thailand includes about 54,000 villages organized into some 6,000 "clusters" of villages known as communes. In the central delta region, for example, there is very little correlation between the village's political and social system and its administrative system. The integrated, self-governing village has largely disappeared, mainly because the commercialization of agriculture and the rapid increase in population have resulted in large farms that straddle more than one village.[6] Charles Keyes, who has noted the poor articulation between peasant and administrative systems in Bang Chan in central Thailand, says that as a result of this lack of correlation, the headman is not as effective a leader as in those areas where the social and administrative systems are isomorphic. The "natural community" of Bang Chan consisted of seven headmen who were under two different commune leaders.[7]

In the northeast and north the natural peasant social and economic communities appear to be isomorphic with the administrative structures. In those areas the headman is a more influential figure. At one time, each village represented a truly sepa-

[6] John E. deYoung, *Village Life in Modern Thailand* (Berkeley and Los Angeles: University of California Press, 1963), p. 148.

[7] Charles F. Keyes, "Local Leadership in Rural Thailand," in Fred R. von der Mehden and David A. Wilson, eds., *Local Authority and Administration in Thailand*, Report No. 1 (University of California, Academic Advisory Council for Thailand, 1970), p. 103.

rate community, centered on the Buddhist temple.[8] Today, however, the village appears to be an arbitrary subdivision of a peasant community.

The Village Headman

Lack of clear differentiation between social and political spheres makes it difficult to analyze the power structure of Thai villages. The village headman potentially is in an influential position because he holds a position of authority and is often a relatively wealthy and educated member of the community.

The headman is usually elected to his position by the villagers. Any male between the ages of 21 and 60, who is neither a priest nor civil servant and who has lived in the village for at least six months, is eligible. The election of the headman appears to differ from village to village. In Ban Ping, a village of Thai Lue in the north, villagers do not seek the position. It is the duty of the officials and village elders to convince potential candidates to stand for office. An informant in Ban Ping explained:

> Having been warned by friends in the police that the officials favored him as headman, he went to his close kinsmen to tell them not to vote for him. . . . only those without close friends who can be asked to vote for others are elected to the office.[9]

This campaigning-in-reverse contrasts markedly with elections observed elsewhere in which candidates compete for office.

In Bangkhuad in the central plains, the perquisites of the headman's position are greater so that the candidates do campaign:

> [The candidate] may go about from house to house and tell them what he will try to do for the hamlet should he be elected. He may give a big feast at his house. He may try to buy votes, and may even try to bribe the district office to miscount the votes in his favor. The farmers will discuss casually the various candidates

[8] Konrad Kingshill, *Ku Daeng, The Red Tomb* (Bangkok, Thailand: Bangkok Christian College, 1965), p. 78.

[9] Michael Moerman, "A Thai Village Headman as a Synaptic Leader," *The Journal of Asian Studies*, VII(3) (May, 1969), p. 538.

among themselves, speaking of such merits as character, wealth, and willingness to help others.[10]

In Pang Kwan near Chiang Mai Province, the district officer called the villagers together without prior notice to elect a new headman after the former headman resigned because of the pressures of the office. There was no campaigning; the district officer, who was not acquainted with the new headman, did not attempt to influence the vote. Nor was there a victory celebration. Following the election the new headman stated, "I must accept my duty and my burden even though I will lose my popularity."

The new headman's concern stemmed from the middleman role he would have to play between his village and the district officials. His position as the representative of the village to the district authorities conflicted with that as representative of the officials to his village constituency. As a middleman, the headman is constantly subjected to conflicting pressures and is therefore in a most unenviable position. One headman explained:

> It's hard to be headman. One must listen to the officials and listen to the villagers. If one says "no", the villagers scold; if one says "yes", the officials scold. One is neither a villager nor an official. One is in the middle. It's hard and the money is small. No one wants the job.[11]

The headman performs a multitude of functions in addition to his middleman role. He attends monthly meetings at the district office, and for many headmen in the more isolated areas, a trip to the district office is a full day's journey. The headman has authority to make arrests in cases such as illegal gambling, buffalo theft, and homicide, and is often called on to arbitrate civil disputes. He must keep records of everything from animal slaughtering to births. He plans festivals and acts as patron in weddings. He is responsible for reporting calamities such as flooding and for obtaining help in emergencies. The headman

[10] Howard Kaufman, *Bangkhuad: A Community Study in Thailand* (Locust Valley, New York, 1960), p. 160.
[11] Moerman, "Village Headman," footnote 7, p. 547.

receives a monthly remuneration of 300 to 435 baht, depending on his length of service. (One baht equals five cents.)

The Commune Leader and the Commune Council

The village headmen choose one of themselves to be the commune leader, whose role once more varies according to region and circumstances. In the northeast a particular headman is not elected as the commune leader, rather the headman of a designated village serves as the commune leader. In the central region commune leaders generally play an insignificant role in the sociopolitical structure, but in northern Thailand they usually are influential persons, both because of their position as headmen in their own villages, and their positions as leaders of the headmen.

In addition to his headman duties, the commune leader carries out a wide array of functions. He must submit periodic reports to the district officials on births, deaths, movement of persons in and out of the commune, land surveys, diseases, taxation, military conscription, marriages, and divorces. He is responsible for calling meetings of the commune councils and deciding how to spend tax funds allocated to the councils.

The commune leader, though not a civil servant, is entitled to wear a uniform, receive some official benefits, and be paid an honorarium for his services. His monthly renumeration is 580–715 baht. In addition, he receives special allowances for delivering mail, attending santiation district meetings, and collecting taxes.

VILLAGE POLITICS IN NORTHERN THAILAND

Thai village politics have been characterized by a dichotomous view of apolitical villagers and all-powerful officials. This view, however, ignores the considerable political activity within the village. In addition, it does not consider the possibility of a middle group acting as a bridge between most villagers and the authorities. Clearly, those who are in contact with the officials, who join special-interest groups, and who participate in political activities cannot be classed with apolitical villagers. Teachers, priests, merchants, wealthy landowners, middlemen, commune leaders, and headmen have ties to the village, as well as interests and ties that go beyond it. This middle group looks beyond their village to their communes and district, and often to urban centers, and thus plays an important role in national integration and development.

The notion of a two-class society must be discarded. The economic and social self-sufficiency of the Thai village has tended to mask a complex pattern of interactions extending to the district, provincial, and national system. Many Thai villages have a competent group of individuals—the "politicals"—who have the capacity to carry out necessary changes for the system to survive and develop.

In northern Thailand three groups of villagers, the "apoliticals," the "politicals," and the village elites, can be more or less distinguished on the basis of the following criteria: contact with officials, group membership, participation in the planning of development projects, and knowledge of the political process. The apoliticals, who comprise some 90 percent of the rural population, have had no direct contacts with district officials and are not members of organized groups. They have not participated directly in project formulation, and are generally inarticulate in describing how projects are devised and implemented. The politicals include villagers who have a high degree of contact with officials and are members of structured organizations, such as commune councils, farmers' groups, irrigation associations, village temple-committees, and cooperatives. The politicals participate in various village and commune programs and have a rather clear understanding of such projects.

An upper stratum of the politicals comprises the three or four members of the village who are directly involved in authoritative decision-making, and who are perceived to be leaders. The members of this small group function as the interest articulators and aggregators, as links between villagers and officials, and as actual decision-makers. In their roles as patrons and in their official capacities, the members of this elite are involved in almost every aspect of village politics.

Keng Village, Sung District

Three villages in northern Thailand, Keng, Maimeerai, and Klang, provide data for an analysis of rural political activity.

Keng village is located in Sung District, on an all-year road, 15 miles from the district administrative center, and 23 miles from Chiang Mai. Daily bus service to the district office costs four baht round trip.

Keng is surrounded by lush rice fields and consists of some hundred houses built on stilts in order to remain above the water line when the monsoons flood the plains. The houses are often grouped in compounds with extended families living together. Most homes are surrounded by coconut and banyan trees. Chickens and water buffalo escape the heat by remaining in the shade under the houses. The men, women, and older children of the village are in the rice fields during most of the day; older residents and the very young stay at home.

In the outskirts of Keng is the Buddhist temple which serves as the religious, educational, and social center of the village. Two ordained monks serve the temple, and eight young novices live in the temple and serve the needs of the monks. There is no electricity in Keng, and water must be fetched from a well about one hundred yards from most of the houses.

Villagers and district officials consider Keng exceptionally progressive and developed. The following projects were in progress during the two-year period from June 1967 to June 1969: excavation of an artesian well for drinking water, construction of a school building, establishment of a generator for electricity, establishment of a midwife center, construction of a rest home for monks at the local temple, development of a marketing scheme through the farmer's group, and repair of feeder roads.

The vast majority of Keng inhabitants contact the village headmen and commune leader only for specific and routine matters, such as settling personal disputes, registration and tax procedures, and ceremonial activities. Since all of these concerns are of a personal nature, they can be dealt with by the headman or commune leader. The apolitical majority does not express the desire for authoritative action even though it may be able to identify needs. Interview responses reveal that the apoliticals perceived as "needs" the very problems with which the political stratum, their patrons, and the district officials, were already attempting to cope.

The political stratum in Keng consists of the other ten percent of heads of households. This political stratum is made up of the village headman, a teacher, canal chiefs, temple committee members and commune council members, selected farmers' group members, irrigation association members, and the owners of large tracts of land. The members of this stratum perceive the needs of the people and are able to communicate these needs to the village elite and the district officials.

The politicals become involved in this process because they are aware of village conditions and because the apolitical stratum expects them, as active members of the village and as clientele leaders, to tell the authorities of their needs. Moreover, unlike the apolitical stratum they are able to articulate a connection between a need and a solution, and a further connection between a solution and the role of the district office. Finally, they are involved in various activities where their purpose is to meet the needs of the people. The requests for a new school and electricity generator, for example, were channeled through the village headman and commune leader, while the road repairs came under the jurisdiction of the commune council. The farmers' group took over the problems of marketing, and in the near future the irrigation association may handle water distribution.

Keng Village Headman.   The Keng headman, Mr. Peng, owns more than 25 *rai* (ten acres) of land. As the elected and recognized leader of his village, he has extensive contact with the commune leader and district officials. He is an ex-officio member of the commune council and the village temple committee, as well as a member of the district irrigation association, the commune farmers' group, and the local loan cooperative.

Headmen initiate, plan, and implement village projects, but Mr. Peng owes his reputation and influence to several factors: his unique personal qualities, his extensive list of clients, the resources he controls, his official role of authority, and his subordinate relationships with powerful patrons. Villagers consider that, within the limits of his role, the headman's actions are authoritative. In this case, however, it is difficult to distinguish between the villagers' attitude toward the office and the man, since he so nearly personifies the ideal headman in most of their minds.

Mr. Peng estimates that he spends an average of two to three hours per day carrying out his duties, much of it occupied in attending commune and district meetings, settling private and public disputes, planning and officiating at the temple fairs, entertaining visiting officials, and advising villagers on registration and tax procedures. In addition, Peng spends considerable time consulting with other members of the elite who hold leadership positions. They are the headman's consultants. More than any other Keng resident, Mr. Peng acts as demand initiator and aggregator. He conceives of his role as a link between villagers and district officials. He identifies himself as the representative of the people, and does not consider himself an agent of the government.

Interviews with Mr. Peng and other headmen suggest the following pattern: the more secure the headman's leadership and social position, the more he will identify with his villagers. Leaders who lack local social and political influence will be more likely to identify with the district government in order to strengthen their status.

The Keng headman gives a focus to the political process by representing not only the structural leadership position but also the functional leadership role. He is able to carry village demands directly to those who have the authority to implement or provide support for projects. For example, it was the headman who met with the district officer to consider the need for a school building and an electric generator. In return for the district officer's financial assistance for the generator, Peng arranged for a large group of villagers to present to the governor a letter of appreciation. The provincial papers headlined the story thus bringing prestige and status to the district officer.

Mr. Peng made sure the commune council arranged for the road repair program and he relayed the need for marketing outlets to the farmers' group. He arranged financial assistance for the farmers' group in return for their labor and support in the marketing project. He also met with various members of the village elite about the formation of a youth group and the construction of a midwife center and a rest house for monks at the local Buddhist temple. The headman cleverly managed to have the rest house named after the leading financial contributor.

Maimeearai Village, Tam District

Maimeearai, in Tam District, has a population of 424, comprising 80 households. This settlement is located on an almost impassable road 15 miles from the district office and some 50 miles from Chiang Mai. There is no public transportation, so that contacts with officials require a walk of approximately six hours. This village has no markets and no dry-goods stores. The thatch-roofed huts are simpler, less sturdy, and far poorer than those in Sung district.

In Maimeearai the apolitical stratum comprises all but the village elite. Except for occasional visits by officials, the residents do not contact district officials. Nor do the villagers join groups; there are no groups to join. Interview responses made clear the villagers' limited awareness of village and district programs.

The village elite consists of the headman, Mr. Dee, his assistant, and a wealthy landowner who is also the local moneylender and employer. The headman and the landowner act jointly as the link between villagers and officials. Mr. Dee spends only one or two hours per week on the routine duties his position requires. His primary task consists of performing services at the district office; because of the great distance, villagers prefer not to make the trip. Once a month on the day before the district meeting of the commune leaders and headmen, Mr. Dee travels to the office to take care of requests. For example, on one trip he registered four guns, obtained three permits for cutting wood, and settled a tax dispute. On the day following the meeting, the headman informally called the heads of households to inform them of the district announcements.

In contrast to Mr. Peng, Mr. Dee is not an active leader. He is an older man, aged 58, who is growing tired of the burdens of the headman position which he has carried for 18 years. Instead of setting up a separate leadership structure independent of the headman, the villagers exert pressure on Dee to fill the leadership vacuum. They will not force or ease him out because of their reluctance to engage in public disputes and to offend Mr. Dee.

No development projects were in process in Maimeearai throughout the year preceding the interviews, despite the very obvious poverty. The demand base is considerably narrower than in Keng, where the political stratum consists of ten percent of the household heads. With fewer persons involved in demand initiation and articulation, there are correspondingly fewer communication channels to officials.

There are several reasons why the substantive demand process does not function in Maimeearai. First, the local elite has a very low expectation that the demands will be fulfilled. In contrast to Sung, where the district's considerations of projects is to a great extent based on the recommendations of the elite, projects in Tam district are initiated after consideration of budgetary limitations. Resources are minimal; so are the projects. Furthermore, yearly labor and monetary contributions and district financial support are allocated to one mandatory project—the repair of the road to the district office (the road is completely destroyed during every rainy season and must be repaired annually to retain communications with Chiang Mai). An additional factor affecting the very low rate of demands is the subsistence economy of Maimeearai. Since 80 percent of the farmers own less than eight *rai*, they have limited marketing requirements and correspondingly fewer needs for outside communication.

As in Sung, Tam villagers do not make a conscious connection between deprivations and the need for a solution. Maimeearai appears to be caught in an unending cycle in which the absence of demands is paralleled by the lack of finances and leadership at the district level.

Furthermore, the headman of Maimeearai has not established the kind of relationships with superiors that would result in reciprocal benefits for himself and his constituents. In contrast, Sung district officials have established patron-client relationships with the headmen of Keng and other villages so that mutual benefits pervade the rural political process there. In sum, personal considerations rather than institutionalized positions and structures account for the way in which most political decisions are made.

Klang Village, Rawang District

Klang village in Rawang district is 14 kilometers from the district office and 58 kilometers from Chiang Mai. The road to Klang is passable except at the edge of the town where it crosses the Mae Ping River. A bridge is built each year, but the yearly floods wash it away, and the road is without a bridge for about three months. Ten dry-goods shops and a noodle restaurant serve the 650 village inhabitants. The center of the village is dominated by a life-sized statue of Klang village's founder, and by a large, concrete, Western-style house belonging to the founder's grandson, Mr. Prida, who stands at the apex of the Klang patron-client pyramid.

Mr. Prida is undoubtedly the leading figure of Klang. He is the elected chairman of the district irrigation association, the elected representative to the provincial council from Rawang (before the councils were suspended following the 1971 coup d'etat), an elected member of the sanitation district committee, and a close confidant of the district officer. He owns over 30 *rai* of land, the market, and the major dry-goods store and is the spokesman for the area's dominant kinship group. He was educated in Bangkok, is wealthy, and an excellent organizer. Every interview unhesitatingly listed Mr. Prida as Klang's most influential citizen.

The political stratum consists of those villagers who contact and are contacted by Mr. Prida, and who belong to the farmers' group, irrigation association, or the commune council. It is not possible to measure the exact percentage of villagers included in the political stratum because of Mr. Prida's towering presence. Approximately ten percent of the heads of households contact him on a regular basis and belong to the major groups.

The role of the political stratum as demand articulator is difficult to assess precisely. Mr. Prida often discusses possible projects, particularly those concerning irrigation, marketing, and farm improvements, with them, and they in turn express their preferences to him. Village needs are articulated to persons and groups which have the capacity to channel demands to authorities—and the officials are able to comply.

Because of his very close relationship with the district officer and the commune leader, Mr. Prida acts as a general spokesman. The district officer utilizes his financial resources and considerable leadership abilities to support Mr. Prida's proposals. Mr. Prida's influence in his community and his reputation as a master organizer among the district and provincial officials place him in a unique position. It appears in many respects that Mr. Prida has been the patron and the district officer the client. Without his support, for example, the district officer could in no way establish a functioning irrigation system, a project crucial to the success of his career. Yet, because of the district officer's political position, it is he who appears to receive the most deference.

Klang Village Irrigation Association. The Rawang district officer initiated plans for an irrigation association in 1967. He appointed himself chairman of a planning group and named Mr. Prida treasurer. By 1969 the association had 2,600 active members (ten percent of the farmers), a circulating capital of 164,000 baht, and a government loan of 420,000 baht for the purchase of heavy equipment and fertilizer.

The irrigation association existed only on paper during the first year. In March 1968 the district officer requested Mr. Prida to take over as chairman. He first called together the members of the political stratum and explained his conception of the purpose of the association. Not all of these "politicals," of course, were members of Mr. Prida's personal patron-client entourage. He realized that each of the politicals had some degree of influence with a particular group of villagers and was eager to include them in his project so as to have maximum participation. He carefully calculated how projects were planned and implemented.

Mr. Prida's primary goal was to create interest in the idea of an irrigation association among the village political stratum. He noted that the organization would be managed by local leaders familiar with the needs of the area and that it might provide modern tools, fertilizer, marketing outlets, improved irrigation facilities, and credit opportunities.

Those present at the meeting mentioned a number of major problems, each of which could lead to severe factional disputes. First, the association's purposes matched those of the already existing farmers' group. Mr. Prida replied that the farmers' groups were narrower in scope, at least in Rawang where they were organized at the village level and were concerned exclusively with the purchase of fertilizer. The irrigation associations would be established at the district level to enlarge the base of support and resources. The groups would be complementary rather than competitive.

A second objection was that the traditional canal chiefs would no longer have a function. Mr. Prida explained that the association would only manage major dams and that the present canal chiefs would retain their positions within its framework. Mr. Prida admitted privately that in the long run the role of the canal chief would be reduced considerably. He felt that the farmers, who were too often slaves to the canal chiefs, would enthusiastically support the association if irrigation fees and labor obligations were minimal. He said that at the meeting he had not wanted to alienate the canal chiefs.

The third objection concerned the membership fees which precluded poorer farmers from participating. Mr. Prida answered that he felt such fees should be minimal (about ten baht per *rai* of land to be irrigated), and that members could pay for services such as the rental of equipment according to what they could afford. He noted that many farmers in the first year would be financially ahead since they would pay the irrigation association ten baht per *rai* to manage the dams rather than pay the canal chiefs one bucket of rice (worth 15 baht) per *rai*.

The objections raised by the farmers were suggestive of potential factional disputes between members of the farmers' groups and the irrigation association, between the traditional canal chiefs and the members of the association, and between poor and wealthier farmers. In the first case, the great majority of farmers' group members joined the irrigation association thus reducing friction between organizations. Group members in northern Thailand were generally part of the political stratum and, as such, this minority segment of farmers was able to see the potential benefits of joint membership. In addition, they had sufficient resources to afford membership obligations and the risks involved.

The second issue raised more serious problems. At the time of this writing, two of the leading commune leaders have refused to participate because they are canal chiefs of large irrigation projects. These chiefs, who are members of the village elite, strongly denounced the association and the intrusion of outsiders. Users of the canals were reluctant initially to join the association and to incur the wrath of their patrons. However, by June 1969 the farmers using the two canals indicated that they would join in order to be free from communal labor obligations. The conflict between the canal chiefs and the association was to a great extent mitigated when the district officer and Mr. Prida requested that the chiefs continue to manage the dams for a salary under the auspices of the association.

The third objection pointed to perhaps the most significant issue of all. The rise of interest-aggregating groups in rural northern Thailand has great potentialities. Since members of the political stratum have joined these groups, the gap between rich and poor may well grow wider. The average holding of crop land for members is 14 *rai*, compared to 5.5 *rai* for nonmembers and 7.5 *rai* for the general district population. Whereas association members are all landowners, nonmembers are more frequently tenant-farmers. The farmers most in need of the services provided by the irrigation association are either unable to join or wary of joining.

Many nonmembers resent the government's providing support for farmers' groups and giving irrigation association members loans, fertilizer, and rice seeds while ignoring the needs of the poor.* At a meeting of the Chiang Mai provincial assembly in October 1968, an elected representative assailed the provincial section chief in charge of rice for favoring farmers' group members over nonmembers. The reply was that the Ministry of Agriculture had limited resources of fertilizer, insecticides, and agricultural equipment and had to assign priorities. The Ministry opted to serve farmers' groups because they were organized and could more efficiently be contacted by officials. The section chief suggested that those who felt ignored by the government could join the groups. It is significant that the rise of interest groups was perceived by the elected representative as a cause of cleavage within Thai society. It seems conceivable that the cleav-

---

*The irrigation association adopted a plan to include the following important measures: (1) arrange for loans to association members at a low interest rate; (2) arrange for new marketing outlets in Bangkok and Chiang Mai for surplus crops; (3) arrange for the purchase of potato and other second-crop seeds at a reduced rate; (4) contact the provincial governor for a loan from the Ministry of Interior for the purchase of heavy equipment, fertilizer, and land (the governor announced a 420,000 baht loan from the Ministry in 1969, including 100,000 baht for the purchase of two tractors, 62,000 for crop land, 40,000 for insecticides, and 210,000 for fertilizer; equipment was to be owned by the association and rented out to members on a daily basis); (5) arrange for the transfer of major canals to the irrigation association (the association would pay a monthly salary to the canal chief, while association members were to be relieved of the communal labor obligations and the association would hire laborers to maintain the dams); (6) arrange for fee collections. With membership fees at ten baht per *rai* the association projected an operating fund of 364,000 baht.

age could be exploited by politicians and used as a base for popular support.

Michael Moerman notes that in Ban Ping in northern Thailand "those who save, invest, expand their production, and use the market more efficiently than their neighbors are the villagers who . . . are critized as calculating, aggressive, and selfish."[12] Those "who perceive and respond to economic opportunities more acutely than others" frequently fail to maintain the peasant values of equanimity and loyalty. They upset the patron-client milieu by choosing workers by affective rather than ascriptive criteria. The political stratum which joins the new functional associations is widening the gap between itself and the great majority of villagers. Thus, the stability of rural Thailand is increasingly jeopardized as the "constant flux" of patron-client groupings radically changes.

LOCAL-LEVEL INSTITUTIONS AND VILLAGE LEADERSHIP

The emergence of local-level institutions with new resources has created potential bases for new patrons in northern Thailand. The rise of new patrons, however, does not necessarily mean a decrease in the number or strength of the established patron-client relationships although the survival of these patrons will depend on their ability to make use of the new resources. As resources increase, so will the possibility that clients will move to groups with better access to institutional resources. In Keng village, following the establishment of the farmers' group, patron-client clusters did not change dramatically because the patrons moved into leadership positions in the new institution, which enabled them to retain control over resources. This meant access to district and provincial authorities and commodities such as fertilizer, water pumps, and tractors. In addition, the patrons' personal influence developed into legitimate authority, as perceived by the district and provincial officials.

The rise of local-level institutions thus far affects only a mi-

---

[12] Michael Moerman, *Agricultural Change and Peasant Choice in a Thai Village* (Los Angeles: University of California Press, 1968), p. 144.

nority of rural Thai. In most cases village demands are not channeled through structured groups but directly through the village elite to the district authorities. The function of the patrons has been similar to that of the structured groups: to aggregate the villagers' needs, convert them into recognizable issues, and present the demands to the authorities for decision.

The change in leadership patterns has been accentuated by the rise of various local-level institutions. The increased importance of the farmers' groups and irrigation associations and the concomitantly enhanced authority of the group chairmen, for example, have changed the means by which resources are allocated. The result has been an increase in the interaction between group leaders and governmental officials and a growth in the resources allocated to group leaders and their clients. The new authority of the group leaders goes considerably beyond that available in the past.

Local-level institutions do not yet perform their functions flawlessly. To some extent the cultural mechanisms affecting superior-subordinate communication and inhibiting group memberships are responsible for institutional weaknesses. Because these organizations have only recently been established, communication patterns and channels are not yet adequately developed. Also, they are manged by members of the political stratum for their own needs, and herein lie the seeds of increased factionalism. In rural Thailand the demands that reach the district level emanate from a small proportion of the population. For the vast majority, the political system bears no meaningful relationship to their daily activities. No mass grass-roots agricultural organizations have been created to meet the needs of villagers. Hence it is not surprising that less than ten percent of the rural population has responded to the establishment of new local-level institutions. Traditional Thai society has been characterized by a highly undifferentiated political process. The villagers' isolation and inertia have resulted in little need for a highly structured political process. The widening of channels of communication, the increase of societal differentiation (as exemplified by the three distinguishable village strata: the apoliticals, politicals, and the elite), and the rise of newly formed local institutions have all contributed to significant changes. As these groups continue to grow, the village political process will be transformed from the traditional type with few organized procedures, to one where politics is both more institutionalized and more differentiated.

BEYOND THE VILLAGE

The overwhelming majority of the Thai do not participate in national political activities. Indeed, a large portion of the populace has very little to do with officials or representatives from the national level. Authoritative decisions agreed to by the governmental leaders rarely affect the lives of the people directly. For most Thai, village and local environs determine their essential political, social, religious, and economic horizons. Although the central government indirectly taxes the rice farmers, and although the government is increasingly involved in developmental activities such as road, irrigation, and education projects in the rural areas, the Thai remain an unmobilized people only slightly aware of their government. Very few make a connection between their perceived needs and the capacity of the central government to meet them.

Villager-Official Interaction

At one time Thailand was a state of isolated villages; today, however, very few villages are totally isolated from the national society. Nevertheless, in many cases officials have neither the time nor the inclination to make a full day's trek to villages located far off passable roads. Nor do villagers have the money, time, or confidence to go to the district office. The villagers are *kreng jai* (considerate and shy) and therefore reluctant to disturb officials. Instead, headmen and politicals are the middlemen who represent and interpret the officials to those who care to listen. The middleman role of the political stratum is an important factor for integration because these leaders travel to nearby towns, speak with persons outside the village environment, and relay back their impressions of district, provincial, and central government officials. These middlemen are the "brokers" who "stand guard over the critical junctures and synapses of relationships which connect the local system to the larger whole."[13]

---

[13] Eric Wolf, "Aspects of Group Relations in a Complex Society: Mexico," in Dwight Heath and Richard Adams, eds., *Contemporary Cultures and Societies of Latin America* (New York: Random House, 1965), p. 97.

At the district level there is very little outside money to allocate. Only the most critical projects can be funded, and for the most part, labor and money come from the villagers themselves rather than from the government. Moreover, a lack of sufficiently trained officials at the district and provincial levels compounds the problems of scarce resources and slight villager-official interaction. The low level of expectations realistically correlates with a minimum of governmental goods and services.

Thai politics has never featured group structures that articulate the interests of the people for eventual processing by governmental decision-makers. In societies with much group activity, the interaction of members is likely to lead to the expression of otherwise unarticulated opinions. It also intensifies attitudes and encourages political participation. Without such formalized group structures the burden of villager-official contact is placed on personal relationships and is restricted to a small minority—the politicals. As institutionalized groups have been introduced, it appears, at least initially, that they have not fundamentally changed traditional patterns. The politicals continue to play the most important role in the groups and leaders devote much of their time to interceding with the proper officials on behalf of their own clients.

Patron-Client Ties and National Integration

Despite these cleavages a large and diverse communications network integrates the rural Thai into the larger political scene. Patron-client relationships help shape the society into a national whole. They are not separate and isolated relationships but connecting parts of a whole system of groupings. A patron becomes a client to a group higher in the hierarchy. Theoretically, it is possible to chart a chain of patron-client bonds from the peasant farmer to the highest reaches of the power elite.

At every level, patron-client entourages carry out the political functions of disseminating information, allocating resources, and organizing people, cutting across bureaucracies and extra-bureaucratic structures. In some cases a patron-client grouping will be complete in and of itself, whereas in other cases such ties will run through the entire governmental hierarchy.

The bases for the patron-client relationship differ at each level. The prime minister, for example, controls the apparatus for decision-making at the highest levels of the central government. His resource is power. Let us suppose that the finance minister in return for a share of that power promises total loyalty to his superior. As finance minister, he has responsibility for determining the terms of the sale of government-owned land. This power might be the basis for a patron relationship to the owner of a construction company in the market for property. The contractor presents the finance minister with the proper "gifts," usually monetary, and in return controls the buying and selling of property in an outlying province, gaining influence over marketing, land ownership, and building construction. The provincial governor, to maximize his own resources, might become client to the owner of the construction company since that company has been assured monopoly control in his province. The governor is willing to support the monopoly in return for suggesting the names of his own clients for special favors. From the prime minister to the governor, a web of patron-client relationships cuts across various levels to form the political system into a whole.

Governors in Thailand enjoy considerable administrative powers over the affairs of their provinces, including judging district officers for promotion. They also have ultimate control over the plans for irrigation canals and dams. District officers and irrigation association chairmen have their own sets of resources, in the form of influence, access, money, contracts, jobs, or assistance. Village headmen, district sections chiefs, merchants and moneylenders, and members of the political stratum all have favors to ask, and district officers and irrigation association chairmen have the power to grant them.

All of these relationships are more personal than institutional. Not all village headmen are clients to district officers, but those who are enjoy advantages over those who are not. Headmen might attach themselves to wealthy landowners, chairmen of farmers' groups, village priests, or any others who can meet their needs. As district officers are transferred, new local-level institutions are established, and as government resources are increasingly introduced into the rural environment, the patron-client bonds change to meet the new situation. This constant flux strengthens the integrative function of the relationships by bringing those who are lower in the hierarchy into contact with a diverse and continually expanding group of higher-status individuals.

Village-District Interaction

The communication process in all societies is affected by the structures of the government. When political authorities are reponsible to the citizenry for their position, the former will attempt to maximize the support of their constituents. In Thailand officials are not responsible to the people whom they govern but rather to the central government. Politics has traditionally been an adjunct of the central government; bureaucrats simply implemented the decisions of their superiors. In the last decade, however, largely because of the threat of Communist insurgency, the government has made a concerted effort to reverse this pattern. The government's new policy rests essentially on the assumption that increased villager support for local authorities will be translated into increased support for the central government. Interpersonal communication has only recently come to be considered an important element in Thai rural administration.

There are other important links to integrate the national society. Indirectly the villagers learn about district, provincial, and national politics from the elites. Some have face-to-face contact with higher officials as they register to vote, pay taxes, obtain licenses, receive health care, or request information and other services. Women travel to marketing towns to sell or buy goods and hear the news of surrounding areas. There is a continual movement as persons marry, seek new land, or travel. Entrepreneurs, who come from the larger towns to buy surplus rice, also bring information about the wider world. Finally, officials themselves travel directly to the people to give them information and to explain government policies.

The marketing channel appears to have played a minor role as an integrating factor since only a small percentage of household heads used the district center for commercial purposes. Isolated villages in particular enjoy comparative independence from urban centers for the purchase of farm tools. Almost all the tools of plow agriculture are made by the farmers themselves.[14] The extraordinary increase in the number of roads and highways and in the diversification of crops has caused once-isolated settlements to become more and more a part of a vast, interrelated

[14] Moerman, *Agricultural Change*, footnote 14, p. 57.

economic system. Still, most of the farmers sell their rice directly to mills in the commune center or in their own village. Farmers with a surplus or second crop are contacted by "middlemen" from marketing towns who drive to the villages. The district center, however, plays only a minor role in the marketing process.

More important than economic considerations or administrative directives as integrating factors are the activities of various individuals. Mobility provides an opportunity to rise above the isolation and localism of the village and to become integrated into a larger system. Increasingly, younger villagers migrate to provincial centers or to Bangkok for work or excitement. The move is permanent or temporary depending on individual considerations and experiences. In Keng and Maimeearai villages in northern Thailand, 32 percent and 8 percent respectively of household heads had traveled at least once to Bangkok. In the northeast even higher percentages of the villagers migrate to the capital.[15]

One obvious reason for this difference is the relatively lower standard of living in the northeast, which strengthens the desire to leave and to achieve status outside the village. For some the desire for change is intense, and emigration casts off ties to a settled way of life. For others the trip to Bangkok is seen as only a temporary means of accumulating capital; they fully expect to return to their village. For still others it is simply the manifestation of the Thai desire to travel around for fun with friends.

The provincial capitals are playing an increasingly more important role in the integration of the Thai nation. These towns, ranging in population from 10,000 to 100,000, are the administrative, economic, and cultural centers. As land becomes more scarce (forcing rice peasants off the fields), as higher levels of education are desired, and as subsistence farmers become surplus farmers with capital to spend, the provincial towns increase in importance.

Thai society is more and more based on a town culture:

> Thailand is not an expanse of completely self-contained villages. On the contrary, the life of the villages and that of the towns

[15] Charles F. Keyes, "Ethnic Identity and Loyalty of Villagers in Northeastern Thailand," *Asian Survey*, VI(7) (July, 1966), p. 364.

are interdependent, not only economically but also, less tangibly, in terms of information, authority, and consolation. The importance of these links and their configuration, both in active institutions and physical locations and movements, is difficult to over-estimate.[16]

PEASANT REVOLT IN THE PHILIPPINES

One of the largest and most important peasant rebellions in contemporary Southeast Asia took place in the Philippines during the decade following World War II. This peasant movement, known as the Huk rebellion, had roots in smaller uprisings in the past and still today plays an important role in Philippine politics. The Huk rebellion, which took place in Central Luzon, illustrates why many thousands of peasants opted for revolt against the established forces.[17]

The Huk rebellion grew directly out of the Japanese occupation of the Philippines beginning in December, 1941. As soon as the Japanese invaded, small groups of Filipinos began meeting to plan anti-Japanese strategies. The Hukbalahap anti-Jananese resistance movement became the core of the Huk rebellion that continued after the Japanese defeat. The repressive and ruthless Japanese occupation in conjunction with nationalist motives brought about almost universal peasant support for the Huk-balahap movement and greatly increased the numbers of peasants actually involved in rebellion.

When the war ended, Philippine government and American forces began arresting the Hukbalahap, an action which galvanized many of the movement's members into further resistance, this time against the Philippine government. In addition, the economic situation throughout the nation deteriorated following the war because of extensive bombing damage of fields, canals, and dikes. The land-tenancy system continued unreformed, so that more and more peasants were landless and increasingly exploited. Following the April 1946 election six congressmen-elect with ties to the Hukbalahaps were prohibited

[16] David A. Wilson, *The United States and the Future of Thailand* (New York: Praeger, 1970), pp. 77–78.

[17] This case study is based on Benedict J. Kerkvliet, *The Huk Rebellion, A Study of Peasant Revolt in the Philippines* (Berkeley: University of California Press, 1977).

from taking their seats. The refusal to seat the congressmen, along with the Philippine government's zeal for military force, resulted in even more peasants going underground. The underground movement eventually became known as Hukbo ng Mapagpalaya ng Bayan (People's Liberation Army) or simply Huks.

The Huks did not make radical or revolutionary demands for a total restructuring of the society. Their propaganda and publications stressed support for "the side of the little people, the poor people, and aginst the big people and the soldiers;" it wanted "better conditions for the peasants, a larger share of the harvest for them;" it wanted landlords to be fair, peasants to have their own organizations, and tenant-farmers to receive a higher proportion of the crop yields.[18]

Violence was not a part of the Huk policy until the "iron fist" policy of the government compelled them to react in kind.

> [For two years] Companies of Philippine constabulary troops, civilian guards, and municipal policemen used heavy artillery, armored cars, tanks, and airplanes against bands of rifle-toting peasants in the barrios and fields of Central Luzon. In the process, they destroyed villages and killed many people not directly involved with the rebellion.[19]

The rebellion reached its peak in 1951 and then gradually declined. The rebels were suffering from exhaustion after years of revolt which had led to only limited success. Moreover, the government's campaign against the Huks grew more sophisticated and disciplined and therefore more effective in capturing Huk leaders. The result was increasing distrust among the rebels and more moves made out of desperation which worked against their interests. The Huks declined after the election in 1953 of President Magsaysay, a reform-oriented government leader who had been an anti-Japanese guerrilla himself, and an effective secretary of defense from 1950 to 1953. He ended the repression and initiated economic reform programs thereby undermining forces which had both alienated and galvanized the rebels. Villagers who had formerly given their allegiance to the

[18] Ibid., p. 164.
[19] Ibid., p. 189.

Huks believed that Magsaysay's reforms should be supported, in particular his vow to reduce tenant-farmers' rents. Such reforms, along with Magsaysay's charisma, persuaded many peasants that rebellion was no longer necessary.

The United States government provided sizable support to the Philippine government's efforts to suppress the Huks. American officials feared Communist domination of the Huk movement (although in reality the core of the leadership was non-Communist and indigenous) and the eventual takeover of American economic investments. The United States buttressed the Philippine economy with huge aid programs that totaled over a billion dollars between 1946 and 1956. By 1956 the Huk rebellion had been repressed except for a few scattered remnants. The others had been killed by government forces or assimilated into village life.

In his analysis of the Huk rebellion Benedict Kerkvliet sets forth several conclusions which are important for an understanding of the Huk revolt as well as for what they say about Southeast Asia peasant movements in general.[20] Kerkvliet first argues that a major cause for the unrest in Central Luzon was the dramatic deterioration of traditional ties between local elites and peasants.[21] For centuries traditional patron-client ties had bound together the rich and the poor. When these ties broke, the Philippine peasantry remained poor and without any source of security or assistance. Traditionally, patrons had provided a wide array of services including sponsorship at weddings and financial support. Clients, in return, provided labor for the patron. Clearly, these ties were one-sided with the client in a subordinate position barely able to subsist. The landlords no longer practiced *utang na loob*.

> A strong patron-client relationship was a kind of all-encompassing insurance policy whose coverage, although not total and infinitely reliable, was as comprehensive as a poor family could get. Consequently, what peasants did for landlords was balanced off,

---

[20] For parallels with other Southeast Asian societies, see James C. Scott and Benedict Kerkvliet, "The Politics of Survival: Peasant Response to 'Progress' in Southeast Asia," *Journal of Southeast Asian Studies*, IV (September, 1973), pp. 241–268.

[21] Kerkvliet, *The Huk Rebellion*, p. 250.

in their eyes, by what landlords did for them. The balance of exchange made the relationship legitimate and just, as far as villagers were concerned, however exploitative it might seem to those on the outside.[22]

As new conditions came about the traditional patron-client relationships changed. Patrons increasingly needed laborers, not clients, without the personal bonds and values of reciprocity. When patrons opted out of these ties, the clients viewed the landed elites as having violated their customary obligations of support during crises and a fair share of the harvest. The clients' perception of a dishonorable elite justified the Huks' rebellion against those elites.

Kerkvliet concluded that the Philippine peasants did not want to overthrow the entire system; instead they sought to reform the tenancy system. The basic objective of the peasants who joined the Huk movement in the 1940s was to regain the economic and political security that the traditional tenancy system had previously provided. They demanded fair rations, low-interest loans, and a larger share of the harvest.[23] The rebels in Central Luzon wanted an end to the repression against the Huks. These were moderate reforms, a call for a return to an earlier traditional system. Only a minority called for the taking over of land for themselves. Only when it became clear that the elites were not willing to meet the needs of the peasants did they begin their aggressive rebellion.

What finally moved the peasant from a situation of protest to one of revolt was the government's repression. No other path was open. The peasantry were reacting to a crisis of survival against a strong government force supported by the richest country in the world. Many persons in 1945–46 joined the movement because of repression rather than their desire for better economic conditions.[24]

Kerkvliet places considerable responsibility for the growth of agrarian unrest on colonial policies which strengthened the hand of the elites while simultaneously making the elites less

[22] Ibid., p. 252.
[23] Ibid., p. 254.
[24] Ibid., p. 262.

dependent on villages for support.[25] The colonials established a cash-crop economy that relied on impersonal economic mechanisms for its success rather than personal patron-client ties. Agriculture became less labor-intensive as capitalist landlords sought to maximize their profits. The result was increasing desperation for the peasants and a turn to rebellion.

The Huk rebellion did not lead to any fundamental reforms. Land reform, for example, both before and after President Marcos' declaration of martial law, never really got off the ground. Power in the Philippines has remained in the hands of large landowners. Land tenancy in the rice-growing areas of Central Luzon remains at 70 to 80 percent. In one province of Central Luzon the top ten percent of the landowners owned 72 percent of the total land.[26] In recent years the gap between the rich and poor in the Philippines has actually widened. When Kerkvliet studied the impact of the Huk rebellion in the village of San Recardo in Central Luzon, he found that the village had little to show for its labors and that the villagers find themselves today in many ways worse off than before.[27]

[25] Ibid., p. 265.

[26] George Rosen, *Peasant Society in a Changing Economy* (Urbana: University of Illinois Press, 1975), p. 39.

[27] Benedict Kerkvliet, "Agrarian Conditions Since the Huk Rebellion: A Barrio in Central Luzon," in Benedict Kerkvliet, ed., *Political Change in the Philippines: Studies of Local Politics Preceding Martial Law* (Honolulu: The University Press of Hawaii, 1974), p. 2.

6
Political Dynamics in Southeast Asia

The postindependence period in Southeast Asia has witnessed four categories of political regimes that represent loose and sometimes overlapping types, rather than pure classifications. The four categories are military-authoritarian, civilian-authoritarian, Communist-authoritarian, and democratic. The principal style in postindependence Southeast Asia is authoritarian.

Only Singapore, Malaysia, and the Philippines have experienced long periods of democratic rule, and the latter moved to civilian-authoritarian rule in 1972. Thailand had only a three-year democratic experiment, between October 1973 and October 1976, and then returned to military rule and once again to democratic rule under military tutelage. Indonesia moved from an unstable democratic government to Sukarno's "guided democracy" and then to Suharto's military government in 1965. Burma experienced a coup d'etat in 1962 that transformed the government from an unstable democratic civilian form to military-authoritarian.

The Democratic Republic of Vietnam was declared independent at Hanoi on 2 September 1945, with Ho Chi Minh as president. The declaration was followed by war between the French and the Vietnamese. The Communist leadership continued to control North Vietnam from the time of independence to the present. South of the 17th parallel in 1954, a new government evolved into an "independent" state led by Ngo Dinh Diem, with its capital in Saigon. The autocratic Diem was overthrown in 1963 by his armed forces. Between 1963 and 1975 military rule alternated with civilian rule in a succession of unsta-

ble administrations, but power was in the hands of the South
Vietnamese military. South Vietnam was taken over by the Communists in 1975 and merged with the North.

Cambodia (Kampuchea), under King and then Prince
Sihanouk's one-man rule, first fought for its complete independence from the French, finally winning sovereignty in 1954 at
the Geneva Conference. Sihanouk dominated every aspect of
political life until 1970, when the nation moved to military
dictatorship and then, in 1975, to Communist government.

In 1953 Laos was granted independence by the French (within
the framework of the French Union). From then until 1975,
Laotian leaders in the administrative capital, Vientiane, attempted to fashion a viable political entity. The leaders, who
were drawn largely from the royalty, dominated Laotian politics
of the right, left, and center up to 1975, when the Communists
took over.

The Philippines, on the other hand, featured a vibrant, competitive, formal democratic system based on the American
model. The rulers were drawn almost exclusively from a small
elite group of economic notables. However, civil liberties flourished and political parties competed for power. The democratic
era ended when, in 1972, President Marcos declared martial law
and took all power for himself. His essentially civilian rule was
characterized initially as reform-oriented and subsequently as
repressive. He was ignominiously removed from power in February 1986 and replaced by President Corazon Aquino.

Singapore and Malaysia did not receive total independence
from Great Britain until 1963 and 1957 respectively. The two
nations were merged into the Federation of Malaysia between
1963 and 1965 and then separated into sovereign states. Both
nations have been ruled by democratic governments throughout
the postindependence period, although each has restricted certain rights of the citizenry. Malaysia declared martial law in
1969, following communal demonstrations. However, the government returned to normalcy in two years' time, albeit with
restrictions on political liberties. Malaysia's neighbor, Singapore,
continued its postindependence democratic rule. Lee Kwan Yew
leads a one-party-dominated government in Singapore, with
restrictions on political freedoms. However, elections are regularly held and various points of view are allowed. Brunei has

been ruled since its independence in 1984 by an all-powerful hereditary monarch.

Authoritarian governments are likely to prevail in Southeast Asia for a number of historical and cultural reasons. Centralized rule is congruent with the cultural patterns of Southeast Asia nations that have experienced Hindu and Confucianist cultures. The rapid changes in Southeast Asia have not obliterated the heritage of god-king or mandarin rule. Indeed, the Communist regimes in Vietnam, Laos, and Cambodia, and the military governments in Thailand, Indonesia, and Burma, may be more compatible with the cultural traditions of these nations than is a liberal democratic government.

The colonial period in Southeast Asia also encouraged the growth of non-democratic regimes. The colonial powers systematically curtailed the growth of popular political parties and repressed most peasant demands for change. At the same time, they encouraged the growth of centralized bureaucratic structures that today are the bedrock of stability and authoritarian rule in Southeast Asia.

Military regimes have been dominant in Southeast Asia since the 1960s. Thailand, Burma, Indonesia, Cambodia, and South Vietnam have been led by military governments, with the latter two nations becoming Communist in 1975. A number of reasons have been advanced to explain the prominent role of the military in Southeast Asia and other Third World societies. The many military coups in Southeast Asia and elsewhere, however, suggest that almost all combinations of political, economic, and social situations have been related to military takeovers. Thus far, scholars of military rule have not provided a satisfactory base for development of a theory of military intervention.

Each Southeast Asia nation will be analyzed by looking at the historical perspectives that provide a context for understanding political regimes. The focus is also on the dynamics that operate under different kinds of political regimes.

THAILAND

Military leaders have long enjoyed a preeminent position in Thai society. The roots of a military class go back to the Sukhothai kingdom, but it was during the Ayuthayan era that military leaders were given significant political positions. In the Ayuthayan period, all officials were concurrently soldiers in times of military threat.[1] Many of Thailand's most illustrious monarchs were soldiers, including the founder of the kingdom of Sukhothai, King Rama Khamhaeng. As with many societies, the military in Thailand flourished during times of war and declined in importance during long periods of peace.

It was not until the reign (1865–1910) of King Chulalongkorn that the military was modernized along European lines, although the royalty remained dominant within the officers' corps. In 1886 a ministry of defense and a military cadet school were established, and a larger share of the nation's budget was allotted to military expenditures.[2] The purpose of these changes was to revitalize the heretofore undisciplined and ineffective Thai military to assure that the French and British would have no excuse to interfere in Thai affairs and expand their imperialistic designs.

The Thai military was further strengthened by King Vachiravut's (1910–25) conscious policy to link the military with a nationalist ideology. When a group of civilian and military men brought about the 1932 coup, the military was a natural beneficiary of the new recruitment policies and thereby attained high offices in the government. The military filled the positions formerly held by members of the royal family. Because the Thai military had never had a tradition of apolitical activities and, therefore, there were no separate spheres of authority for civilian and military officials, the military fitted easily into a political role once royal controls were loosened.[3]

From 1932, when the absolute monarchy was overthrown, to the present, the Thai military has played the dominant role in Thai politics. This is due at least partly to historical conditions that make military rule less an anomaly than a natural outgrowth of traditional authoritarian rule.

---

[1] Claude E. Welch and Arthur K. Smith, *Military Role and Rule: Perspectives on Civil-Military Relations* (N. Scituate, Mass.: Duxbury Press, 1974), p. 84.

[2] J. Stephen Hoadley, *Soldiers and Politics in Southeast Asia: Civil-Military Relations in Comparative Perspective* (Cambridge, Mass.: Schenkman Publishing Co., 1975), pp. 10–11.

[3] Welch and Smith, *Military Role and Rule*, p. 85.

Military rule in Thailand has been at least partially a function of ineffective civilian rule. The 1932 coup, which replaced the absolute monarchy with a constitutional monarchy, occurred when the competence and fortunes of the kingdom's leaders were at their weakest. King Prachadipok (Rama VI) desired reform that would move Thailand in the direction of a quasi-democratic state. He was surrounded and influenced, however, by conservative royalists who feared that reform would jeopardize their position. King Prachadipok's royal predecessors had initiated changes that fundamentally altered Thai society, whereas Prachadipok's reign appeared to the 1932 coup leaders to be a retrenchment and hence a threat to their chances for advancement and power.

Although the civilian and military coup leaders had discussed the prospects for a revolution against the absolute monarchy prior to the worldwide depression, this event acted as a precipitant for the coup d'etat. The depression caused huge budget deficits that the king attempted to curtail by cutting government expenditures. A large number of civilian and military officials were forced out of office, and hundreds of college graduates and trained military personnel found their chances for high-status positions blocked. To the coup leaders, the government appeared to be incapable of coping with the deterioration of the Thai economy. Prachadipok's reluctance to wield power brought about a leadership vacuum that was eventually filled by the Thai military.

Similarly, Marshal Phibun's return to power in 1947–48 (after his humiliating ouster from the prime minister's position when Japan was defeated) followed a period of civilian rule that was characterized by instability and drift. The civilian government, under Pridi, lost legitimacy and authority when King Ananda was found dead and Pridi was linked with the alleged regicide.

Thailand's longest experiment with democratic government occurred between October 1973 and October 1976. The civilian leadership vacuum during those three years provided the opportunity and rationale for the military takeover in 1976. Fundamental reforms were not initiated during the democratic regime largely because of the entrenched interests of the top-level bureaucrats and legislators who dominated policymaking. The military contributed directly to the downfall of the democratic government by supporting extreme right-wing youth and border police forces who desired to undermine the authority of the civilian government.

As with the 1932 coup leaders and Marshal Phibun, the military coup leaders of 1976 claimed their administration would end corruption and the nation's drift toward economic stagnation. Just as the 1932 coup leaders took advantage of the worldwide depression and Phibun capitalized on the postwar recession, the 1976 army leaders claimed that the recession and inflation of the mid-1970s could be solved only by strong military leadership. Seni Pramoj's administration appeared indecisive when Generals Prapat and Thanom returned from exile. The military grew more and more restive when Seni initiated foreign policies that were thought by the military to show weakness detrimental to the kingdom. Indeed, the majority of the Thai population breathed a sigh of relief when the military removed Seni and set up its own "strong" government.

The "civilian problem" is related to the assessment of the Thai political system in its lack of extrabureaucratic institutions. The military is likely to predominate in countries where extrabureaucratic political organizations such as legislators, political parties, and interest groups are weak. In the Thai political system, the arena of politics is within the government itself, and little or no competition for political power emanates from outside the bureaucratic institutions. Military leaders have seized power in the absence of countervailing institutions. Thailand is a superb example of a nation with the proper preconditions for military rule. Since high political posts are held by only a very few people and since governmental participation is concentrated in the bureaucracy, it is possible to dominate the entire political system merely by controlling the bureaucratic structure. And since extrabureaucratic institutions have been inconsequential, they are easily bypassed.

The military is the best-organized group in the kingdom, and in terms of discipline and hierarchy has no rival. Thus the national emphasis on hierarchy, deference, and status is congruent with the military's organization, which is based on superior-subordinate relationships. In addition, the army can count on the loyalty and obedience of its followers to a much greater extent than ad hoc groups of politicians can count on theirs. The record of civilian rule during the constitutional period has been neither long nor illustrious. By decrying civilian ineptness, corruption, and malfeasance, and by proclaiming the threat of Communist-led insurgency and the inability of civilian regimes to cope with the threat, the military leaders have been able to persuade the bureaucratic polity that they can do a better job of governing the nation.

The success of the military has also been due to its capacity to meet the demands of the elite. Since 1932 the military regimes have allocated the nation's meager resources (which have been supplemented by massive United States aid) in such a way as not to alienate any potential opposition group. In some instances the military has relied on heavy-handed tactics to stay in power, and the fact that the military controls the weaponry of the nation has ensured its monopoly of the use of force. Moreover, Thailand has been independent of foreign influence that opposes the means or the results of the coups d'etat. Since World War II, the United States has had pervasive influence in Thailand but has not opposed the leaders of coups, principally because the latter have consistently proclaimed anti-Communist and pro-American sentiments.

Since a scarcity of resources in terms of wealth, prestige, and power is available to the elite, the tendency in Thailand is to eliminate as many of the elite as possible, thereby preserving the exclusive nature and maximizing the benefits of the ruling class.[4] Those who constitute the elite are willing to share the perquisites of power with others only if the sharing will result in a favorable quid pro quo. Elite domination of Thailand's politics also results from the passivity of the citizenry vis-à-vis politics; from the socialization process, which has fostered specialized political skills and the desire of a few to use these skills; and from the traditional attitude that those in power have the right to rule while those who are not in power have the duty to obey.

In spite of the personal and elite nature of Thai politics, there has been an institutional context for the study of Thai politics

---

[4] This section is a revised version of the author's chapter on Thailand in Robert N. Kearney, ed., *Politics and Modernization in South and Southeast Asia* (Cambridge, Mass.: Schenkman Publishing Co., 1975).

throughout the kingdom's recent history. These institutions have included constitutions, elections, parliaments, and separation of powers, but substantial changes have been made in these elements as they were adopted from the West and integrated into the national culture. These structures, although superficially Western in form, are distinctly Thai and can be only partially understood in a Western framework of analysis.

Since the 1932 revolution and overthrow of the absolute monarchy, Thailand has been governed under 13 constitutions, six provisional and seven "permanent." Indeed, the Thais' propensity for changing constitutions has been referred to as "faction constitutionalism,"[5] whereby each successive constitution has reflected, legitimized, and strengthened major shifts in factional dominance. Thai constitutions have not been considered the fundamental law of the land; rather, they have functioned to facilitate the rule of the regime in power.

Since the 1932 revolution the major political institutions have been organized on the principle of an unequal separation of powers. Although the central government has been composed of separate executive, judicial, and legislative branches, the major source of power has been the executive branch.

Above these three branches, and theoretically and legally above politics, is the monarchy. Indeed, it is difficult to conceive of Thai politics without the magnificent pageantry that surrounds His Majesty, the Lord of Life, the King of Thailand, who is revered by his subjects as are few other modern monarchs. Even today the king is the national symbol, the Supreme Patron who reigns over all, and the leader of the Buddhist religion.

The prestige and influence of the monarchy, moreover, has increased since 1950 with the coronation of King Phumipon Adunyadet, who with his wife, Queen Sirikit, has traveled throughout Thailand and abroad on good-will trips. Each of Thailand's prime ministers has encouraged the king's endeavors to be closer to his subjects as a means to increase the legitimacy of the regime in power and to decrease the potential for insurgency by providing the people with a symbol of Thai unity.

---

[5] David A. Wilson, *Politics in Thailand* (Ithaca, N.Y.: Cornell University Press, 1962), p. 262.

Nevertheless, the direct impact of the monarchy on politics has been slight, as was shown by the king's inability to prevent coups d'etat and by his silence on issues before the government. His indirect influence is difficult to assess, although the various governments have hesitated to set forth any program that would contravene the values of the king. Thai leaders have not been willing to precipitate a confrontation between themselves and the monarchy, and in that sense the king acts as a moderating influence.

When the military took power from the democratic civilian government in October 1976, the king supported the coup and hand-picked the new prime minister, Thanin Kraivichien. The king's supportive role disillusioned many intellectuals and democrats who heretofore had admired his decision to remain above politics. Thanin proved to be rigid and unwilling to follow the military's dictates. However, the moderate elements of the army, led by Kriangsak Chamonond, were wary of overthrowing Thanin because of his close ties to the throne. Not until the king signaled his acceptance of a change did the military make its move.

The king's involvement in politics reached its peak in 1981 when he supported Prime Minister Prem against Young Turk colonels who had staged a coup d'etat. His strong stance against the coup helped to defuse the crisis and to heighten his prestige and influence.

The king promoted his daughter Princess Sirindhorn to the rank of Maha Chakri, thereby placing her in the line of succession along with her brother Crown Prince Vachiralongkorn. Because the crown prince was criticized in many circles for his lack of serious intent and discipline, while the princess was universally admired for her brilliance and dedication, the Thais feared a future succession crisis. By 1986, however, the crown prince was more involved in ceremonial duties. As the nation prepared for the king's 60th birthday celebration in 1987, he continued to be venerated by virtually all Thais for his efforts to improve the conditions of the kingdom.

The executive branch of the government, as has been said, dominates the political scene. Since 1932 the prime minister has wielded great authority as the leader of both the cabinet and the military, which in turn has provided the executive for 41 of the

46 years of constitutional government. During most of this time the executive branch has consisted of the prime minister and other cabinet-level ministers. Next to the prime minister, the ministers of interior and defense have the greatest power. The Ministry of Interior controls local-level administration, as well as the Department of Finance, while the Defense Ministry is responsible for all military matters. Traditionally, however, these positions have been retained by the prime minister or entrusted to one or two of his closest confidants. The other cabinet-level ministers are often experts in their field, as well as politically influential individuals.

Serving under the various cabinet ministers are some 260,000 regular (nonmilitary) civil servants, who comprise the official bureaucracy. The top civil service employee in each ministry is the undersecretary. In keeping with the 1971 reorganization of Prime Minister Thanom, the undersecretaries function both as nonpolitical leaders of the ministry (as in the past) and as political leaders with significantly increased powers. Below the undersecretaries are the various departments, which are headed by directors general and divided into divisions and sections.

The Thai bureaucracy, like Thai politics in general, cannot be adequately analyzed in terms of the Western model of an impersonal or legal administrative system. In his standard work on the subject, William Siffin has noted that the Thai bureaucracy should be viewed as a social system—a collection of basic rules and relationships that sets the standards for the behavior of those within the system.[6] Hierarchy, personalism, and security are the dominant values of this social-bureaucratic system, and the actions of bureaucrats must be judged in the context of these values rather than on the basis of productivity or efficiency, which are secondary rather than primary values. The bureaucracy's primary objective is not to produce services for the general public; rather—according to Siffin—the function of the bureaucracy is to provide personal security, to secure personal status, and to establish the guidelines for reciprocal patron-client arrangements. Thus the system is concerned primarily with its

[6] William J. Siffin, *The Thai Bureaucracy: Institutional Change and Development* (Honolulu, Hawaii: East-West Center Press, 1966), p. 160.

own officials, but in fulfilling its self-serving functions it necessarily relates to the general populace. The secondary functions
of resource procurement, allocation, and utilization make sense
only when they are seen in light of the values of the Thai social
system.

The legislature has only recently been a politically powerful
branch of the national government. On the contrary, the legislative branch has regularly been used to enhance the power of
the executive. The resources available to the legislative branch
have been minimal, and hence legislators have had to rely on the
executive branch for favors. The executive's control of the legislature has come about partially through the government's power
to appoint half of the legislative body and partially because the
representatives hold office only by the sufferance of the army.
Also, the ever-present threat of a coup has prevented legislators
from performing their constitutional duties. When the legislature has attempted to perform its proper functions, as in 1971,
it has been disbanded by the army.

In a Western framework of analysis, elections provide the
populace with both the opportunity to make their views known
to the decision makers and to change the government if this is
deemed desirable. Parties aggregate the demands of the people
by synthesizing diverse desires that are presented to the government. Also, representatives in most Western political systems
provide an integral link between the rulers and the ruled as they
process the citizenry's demands and provide their constituents
with information, services, and resources. But the Thai notion of
elections is in sharp contrast to, say, the American idea that
elections are held essentially for providing the opportunity to
make changes in the government. In Thailand, elections are
held when the ruling groups become convinced that elections
will enhance their power.

Although elections are not held for the purpose of expressing—or finding out—the views of the citizenry and then acting
on the information, national elections have played an important
integrating role. During National Assembly elections, for example, many villagers are told about an environment far different
from that of their self-contained villages. District officials, National Assembly candidates, commune leaders, village headmen,
village elites, school teachers, and ordinary citizens interact in a

common election-time phenomenon. If only for a brief moment in the election booth, almost 50 percent of the adult Thai villagers make a positive act that transcends their daily and routine activities. Moreover, Thai villagers have few such opportunities.

Until the past decade, Thai political parties have had the most rudimentary organization, almost devoid of programs or issues. Party lines were not based on ideologies but on the personalities and aspirations of political leaders. Even when political parties have been allowed, they have acted essentially as a vehicle for a particular leader and his close associates. A further indication of party impotence is the fact that legislators of one party easily shift to other parties when their interests are better served.

The military-dominated parties have traditionally had considerable advantage over opposition parties in recruiting members because the ruling group has had control of the state machinery and patronage appointments. Supporters of a party could be promised hundreds of bureaucratic and political positions. In addition, the government has controlled the distribution of a wide array of resources to various groups. Because of extensive ties with the business community, government leaders have been able to provide opportunities to party members for corporation directorships, or merely for useful contacts, and the government party has generally been able to give its candidates considerable financial help during campaigns.

In the past, it would have been a mistake to view elections as an indication of public support for either the party or governmental policies. Political ideologies have not been significant in determining party affiliation or campaign practices. In general, the personality of candidates was much more important than their party affiliation. Thailand's election in April 1976, however, indicated that party affiliation might have played an important role in voting behavior. In all, 2,369 candidates representing 55 parties contested the elections. About 29 percent of the eligible voters in Bangkok and about 40 percent of the 20.9 million eligible voters throughout the country cast ballots. The Democrat party swept Bangkok, and defeated even Prime Minister Kukrit Pramoj in his district. The socialist parties were almost totally defeated in every section of the country, winning only six seats. The Democrats won 41 percent of the seats, and three other parties, all right wing, shared the bulk of the remainder.

The defeat of candidates in the socialist-oriented parties was interpreted as a rejection of policy rather than individuals. The government's campaign against communism and the horror stories of refugees from Laos, Cambodia, and Vietnam about repression in their Communist homelands struck a responsive chord. The Democrat party portrayed itself as middle of the road. The voters' rejection of both left- and extreme-right-oriented parties and the overwhelming victory of the Democrats suggest the voters consciously sought a middle or right-middle path.

As with most of the preceding 11 elections, the April 1979 election was designed to perpetuate and strengthen the rule of those in power. The accomplishment of that aim assured the continuation of the political dominance of the military-bureaucratic-business elites. Voters, especially among the Bangkok citizenry, showed an increased propensity to choose according to party lines rather than to vote for individual personalities. The nation continued to choose conservative candidates and reject candidates affiliated with socialist parties. In Bangkok, the Democrats, the nation's longest established and previously most successful party, were overwhelmed by a new party, Prachakorn Thai. For a combination of reasons, Bangkok voters stayed home. Only 19.5 percent of the capital's eligible voters cast ballots.

The new constitution deliberately emphasized continuity of existing power structures rather than democratic institutions. The bicameral parliament, for example, featured a Senate appointed by the prime minister (in the king's name) consisting of three fourths the number of the elected representatives in the lower house. The Senate was given extensive powers in order to appease the military who knew they would dominate the upper house. Indeed, the president of the appointed Senate, instead of the speaker of the elected House of Representatives, was given the power to nominate the prime minister. Moreover, the constitution required joint sessions of the parliament for general debates, votes of confidence, and budget and appropriations bills. The constitution also empowered a joint session for all bills considered "to be vital to national security, the throne, or the nation's economy."

The military's insistence on an appointed and powerful Senate was predicated on the assumption that the prime minister would name military figures to the upper house. On election day the ruling prime minister, General Kriangsak, did indeed appoint 114 army, 37 navy, 34 air force, and nine police officials to the 225-seat Senate. Only 31, or 14 percent of the total number of senators appointed, were civilians. All of the leading military figures were appointed except for those few in line for cabinet positions. The military's dominance of the Senate assured that no major parliamentary act could be promulgated without military approval. In those cases where the parliament meets as a joint body, the new prime minister needs only 39 votes in the 301-seat House together with the 225 senators to give him a majority (264 out of 526).

Kriangsak and his military colleagues had insisted that the prime minister-designate need not come from the elected House. Kriangsak himself chose not to run for an elected seat. In that way he retained certainty that he would be chosen prime minister again while not risking a humiliating defeat at the polls.

Despite Kriangsak's decision to remain "above" the campaign by choosing not to run for a seat, his administration became a central issue. Some 1,630 candidates including supporters and critics of the general campaigned in electoral constituencies throughout the kingdom. Candidates supporting Kriangsak emphasized his foreign policy of "flexibility and neutrality" and his success in improving relations between Thailand and its Communist neighbors. His supporters contrasted his tolerance and moderate policies with the more rigid and extreme policies of his predecessor Prime Minister Thanin Kraivichien. Pro-Kriangsak candidates argued that he had adequately demonstrated his concern for the rural citizenry by proclaiming 1979 the Year of the Farmer with new and innovative development programs for rural poor.

Kriangsak's critics came both from right-wing and left-wing parties. The former portrayed the prime minister as soft on communism and called for more vigorous action against Communist insurgents and against nations supporting the guerillas. Critics from more liberal parties pointed out the absence of meaningful domestic reform programs designed to alleviate the growing gap between the rich and the poor in Thailand. They pointed out that double-digit inflation has continued to reduce the standard of living of the Thais for the past five years. Critics from both the left and right complained that the administration did not have a coherent energy program. The only tangible response to the oil shortage, critics charged, was Kriangsak's order to shut off air conditioning in all public buildings. Of Thailand's 21 million eligible voters, 9.5 million (45 percent nationwide) chose to cast a ballot at one of 28,873 polling booths. Citizens could vote for candidates from 38 parties as well as for independents with no party affiliation. Nine women (three percent) were elected and 63 of the 301 members were former representatives.

Political party affiliation was an important determinant of voting in the capital. Bangkok voters overwhelmingly supported the candidates belonging to the Prachakorn Thai party. Samak Sundaravej, a controversial right-wing populist with superb oratorical abilities, led the party to a surprising sweep of 29 of Bangkok's 32 seats in the House. Many of Samak's 28 colleagues were virtually unknown before the election, yet they triumphed over some of the biggest individual names in Thai politics.

The Democrats' demise was due to a number of causes. Their factionalism and mediocre performance during Seni Pramoj's administration in 1976 and their inability to stop the military coup d'etat in October 1976 presented a picture of a weak party. Moreover, the Democrats' campaign speeches continually stressed their desire to be an opposition force rather than the ruling administration. Their campaign was largely negative in tone and substance. Hence, most potential Democrat voters stayed home.

In contrast, Samak Sundaravej's Prachakorn Thai party proposed numerous programs designed to please the laboring class and low ranking officials, especially policemen, in Bangkok. Samak, as Thanin Kraivichien's Minister of Interior from October 1976 to October 1977 had developed a reputation for active support of these groups. He was famous as an ardent anti-Communist and was accused by the Bangkok press of being an oppressor of civil liberties. The press's furious attack on Samak may have encouraged a backlash by sympathetic voters who saw him as a spokesman for both the underprivileged and the traditions of the kingdom.

The Social Action party leader Kukrut Pramoj was able to

break the Prachakorn Thai's monopoly in Bangkok. Kukrit's campaign stressed his own potential as an alternative to military rule in Thailand. In contrast to the Democrats who stressed their role as an opposition, Kukrit asserted that he himself and his party were a viable ruling force. Moreover, his program of direct subsidies to every commune in the country had popular appeal and was largely responsible for the Social Action party's winning the largest number of seats from the rural areas.

All 45 candidates of the newly formed Social Democrat party were defeated. This party was an amalgam of the various socialist parties that had once won impressive numbers of seats in Thailand's impoverished Northeast. The perceived threat from Communist Vietnam, the border disputes with Laos and Kampuchea, and the attempt of opposing candidates to portray the socialists as left-wing extremists all contributed to the poor showing.

The voter turnout was one of the lowest in Thai political history. For many voters, the election was a fraud carried out in the context of an undemocratic constitution. Many voters believed that no matter the outcome, the present regime under Kriangsak would remain in power. These nonvoters were more cynical than apathetic.

Also contributing to the low turnout was a stipulation in the election law requiring Thais with alien fathers to meet certain conditions before being allowed to vote. The law was clearly aimed at Thailand's Chinese and Vietnamese minority groups and succeeded in infuriating and alienating large numbers of citizens especially in Bangkok.

The low turnout was due at least partially to the complicated procedures potentially eligible voters had to complete. Citizens had to go to their district officers prior to the election to ascertain whether they had been properly registered. Those persons who did not check and who came to vote on election day were often turned away if their name was not on the list. The high degree of mobility in Thailand and negligence by many district officials in setting up the original registration list help explain why so many citizens would not vote.

As expected, on 11 May 1979, Kriangsak was selected Thailand's prime minister. He received the support of 222 of the 225 Senators in addition to 89 votes from the 301-member

House. The total of 311 gave him a majority of the combined parliament. Kriangsak received support from several small parties including the Seritham and New Force as well as from the bulk of the independents. Originally Kriangsak had hoped to bring larger parties into his coalition but negotiations between party representatives and Kriangsak broke down over monetary and cabinet position demands.

Kriangsak was unable to mobilize major parties into his coalition. The opposition Democrat, Prachakorn Thai, Social Action, and Chart Thai parties continued to control a majority of the House seats. As the economy deteriorated, the opposition called for his resignation. He was replaced in March 1980 by his army commander-in-chief and defense minister, General Prem Tinsulanond.

The elite in Thailand's national politics are top-level bureaucrats, high-ranking military officers, the royalty, distinguished journalists, directors of large business operations, intellectuals, and politicians with mass constituencies. Indeed, the formally installed government elite comprises a very high percentage of the available elite. The effect of this form of oligarchy is to reduce the number of persons engaged in politics and to narrow the range or scope of political activity. Yet top-level politics in Thailand, as in more diffused systems, is characterized by competition and conflict, cleavage and manipulation. Power struggles are at the heart of national-level politics as groups compete for what there is to get: power, wealth, position, and perquisites.

To maximize the chances of achieving these ends, patron-client groupings amalgamate into what are usually referred to as cliques, and the workings of these factional groups are probably best understood in the context of patron-client relationships. The society's sharp status differentiations and lack of more institutionalized groups are reflected within the cliques, which—like their smaller subunits, the patron-client groupings—are held together by bonds of personal loyalty and reciprocity, so that the alliances are mutually advantageous.

National-level politics are primarily concerned with the cliques' competition for additional power and for all that accompanies the possession of power. Invariably, the leader (patron) of a clique is a person who has power, or access to power, or potential power. The members (clients) of a clique represent constituencies (the army, Chinese business interests, the police, etc.) that are sufficiently strong and well organized to ensure perpetuation of their leaders' and their own positions. Each member of a clique is a patron to his subordinates, so that reciprocity works both upward and downward.

Once in power, and therefore concerned with maintaining its power, a clique must dispense the prerogatives of office in a judicious manner, and since the clique's leaders are also the highest governmental officials, the political and the administrative elites are one and the same. Thus personal loyalty and other ascriptive criteria are more highly rewarded than administrative know-how. As a minister of state, a clique leader uses the resources of his ministry to strengthen his clique and to ensure the perpetuation of his position and power. One way to judge the power of a top official who is a member of the ruling clique is to measure, over time, the budget allocations for his ministry or department. The more money he receives, the more he is able to distribute to his clients.

The cabinet represents the highest level of political activity because its ministers have greatest access to the government's resources and are closely affiliated with the prime minister. Generally, therefore, cabinet members include members of the dominant clique. Those who are closest to the prime minister usually head the ministries of interior and defense. Ministers who are not members of the ruling clique may be former high officials who gave indirect support to the ruling group.

Cabinet members must cater to major constituencies to retain their position. They must support their patrons, who are usually the prime minister and his associates; they must serve the interests of their particular ministry; and they must provide their clientele with sufficient favors so as to retain their loyalty. The overlapping and at times conflicting claims of these constituencies require great adroitness on the part of cabinet ministers.

Political Dynamics in Modern Thailand

Thailand has not had a strongman as ruler since 1963, when Marshal Sarit Thanarat died. Instead, a number of institutions have arisen with functions that replace the personalistic rule of the past. Personalism, in the form of patron-client relationships, still pervades every level of Thai politics; however, as the process of modernization takes hold, new means for articulating popular demands have been established, and the system's capacity to cope through patron-client behavior has changed.

These new institutions, which include interest groups, political parties, non-governmental associations, and decentralized ministerial units, have achieved a higher degree of legitimacy than in the past. In the face of public acceptance of these institutions, the military would find an attempt at seizing power opposed with strong resistance. The kingdom has accepted procedures for the transfer of political power. These procedures for succession have worked well since 1977, the year of the last successful coup in Thailand. The likelihood of unconstitutional intervention by the military decreases with the rise of such procedures.

Military intervention occurs less frequently in nations with governments that have a high degree of legitimacy. The bulk of the Thai people accept the Prem government as legitimate and as capable of resolving the nation's major problems. Moreover, the king has indicated his support for the present government. His involvement in politics reached its peak in 1981, when he supported Prime Minister Prem against the dissident colonels who staged a short-lived coup d'etat. The refusal of many army personnel to support the coup, in keeping with the wishes of the king, was an indication of his influence. It is true that the king, who is venerated throughout the kingdom, risks losing his aura and prestige as he is brought into the political fray; thus far, however, his support has stabilized the Prem regime and mitigated attempts to overthrow his government.

Political parties today are fewer in number, more coherent in structure, and better able to represent citizens' demands, in contrast to the personal orientation of parties just a decade ago. The civilian-controlled lower house of the national assembly is no longer impotent, and is no longer the puppet of the military-controlled cabinet, as it was during the 1960s and '70s (despite former Prime Minister Kukrit Pramoj's view that Thailand's elected representatives are "shameless and have no concept of sin").

In an unprecedented act of independence, the parliament in

1983 voted against a series of amendments to the constitution that would have enhanced the army's political strength. The vote jeopardized the political future of key army figures, undermined the army's control over parliament, and strengthened the large civilian-based political parties such as the Democrats and Social Action party (traditionally the bane of the military).

Again, in 1984, supporters of Army Commander-in-Chief General Arthit Kamlang-ek urged the national assembly to revise the constitution to allow active military officers to hold government posts. Refusal to acquiesce to the army's wishes was an indication that the legislature wanted to protect its prerogatives, to continue the nation's progress toward civilian democratic rule, and was more and more confident about its higher level of institutionalization and legitimacy. The fact that military officers backed off their demands when they were rebuffed indicates their perception of a government that was not ripe for intervention.

Rural Thais are no longer the passive peasantry one reads about in textbooks. Increasingly, a larger number of Thais are engaging in political activity, have contact with officials, have joined interest groups and participated in village projects, and have some knowledge of governmental processes. Rapid population growth, a scarcity of cultivable land, and the advent of a cash economy have led to increased membership in farmers' groups, more interaction between peasants and officials, greater mobility, and looser patron-client ties.

Thailand's remarkable economic growth in the past decades has also changed the character of the citizenry. An educated middle class has emerged in Bangkok, as well as in the provincial capitals and small towns of the kingdom. With per capita income growing steadily at an average annual rate of over seven percent, to about $800 (compared to $150 just 20 years ago), and with literacy becoming universal among the younger generation, Thailand has joined the ranks of the emerging middle-income countries. The result has been the rise of a vibrant, articulate class that views military rule as an anachronism, unsuited to the nation's well-being.

Related to the rise of the new middle class is the increased sophistication of the nation's agricultural class. Rice, rubber, tin, and teak made up 80 to 90 percent of all exports in the 1950s, but declined to less than half of all exports as Thailand has launched an era of agricultural expansion and new technology. This diversification verifies the view of the Thai farmer as a profit-oriented rational being, rather than as the stereotypical economically naive peasant.

Thailand's fifth five-year development plan (1982–86) emphasizes equity rather than growth, and focuses on the agricultural sector rather than only on industrialization. The plan's emphasis on decentralization has changed the way resources are allocated and bureaucracies organized. Part of the reason for the plan's success is the rise of highly educated and skilled technocrats in the Budget Bureau, the National Economic and Social Development Board, and related ministries. These young and sophisticated technocrats have public-regarding, rather than self-interested, values as they carry out their responsibilities and implement the goals of the five-year plan.

The new middle class, industrialists, bankers, and service oriented personnel, graduates of Thailand's rapidly expanding higher education system, have little patience with the inefficiencies that have characterized military dominated bureaucratic regimes. They are participating in Thai politics so that policymaking is no longer the reserve of the bureaucrats and the military. They desire the stability of a moderate government that encourages technocrats to run the ministries, holds the lid on corruption, restricts the rise of labor organizations, controls the military while continuing to allocate sufficient resources for security, and allows various political and economic forces such as political parties and parliament to participate in the affairs of the state. Thailand's economic growth has brought about a new significant class, concerned with effectiveness and stability, and opposed to autocratic military rule.

Since 1979 there has been a stunning change in the fortunes of the Communist-led guerrilla insurgency that threatened Thai security for two decades. In the past, military leaders pointed to this threat as a primary reason for military dominance, but the virtual collapse of the Communist movement has removed that rationale. By 1985 the movement's United Front had collapsed, most of the cadre and leaders had defected, the guerrilla military bases had been wiped out, and outside support (from Vietnam and China) had all but vanished.

The reasons for the loss of support for the Communist party of Thailand (CPT), while rural-based revolutionary movements have been thriving in other parts of the world, stem from internal and external conditions. Thailand's consistent and booming economic growth and the clear improvement in the living conditions of rural Thais have undercut support for the party. Moreover, the governments of Prime Ministers Kriangsak and Prem have initiated a number of rural development projects, particularly in areas where insurgency had been greatest.

Beginning in 1977, the government offered amnesty to insurgents who would defect from the Communist cause. Some 9,000 (of the estimated 12,000) have taken advantage of the program by surrendering to government officials. The plan calls for the distribution of farmland to defectors, who are called *phu ruam pattana chat Thai* (participants in Thai national development) instead of the more pejorative term defector.

Rivalries internal to the CPT also contributed to the demise of party strength. Because of a major schism among party factions, centering on ideological differences, pro-Chinese and pro-Vietnamese groups were not able to fashion an essentially "Thai road" to revolution.

External variables contributed to the demise of the CPT. Vietnam stopped financial support of the party after it was invaded by Chinese forces in 1978. The People's Republic of China similarly withheld funds after it established diplomatic relations with Thailand in 1979. China attached greater weight to its relations with the government of Thailand than to its relations with the CPT. China's support of Khmer resistance forces in Cambodia required the cooperation of Thai officials. In addition, refugees have poured into Thailand with horror stories of life under Communist rule in Laos and Cambodia, thereby undermining the support that Thais might have given to Communist insurgents in their own country.

Paradoxically, insurgency was at its height during the era of Prime Minister Thanin Kraivichian, the most anti-Communist regime in contemporary Thai politics. Moreover, once the United States removed its counter-insurgency experts and let the Thais handle the situation (by their policy of "politics over military"), counterinsurgency successes increased. Finally, rather than exacerbating the insurgency problem, Thailand's establishment of diplomatic relations with China brought about the withdrawal of outside support for Thai guerrillas.

Each of these points undermines the military's claim that only it has the means and fortitude to secure the nation's security against internal upheaval. Many Thais now see that a program of economic development, generous amnesty, national reconciliation, and a balanced foreign policy may be more effective ways to combat insurgency than the traditional reliance on military force.

The Thailand of 1985 is fundamentally different from the Thailand of just a decade or two ago. The nation's institutions are stronger, more responsible, and less vulnerable to the instability that stems from personalism. Throughout the bureaucracy are highly trained and educated leaders with societal, rather than self-serving, values and goals. The present government is perceived by most classes and interests as meeting their interests, with a minimum of corruption and oppression. Inasmuch as no significant foreign or domestic crises threaten the country, the rationale for military intervention does not exist. Recent Thai governments have shown a remarkable capacity to blend tradition, modernity, and *realpolitik* in a manner that augurs well for the nation's future.

BURMA

As in Thailand, many of Burma's greatest kings were military heroes. Burma's history includes countless wars with neighbors and attempts at expansion of power by force. During the British colonial period, Burma became an administrative subdivision of British India. The British disbanded the Burmese army and recruited ethnic minorities in Burma into the Indian army. The decimation of the Burmese army infuriated Burmese nationalists, who felt humiliated.[7]

The Japanese threat caused the British to reverse their policy of excluding Burmese involvement in the military. However, the Japanese defeated and occupied Burma before the military had sufficient strength to repel the Japanese invaders. Before the

[7] Hoadley, *Soldiers and Politics,* p. 37.

Japanese invasion, a group of Rangoon University students had begun the anti-British Thankin movement. A group within the movement, known as the Thirty Heroes, with the support of Japan organized a Burmese Independence Army that eventually numbered some 30,000 men. This army, which became the Burma National Army, turned against the Japanese, and became the nucleus for the Anti-Fascist People's Freedom League (AFPFL). The military emerged as the core of the anti-British, anti-Japanese nationalist struggle for independence.

Although the Burmese military stayed out of political activities after independence, it retained a reputation for sacrifice, honesty, and nationalism. When Prime Minister U Nu invited General Ne Win to head a caretaker government in 1958, most relevant parties agreed it was appropriate that the military govern the society. The success of the military rulers in stabilizing the political and economic situation in Burma during its caretaker administration caused most Burmese to greet their return in 1962, this time by coup d'etat, with hope and even enthusiasm.

Burma's military, like Thailand's, took advantage of a leadership vacuum during U Nu's civilian era prior to establishment of the military caretaker regime in 1958. U Nu's leadership was based on charismatic qualities and a reputation for impeccable honesty. At the same time, U Nu was a poor administrator of the nation, as well as his own party following. He proved incapable of holding the Anti-Fascist People's Freedom League together, so that by 1958 the coalition had virtually disintegrated. His government barely made a dent in the overwhelming economic problems facing postwar Burma. The war had decimated even the incipient industrial life of the country, and much of the economic infrastructure (roads, trains, ports, etc.) was in ruins. Because the nation was reeling from multiple rebellions among minority groups, a large share of the central budget was allocated to internal security needs.

Premier U Nu's civilian administration did not move decisively to solve these problems. Instead, U Nu concentrated on his program to make Buddhism the state religion. This program was supplemented by his idealistic vision of a Burmese welfare state (Pyidawtha) based on the teachings of the Buddha. U Nu's ambitious goals were not matched by a parallel plan for implementation and administration. The controversy over Burma's declining economic fortunes precipitated a bitter struggle among AFPFL leaders for party control. By spring of 1958 the government machinery came to a halt, and U Nu turned to General Ne Win's army to extricate the nation from the chaotic situation.

The military takeover on 28 October 1958 inaugurated a period of stability in Burmese politics. General Ne Win moved with dispatch to pacify the rebellious minorities. His largely civilian cabinet was made up of competent technocrats, skilled as administrators and mandated to end corruption and malingering. Simultaneously, the caretaker regime clamped down on alleged dissidents and acted with what many Burmese saw as arbitrary authority.

The army allowed elections in February 1960, and U Nu's New Union party won. When U Nu once again duplicated his indecisive tenure, the military looked for an excuse to take power. John Cady, a foremost historian of contemporary Burma, summed up the problems of civilian rule:

> Both politically and administratively, the second Nu government had pretty well run aground. Nu's basic intentions were worthy, but he failed to coordinate his goals and to implement approved policy decisions. Although unable to keep his variegated followers in line politically, he tried to use both democratic means and the force of his own personality to bridge the huge gaps that separated the traditionalists from the minority modernist socialist elements, trying at the same time to conciliate the distrustful ethnic minority factions. His objectives were utopian rather than realistically conceived. He tried to wear too many hats: orthodox Buddhist, champion of religious freedom and minority rights, convinced proponent of democracy, and the enemy of greedy, exploitative and alien-dominated capitalism. He also suffered from the characteristic indiscipline of many of his countrymen, restive under restraint and too impatient to concentrate on detail. In this sense, the democracy which Nu espoused was backward looking and opposed to modernization, while tolerating a surfeit of freedom.[8]

[8] John F. Cady, *The History of Post-War Southeast Asia* (Athens, Ohio: Ohio University Press, 1974), p. 232.

Like the military in Thailand, the Burmese military took advantage of the weaknesses of civilian rule and instituted a highly repressive administration. Unlike the Thai military, however, the Burmese military set forth a socialist and isolationist program that is unique among military-dominated Southeast Asia societies.

Within a year of its takeover, the army produced the official ideological document of the government, "The Burmese Way to Socialism" (BWS), which condemned capitalism, advocated nationalization of production, and called for elimination of foreign and non-Burmese ownership of businesses. Within two years Ne Win's government had virtual control over the major economic enterprises. To some extent the centralized aspect of the rule was reminiscent of colonial rule, while the socialist ideology was an outgrowth of U Nu's economic program.

The Burmese military's effort to engage in socialist policies is counter to the general tendency of army rulers to favor more conservative policies, but it should be remembered that the Burmese military were initially leaders of the nationalist Burma Independence Army and the AFPFL. The AFPFL leaders were socialists from the very establishment of the party. The present rulers were socialist politicians first and army leaders second. Since the army took over, Burma's economy has continued to lose ground. The economic performance is most clearly seen in the deterioration of the nation's most important product, rice.

> Prior to the 1962 takeover sufficient rice was produced for both domestic consumption and foreign export. The highly favorable situation was drastically altered after the military took on the sole responsibility for purchasing, milling, distributing, and setting the price of rice. Production declined sharply, and real (i.e. black market) prices increased significantly due to the operation's poor planning and monumental inefficiency.[9]

The decline in rice production was paralleled in industrial production. Most small private industries closed their doors because they could not obtain the materials they needed. Tin-ore

---

[9] Eric A. Nordlinger, *Soldiers in Politics, Military Coups and Governments* (Englewood Cliffs, N.J.: Prentice-Hall, 1977), p. 185.

output in the lower peninsula was 6,000 tons in 1939, 1,624 tons in 1951, and zero in 1965.[10] "People's stores" were set up to distribute resources, but they were so inefficient that the public chose to use the black market.

These policies were carried out by the Revolutionary Council (RC), composed of 17 men who were close military associates of Ne Win. The RC was under the absolute control of Ne Win. Its decisions were tantamount to law since there was no legislature, constitution, or public forum. In 1971 the government moved to a more traditional pattern by designating Ne Win as prime minister. He and his military associates controlled all the major ministries.

In 1972 General Ne Win resigned as an army officer, ostensibly to "civilianize" his government. The change made no practical difference in the operations of the government or in the army's dominant role. Ne Win expanded his control by direct and indirect means. The press was subject to censorship, and numerous journalists were imprisoned for "antigovernment" articles. Political party leaders were subjected to imprisonment and harassment. Foreigners were restricted to certain areas and allowed to stay in the country only 24 hours, between flights; in 1974 this restriction was moderated to allow seven-day visits for foreigners.

Because university students were prone to oppose the government, the military dealt with them in an especially harsh manner. Rangoon University was closed on numerous occasions, once for an entire year. The government took control of curriculum design and placed "safe" persons in faculty positions. In December 1974 Rangoon University students defied the government by seizing the coffin of United Nations Secretary General U Thant. In the students' view, Ne Win, who had often feuded with U Thant, had refused to provide proper honors for a man of such eminence. The students buried the remains on the university campus after performing Buddhist rites. The military arrested student leaders and, eventually, over 4,000 persons who were suspected of acts against the national security. Although the incident focused on the burial of U Thant, the riots reflected the

[10]Cady, p. 482.

students' larger discontent with the repressive and incompetent Ne Win administration.

Moreover, prominent personalities, such as former Premier U Nu, were jailed for many years. U Nu was released in 1966 and eventually went into exile, where he organized a rebel army in Thailand with the goal of overthrowing Ne Win. Internal disagreements in 1972 among the rebel leaders caused U Nu to resign, thereby ending his challenge to the established government. U Nu eventually was allowed to return to Burma to work on his scholarly writings on Buddhism.

The military believed that its rule could be strengthened by establishing a mass political party to unify the masses and provide a means to assure electoral support for the army leadership in future elections. The RC announced in July 1962 the establishment of the Burmese Socialist Program party, known in Burmese as Lanzin.[11] The party remained a cadre party until 1971, when it was changed to a mass-based national party.

The military promulgated a new constitution in 1974 that gave supreme power to the Burma Socialist Program party and explicitly stated that the BSPP would be the sole legal party. Because the military holds the positions of power in BSPP, the new constitution reaffirmed and enhanced the military dictatorship. The new name of the nation, Socialist Republic of the Union of Burma, signifies the constitution's emphasis on the socialist nature of the new regime.

A one-house legislature, the People's Assembly, is elected by the people. The BSPP controls the nomination of candidates, so there is no deviation from party policy. Twenty-nine members of the legislature are chosen to the Council of State, the supreme executive authority, whose chairman, Ne Win, serves as president of the republic. The Council of State nominates a Council of Ministers for the national assembly to approve. This council chooses the prime minister and carries out day-by-day governing responsibilities. In the January 1978 elections by the Peoples' Congress Ne Win once again was overwhelmingly chosen president of the Socialist Republic of the Union of Burma.

---

[11] Josef Silverstein, *Burma, Military Rule and the Politics of Stagnation* (Ithaca, N.Y.: Cornell University Press, 1977), p. 101.

The new constitution abolished the Revolutionary Council but, in actuality, little changed in the dynamics of Burmese politics.

> The election of the Council of State gave the first evidence that very little actual leadership would be transferred to a civilian elite. Of the twenty-nine members elected, eleven, or more than one-third, were carryovers from the now defunct Revolutionary Council.[12]

The new government was faced with the same problems confronted by previous Burmese administrations: national unity, Communist insurgency, and economic stagnation. The government's inability to solve these problems has caused dissatisfaction and strains within the ruling sectors and among the general populace. From 1974 to the present, numerous mass demonstrations protesting the declining economic conditions took place. For the most part, however, the government has been unwilling to move away from its rigid, doctrinaire socialism or its isolationist stance.

Intrigues among the top military leadership have brought instability to Burmese politics. In 1977 the BSPP underwent wrenching changes when over 50,000 of its members, including several top leaders, were purged. The purge highlighted the continuing controversy over the deterioration of the economy and the growing disillusionment toward socialist economics. The third party congress met in 1977 amid claims of faulty implementation of BSPP policies and issued a new Four-Year Plan designed to alleviate the country's woes, but the plan did not call for fundamental reforms of policies. The BSPP congress issued an extraordinary report, detailing the decline in economic production, the soaring cost of living, the rise in unemployment, increased corruption, abuses of power, personality cults, and opportunism. Despite these admissions, BSPP remained firmly in control of Burmese politics.

The 1977 purge was followed by others including several which focused on potential successors to Ne Win. Although Ne Win had indicated in 1981 that he wanted to prepare for succes-

[12] Ibid., p. 137.

sion, he refused to promote any particular candidates. On the contrary, as candidates emerged, he purged them and their followers. These purges pointed to the importance of personalism in Burmese politics. Ne Win indicated that he preferred a collective leadership after he leaves office.

INDONESIA

In contrast to Burma and Thailand, the Indonesian military did not play an important political role during most of the nation's history. In World War II the Japanese occupation of Indonesia brought about the establishment of the Fatherland Defense Corps (Peta), which, following the Japanese defeat in 1945, was transformed into the Indonesian National Army. This army was the core of the nationalist fighting force against the Dutch attempt to reassert colonial status over Indonesia.

Initially, the National Army was severely handicapped because no officers above the battalion level had been trained. Various paramilitary nationalist groups (Pioneer Corps, Youth Corps, Student Corps) joined the National Army in its successful war against the Dutch. From the Indonesian people's point of view, the military could claim the primary credit for Indonesia's achievement. As independent Indonesia was proclaimed, the military's prestige was strong.

Factional problems within the army emerged following the truce agreements between the Dutch and the Indonesians. When officers from the disbanded Dutch Colonial Army were incorporated into the Peta battalions, friction arose as various groups jockeyed for power. The result was a number of military rebellions throughout the archipelago and a lack of unity amongst the top command positions. The Peta leadership tended to support the Indonesian Nationalist party, led by Sukarno, whereas the officers who had been trained by the Dutch supported the Socialist and Masjumi (Muslim) parties. The support was essentially nominal; the army had no ideology, program, or defined political goals.[13]

[13] Daniel S. Lev, "The Political Role of the Army in Indonesia," in *Man, State, and Society in Contemporary Southeast Asia,* ed. Robert O. Tilman (New York: Praeger, 1969), p. 288.

Army factionalism kept the military from playing a direct role in political affairs during the period of "liberal democracy" (1949–58). However, the military increased its role in the administration of outer island regions and gradually involved more and more of its leadership directly in national-level politics. Army leaders grew discontent with the instability of the multiparty system, which was manifested clearly in the 1955 election and its aftermath. Military leaders saw themselves as the best organized and most powerful institution in the country, with the ability to bring about stable, effective, and noncorrupt rule.

"Guided democracy" evolved under Sukarno's leadership between the late 1950s and 1965. The army supported the retreat from liberal democracy and deftly moved to become one side in a four-sided pattern of control, with power divided between the army, the Indonesian Communist party (PKI), the rightist Muslims and President Sukarno. Sukarno was in a balancing position, between the other three groups. The PKI had the ability to mobilize thousands of peasants, and to rouse revolutionary fervor, in support of nationalist goals. The army provided the means to control the outer islands and kept the PKI from taking too much power. The Muslims continued to have widespread backing among the masses, as well as among influential intellectuals.

Sukarno's delicate balancing act proved difficult as the competing groups maneuvered for favorable positions. During the guided-democracy period the Indonesian economy declined precipitously, with a high inflation rate and disastrous trade balance. The peasant farmers survived by subsistence agriculture and barter.

The policy structure was also affected by a shift in Indonesia's foreign policy to a Peking-Hanoi-Djakarta alliance. Sukarno proclaimed himself the champion of the New Emerging Forces (NEFOS), with solid support from the PKI and the Soviet Union. His policy of taking over West Irian and of declaring war on Malaysia (Konfrontasi) threw the Indonesian economy into total disarray. The latter struggle, beginning in 1963, won the support of the PKI for ideological and anti-imperialist reasons. The crush-Malaysia policy strengthened the army's claim for increased budgeted funds and enhanced its reputation as a nationalist force.

The struggle between the PKI and the army came to a head when Sukarno agreed to accept arms from the People's Republic of China to equip an Indonesian militia that comprised the peasant class. The PKI saw this program as a means to arm its supporters against its main opposition, the army. The army opposed the establishment of a fifth force because its preeminent position as the only armed group in the country was threatened and because the army feared PKI dominance over the militia. The 1965 Gestapu coup occurred at the height of the controversy.

By early 1965 the army and the PKI were open antagonists and both were potential heirs to Sukarno's power. The Gestapu coup, on 30 September 1965, provided both groups with the chance to take that power. The army, under General Suharto, crushed the plot (after six leading generals in the army high command were assassinated) and then decimated the PKI and all other suspected Communists. The Indonesian military moved rapidly in 1965 to capitalize on the abortive Gestapu coup that originally had been planned to reduce the military's power.

Military rule in Indonesia, as in Burma and Thailand, can be partially explained by the incompetent and corrupt administration of the preceding civilian rulers. When Sukarno was officially deposed in March 1966, inflation was running at an estimated 600 percent a year. The nation was on the verge of bankruptcy. The middle-class bureaucrats resorted to open corruption because their salaries no longer provided for their needs. The nation's infrastructure was in collapse as roads became impassable, gas and oil became unavailable for ships, cars or planes, and industry after industry folded. Cities like Jakarta was inundated by millions of unemployed persons, now forced to live in slum conditions without water or sewage services.

Moreover, Sukarno's balancing act between the left (PKI) and the right (army and Muslim organizations) had ended by 1965, as it became clear he favored policies supported by the Communists. His alliance with the left frightened many of the most powerful elements of Indonesian society, thereby undermining political stability. The skills he had manifested in the first years of his presidency, as an orator, revolutionary, and then solidarity maker, were far superior to his administrative skills, which he now needed to establish economic growth and political stability.

Thus when General Suharto became president, Indonesia was in a state of near anarchy. From October 1965 until March 1967, when Sukarno was forced to sign the "March 11 order" (giving General Suharto emergency powers), Suharto deftly maneuvered Sukarno into political impotence without humiliating him or otherwise rallying his supporters. Suharto moved quickly to destroy potential opposition and to build political support. He set up a triumvirate, consisting of himself and two distinguished civilians, the sultan of Jogjakarta (Hamengku Buwono) and the diplomat Adam Malik, to mask the military character of his regime.

Suharto consolidated civilian support by placing the respected sultan and Malik in high-level positions. He then moved to liquidate the PKI. He approved army participation in mass killings of Communists and suspected Communists on a scale almost without precedent. The PKI leadership and most of the party members and supporters were decimated.

His harsh stand against the Communists strengthened his position vis-à-vis other potential opposition forces, now cowed into inaction, as well as factional leaders within the army. In the years following the 1965 coup, the military comprised a number of competing factions that were eventually divided into pro- and anti-Suharto groups.

The members of Suharto's faction are central Abangan Javanese who served with him in Peta during the Japanese occupation (but many of these officers retained a strong commitment to President Sukarno and were reluctant to discredit him). Suharto's greatest triumph was to dislodge Sukarno from the presidency while retaining the support of the Javanese generals. Anti-Suharto military officers generally have supported Generals Nasution and Dharsono, identify with Islam, and include non-Javanese as well as Javanese. Both of these factions share an anti-Communist ideology. Sukarno's refusal to speak against the PKI eventually rallied the army generals around Suharto. It was not until 20 February 1967, however, that Suharto demanded the total transfer of power from Sukarno. With Suharto as acting president and General Nasution as chairman of the congress, the military were firmly in control of the key political institutions.

Suharto moved swiftly to build cohesion and support within

the army. He jailed or executed military officers considered to be involved in the abortive 1965 Gestapu coup. Officers who were felt to be sympathetic but not directly involved with the coup were transferred to isolated positions. After Suharto was reappointed president and his emergency powers were extended in 1968, he transferred a large number of opposition and potential opposition military officers to peripheral locations or to foreign countries as ambassadors. Suharto also followed a policy of co-opting the opposition officers by giving them advisory roles in the government, thereby preventing them from publicly expressing their criticism. He appointed himself minister of defense and security, with authority to control the activities of all the armed services, and restructured the military hierarchy to limit inter- and intra-service rivalry. His virtual one-man rule for 20 years attests to his success in mitigating the destabilizing tendencies of a highly factionalized and competitive military.

Suharto's commitment to a central political and governmental role for the armed forces is called *dwi-funksi* (dual function—military and civilian functions) and the appropriateness of dwi-funksi has not been debatable since Suharto consolidated his control over the army. In addition, the office of president is enormously powerful. No parliamentary bill can become law without his signature. His influence over the majority of the parliament further enhances his power.

Karl Jackson characterized Suharto's Indonesia as a bureaucratic polity—"a political system in which power and participation in national decisions are limited almost entirely to the employees of the state, particularly the officer corps and the highest levels of the bureaucracy, including especially the highly trained specialists known as the technocrats."[14] Jackson maintains that the president, his personal advisors, a group of Western-trained technocrats, top-level generals, and a few top bureaucrats exercise decisive control over national policy-making. Meaningful power "is obtained through interpersonal competition in the elite circle in closest physical proximity to the

[14] Karl D. Jackson, ed., "Bureaucratic Polity: A Theoretical Framework for the Analysis of Power and Communications in Indonesia," in *Political Power and Communications in Indonesia* (Los Angeles: University of California Press, 1978), p. 3.

president. Elections are held to legitimize, through democratic symbolism, the power arrangements already determined by competing elite circles in Jakarta."[15]

The nature of the bureaucratic polity is not totalitarian, although the brutal purge of PKI and suspected PKI members in 1965 and 1966 shows the government's capacity for force. Jackson points out that "bureaucratic politics usually do not possess the organizational apparatus required for continual systematic terror, and the mobilizing effects of constant mass coercion contradict the nonparticipant nature of bureaucratic polity."[16] Co-optation, rather than coercion, has been the primary means by which present-day Indonesian leaders have sustained their power. Interest groups, political parties, and other extra-bureaucratic groupings are weak and unable to affect the basic political decisions of the elites. It is precisely this lack of social mobilization of the masses and the isolation of the bureaucratic elites that has entrenched the latter in power and kept the former from active involvement in economic and social development.

Once firmly in power, Suharto moved to change the direction of Indonesian foreign and domestic policy. His government banned the PKI, broke off relations with the People's Republic of China, rejoined the United Nations, ended the economically disastrous confrontation policy against Malaysia, and sought needed financial aid from the West. Although Suharto's government retained the Pantja Sila as the basic principles of the state, for the most part the extreme ideological rhetoric of the guided-democracy period was discarded. Indonesia began taking more interest in regional affairs, including sponsorship of the Association of Southeast Asian Nations (ASEAN).

> Turning a deaf ear to Sukarno's plea, Indonesia continued upon its changed course, disengaging from many of his most cherished positions in world and domestic affairs. Internationally, it abandoned his "global strategy"—the crusade to "build the world anew"—, toned down the shrillness of his struggle against "imperialism and colonialism," and generally sought a less isolated, more respected position within the community of nations.

---

[15] Ibid., p. 5.
[16] Ibid., p. 32.

> Domestically, . . . he set about a more moderate, rational and
> pragmatic approach to government, especially in the economic
> sphere. To accommodate these changes a new political vocabulary
> emerged. The less emotive word "struggle" largely replaced the
> somewhat pretentious "revolution" in most official usage, "non-
> alignment" returned as "confrontation" was banished, "peaceful
> coexistence" won favor over "independence at all costs," "eco-
> nomic" interests gained precedence over "political," and "prag-
> matism" before "idealism" in a comprehensive reassessment
> aimed at promoting political and economic stability rather than
> "controlled conflict" and turmoil.[17]

Suharto's success in bringing stability to Indonesia in the time
of national crisis in 1965–66 was followed by a move to further
legitimize his rule through elections. His establishment of a mass
party in preparation for elections paralleled the plans of General
Ne Win in Burma to set up the Burmese Socialist Program party,
and the plans of Generals Phibun and Thanom in Thailand to
assure electoral support for continued military rule. Suharto
sent a bill to the Provisional People's Consultative Assembly in
November 1966 requesting an elections act. The fact that
Suharto had initiated parliamentary debate defused democrats'
criticism of his regime and therefore helped to restore political
order.

However, a long series of delays caused the elections, promised for 1968, to be postponed until 1971. Clearly, Suharto's first
priority was to strengthen his rule and to emphasize economic
rehabilitation. During this period Suharto and his staff expanded a group created in the mid-1960s to establish a quasi-
political party called Golkar, a loose confederation of occupa-
tional groups ranging from civil servants to *betjak* (tricycle-taxi
drivers).[18] Golkar (also referred to as Sekber Golkar) is an acronym for *golangan karya* (functional group). Although Golkar
comprised persons from all walks of life, the military remained
firmly entrenched in the group's leadership positions.

---

[17] Peter Polomka, *Indonesia Since Sukarno* (Middlesex, England: Penguin Books,
1971), p. 118.
[18] For a complete analysis of Golkar and the 1971 elections see Masashi
Nishihara, *Golkar and the Indonesian Elections of 1971* (Ithaca, N.Y.: Cornell University Press, 1972).

Golkar became a highly sophisticated and organized group with branches at every level of administration, down to the village level. Civil servants, in particular, became the backbone of the group as they mobilized the peasantry (over which they ruled) to support the government party. Golkar emphasized its unique Indonesian character—a nonideological group consisting of persons with diverse occupations who used the traditional *musjawarah-mufakat* style of decision-making.

When the elections finally took place, 94 percent of the nation's eligible voters went to the polls, and 63 percent voted for Golkar candidates. The party won 236 of the 360 contested seats. The overwhelming victory for Suharto and Golkar can be explained by a variety of factors. First, Golkar had access to unlimited government funds, which Suharto distributed to his candidates. In contrast, the other political parties were without adequate funds. Second, there appeared to be sincere support for Suharto's generally successful endeavors to bring economic stability and growth to Indonesia. Golkar emphasized its message of *modernisai* and *pembangunan* (development), and contrasted the ideological rhetoric of the other parties with its own pragmatic style.

Golkar's victory is also attributable to the nation's civil servants who used their bureaucratic positions to mobilize the countryside, for they were obliged to join the Golkar bandwagon to assure their job security. In addition, the election law stipulated that candidates could not discuss the basic principles (Pantja Sila) of the government or slander or show contempt or disrespect for government officials. This injunction greatly limited free debate of the issues. Finally, several major political parties, such as the PKI and certain Islamic parties, were banned from participating in the election.

The newly elected parliament (DPR) made up half of the larger deliberative body, called variously the People's Deliberative Assembly or the People's Consultative Assembly (MPR). The other half of the MPR was made up of appointed group representatives and military officials. This assembly, which meets every five years, has the power to appoint the president and set the broad outlines of national policy; it also has the legislative power to initiate and pass bills. Golkar's large majority has assured Suharto's dominance over the parliament.

Suharto, like military leaders in other Southeast Asia nations, used the elections to enhance and perpetuate his military rule. He allowed elections only when he was convinced that he could control the outcome. He took the added precaution of reserving 100 of the 460 parliamentary seats for appointment, thus assuring parliamentary support. Even if Golkar did not win a majority of the 360 elected seats, the pro-Golkar appointed members, 75 of whom were to be members of the armed forces, would safeguard the government's position. With their impressive win, Suharto and his military colleagues gained control over parliamentary politics and legitimized their rule in the eyes of Indonesians and foreign nations alike. The defeat of formerly prominent parties, such as Sukarno's Nationalist party of Indonesia (PNI), which won 20 seats and only 6.9 percent of the vote, meant that only the Nahdatul Ulama party, with strength among Muslim villagers in Java, which won 19 percent of the vote and 60 seats, could provide opposition to Suharto. However, even the Nahdatul Ulama, in return for minor cabinet positions, seemed content to acquiesce to the military's control of the government.

Suharto used his enhanced position to gain more control over army factions and over every facet of political life in Indonesia. His position was sufficiently secure in 1977 to call for a second election. The Golkar strategy was essentially the same: through intimidation, pressure, and persuasion Golkar won 62 percent of the vote, and 232 of the 360 elected seats in the 460-seat parliament. The major opposition Muslim parties, including Nahdatul Ulama, had been forced by the government to fuse into the Unity Development party (PPP); it won 99 seats. The other handful of seats went to minor parties. As in 1971, the army reserved 100 seats.

Despite Suharto's skill at controlling the army's factionalism and manipulating the political organs of the country for his own power interests, there have been a number of crucial problems and displays of dissidence and disillusionment toward his New Order rule. In 1972 a large student demonstration protested Suharto's (and his wife's) alleged corrupt involvement in a government-supported project to construct a "Miniature Indonesia" equivalent to Disneyland. The students protested massive government funding, which they believed could better be spent on development. Suharto responded by banning public demonstrations and arresting student leaders. Like many demonstrations that followed, this protest centered on a particular act (construction of Miniature Indonesia) but symbolized widespread student antipathy toward the military's *dwi-funksi* role in governmental affairs.

The state visit of Japan's Prime Minister Tanaka to Indonesia on 14 January 1974, set the scene for one of the largest and most violent political demonstrations in recent times. Again the target of the demonstrators was narrowly focused on the great influx of foreign capital into Indonesia. During Tanaka's visit, a large number of youths looted and burned all goods thought to be made in Japan, as well as Japanese-owned property. At one time some 20,000 youths surrounded the guesthouse where Tanaka stayed, and there was fear among the Indonesian authorities for his safety. When the rioting ended, 11 youths had been killed and hundreds of homes and cars destroyed.

To defuse the situation, Suharto made several concessions designed to reduce the military's authority in some areas and to moderate corruption. Concurrently, he banned six daily newspapers and arrested protest leaders. Suharto was apparently convinced that his call in 1973 for more communication between government and students had raised their expectations to heights that could not be met. Hence he was determined to clamp down on dissidents and potential dissidents to keep the social and political order intact.

In 1975 the military rulers faced an extraordinary economic problem. In the preceding years Indonesia had produced more oil than ever before and the price of that oil had gone up 430 percent, generating huge increases in government revenues. The unexpected boom was expected to accelerate the government's economic development program. The government's second five-year economic development plan (Repelita II, 1974–79) was a forward-looking and wide-ranging plan that, if carried out, would have had a positive impact on the entire Indonesian population; however, the government's hopes for fundamental change were dashed when Pertamina, the state-owned oil firm, went bankrupt.

Pertamina had expanded far beyond its oil interests into numerous industries. The firm, under the direction of Ibnu

Sutowo, a flamboyant former deputy army chief of staff, mobilized a tremendous flow of investment capital from foreign countries that the firm soon found it could not repay. The Indonesian government was forced to absorb $10 billion in debts, thereby spending money that could otherwise have been used for development. The Pertamina crash was a blow to the prestige and economic fortunes of Suharto's rule. However, he moved effectively to reform the oil monopoly and managed, with the help of foreign creditors, who agreed to reduce the outstanding debt responsibilities, to rebuild the economy.

The Pertamina affair reflected the growing concern of many Indonesians about a national environment of moral decay. The enormous influx of foreign capital and the billions of dollars initially generated by Pertamina had brought new opportunities for massive corruption in the Indonesian bureaucracy and military leadership. The rich in Djakarta and other urban centers were getting richer, but the rest of the society was living at a level of bare subsistence.

This concern was manifested in a letter signed by five prominent Indonesian leaders in 1976, calling for a change in the moral and political climate of the country. The letter claimed that, though economic progress had been made, the country "has in fact degraded genuine morals and [been] led to a morass of sin." The letter was instigated by Sawito Kartowibowo, a retired government official and mystic who claimed he had received a vision indicating that he would become Indonesia's president. Suharto thought the incident serious enough to have Sawito arrested and tried (in 1977–78) for undermining national security.

Suharto's problems with political stability and control came to a head in January 1978, when he banned publication of the nation's leading newspapers and arrested scores of students for "undermining national security and throwing into jeopardy the hard-won gains of the past twelve years." The military's concern was that the mounting criticism of the Suharto government could become unmanageable. However, Suharto was reelected unanimously to a third term by the Golkar-dominated People's Congress in March 1978, despite the fact that university students issued a statement opposing him for another five-year term and detailed the areas in which the government had failed. At the same time, prominent generals criticized the New Order's performance. Suharto dealt with the problem by banning newspapers, "detaining" students, and dismissing the critical generals. His crackdown was a shift from what appeared to be a gradual loosening of the government's dictatorial rule. A government spokesman indicated that "if you have to choose between freedom and authority you must choose authority first, rather than get into a situation of anarchy."

The 1982 election triumph for Suharto confirmed the view that he and his supporters were firmly in control. Suharto had succeeded in having the armed forces institutionalized as the nation's leading political body. His domination of the military, bureaucracy, and presidential office was complete and accepted by the majority of Indonesians. He also succeeded in legitimizing his authority in the eyes of his allies in Southeast Asia and the United States.

Moreover, Suharto insisted that all political organizations accept the state ideology of Pantja Sila, thereby undermining Moslem parties and groups. Indonesia became virtually a one-party state. The succession question remains unanswered in 1986 although no rival or obvious alternative has arisen. Suharto would be 72 at the end of a possible fifth term in 1992.

CAMBODIA

In the twelfth century the Khmer Empire, under the great warrior Jayavarman VII, dominated much of mainland Southeast Asia. Not until the 15th century was the empire reduced in size, to approximately the present boundaries of Cambodia. French colonialism, beginning in 1864, protected Cambodia from invasion by its two aggressive neighbors, Vietnam and Thailand. As the French took control of the country, they filled the officers' positions with Frenchmen and reduced the role of the Cambodian army to ceremonial functions.

The transition from French control of the Cambodian army to Cambodian control evolved slowly. By the time of independence in 1954, the army, consisting of some 10,000 troops, was engaged in domestic operations against insurgency groups. As the threat of insurgency diminished, the military was diverted into civic action and development projects, such as building roads, dams, and schools, and teaching in rural areas. Cambodia's relatively nonviolent transition to independence and the peaceful period during the next decade kept the army from an overtly ideological or otherwise prominent role in Cambodian affairs and politics.

The preeminent role of Prince Sihanouk in every facet of postindependence political life in Cambodia further explains the secondary role of the military. Sihanouk, as supreme commander of the armed forces, decided which military officers were promoted and given the best positions. He provided the army with large budgets in order to reduce potential opposition to his one-man rule. He forbade military personnel to participate in political groups, including the national assembly, thereby decreasing their political role. At the same time, he provided lucrative state corporation positions to loyal military followers to assure their continued support.

In the mid-1960s the military's satisfaction with the established government faded as their budgets and perquisites were pruned. Sihanouk had banned United States foreign aid in 1963 because of alleged American interference in Cambodian domestic affairs, including support of anti-Sihanouk Khmer Rouge guerrilla insurgents. United States aid had underwritten about one-third of the Cambodian budget, and the cutoff of this large amount forced Sihanouk to reduce the military budget, thereby alienating army leaders.[19] Furthermore, Sihanouk's perceived move from a neutral or pro-West position to a pro-Communist foreign policy alarmed the army officers, who generally held anti-Communist views. The army was particularly angered by Sihanouk's apparent acquiescence in the abuse of "sanctuary" privileges by North Vietnamese and Viet Cong troops, which it interpreted as a violation of Cambodia's sovereignty. The army's inability to move against the Vietnamese unified it in hostility to Sihanouk.

The military's dissatisfaction with Sihanouk was paralleled by intellectuals' frustrations at their inability to influence public

[19] Hoadley, p. 132.

policy and their declining economic fortunes. In 1957 there were 914 college and university students; in 1965 the figure had swelled to 7,362, and in 1970 to 12,000.[20] These students could not find jobs appropriate to their training. Their disillusionment strengthened the anti-Sihanouk feelings of the military.

General Lon Nol was named premier in 1969 in a move that many interpreted as the beginning of the end of Sihanouk's total dominance over policy. Lon Nol reactivated Cambodian-United States relations and moved to undo much of Sihanouk's nationalization program. While Lon Nol gathered power, Prince Sihanouk left for Europe, the Soviet Union, and China in an attempt to counteract growing American influence and to seek Soviet and Chinese support against Vietnamese intrusions into Cambodia. While Sihanouk was abroad, General Lon Nol organized a takeover of the government and banned Prince Sihanouk from Cambodia.

No significant opposition arose to the military takeover among the elite sectors of the society; Sihanouk had alienated almost every influential group in Cambodia. And uprisings among the peasantry were quickly and harshly put down by the new government. Few Cambodians could foresee the catastrophic problems that would ensue, following the military's rise to power.

The military takeover was followed almost immediately by the collapse of the economy and by total war when South Vietnam and the United States intervened to destroy Vietnamese Communist sanctuaries in Cambodia. The political system was in a constant state of instability as various factions vied for power. Controlled elections were held by the military rulers in 1972, with opposition parties barred from campaigning. Lon Nol moved toward dictatorial rule and the United States assumed almost complete responsibility for budgetary matters. Despite huge American expenditure, the Cambodian political and economic situation deteriorated. In contrast, the Communist and pro-Sihanouk guerrilla forces grew stronger, until they forced the collapse of the Lon Nol military government in April 1975.

Thus the military came to power in Cambodia amid a chaotic economic, political, and military situation. The army leadership

[20] Ibid., p. 136.

took advantage of the elites' fear of Vietnamese incursions and the masses' dismay at the unparalleled corruption that pervaded every aspect of life. In addition, army leaders received the indirect backing of the American Central Intelligence Agency (CIA) and the American embassy, with promises of aid and military weaponry to use against the Communists.

The military's capacity to meet the needs of the people was never given a fair test, since the country was immediately engulfed in an all-out civil war and war against the Vietnamese. The military mobilized the entire population, which depleted the national budget. By 1971 the United States had given or allocated $194 million of military aid—and that was only a small portion of the total invested in Cambodia by 1975.[21] The military attempted to cope with the war-induced economic, political, and military problems by increasing the scope and intensity of its dictatorial rule.

As each year passed, the antigovernment insurgents gained more and more control of the countryside. The insurgents represented several diverse groups, including the Royal Government of National Union of Kampuchea (GRUNK), first led by Prince Sihanouk from his exile in Peking and later by his rival, Khieu Samphan. The Lon Nol government was incapable of stopping the seemingly inexorable advances of the insurgents. Moreover, Lon Nol's government appeared powerless, or at least unwilling, to stop the spread of corruption and economic deterioration.

Between 1970 and 1975 the highest positions in the government rotated among a number of military officers who headed competitive factions that represented nationalist, liberal, royalist, American, and business interests. These military factions vied for power, especially following the serious stroke Lon Nol suffered in 1971. But none of those who assumed cabinet positions could control the inflationary spiral or the declining value of the Cambodian *riel*. In fact, government control did not extend much beyond the city limits of Phnom Penh, the capital.

Lon Nol attempted to strengthen his regime in 1972 by holding elections. He gerrymandered the districts, to assure that only his followers could win election, and sponsored an "official"

---

[21] Ibid., p. 142.

political party that won every seat in the assembly. Despite American pressures on Lon Nol to broaden the support of his government, he took all power into his hands in October 1972. Nevertheless, the United States, under President Nixon, expressed "admiration for the courage and steadfastness of the Cambodian people under Lon Nol's leadership" and conveyed assurances of continuing American support.[22] However, American support was not enough to reverse the military's incapacity to meet the needs of the people.

In contrast to Indonesia, Thailand, and Burma, where the military gained support among the peasantry, the Cambodian military never was able to inspire the masses or win their support. Cambodian military rule rested on a small group of elites who had everything to gain from keeping the status quo. In addition, United States economic and military aid allowed the military to stay in power longer than it could have done on its own. In spring 1975, even the supporters of Lon Nol began to draw away as they realized the inevitability of the Communist victory and the incompetency of his regime. By April, the Communist takeover was accepted stoically, and even with hope that peace would return to Cambodia after five years of total war.

The extraordinary and extreme policies of Cambodia's new Communist rulers were not predicted by Cambodian or Western scholars. On the contrary, most Western scholars believed that a Communist government in Cambodia would be comparatively gentle, given the cultural conditioning of the guerrilla leaders. Thus it came as a shock when the first news about the new regime indicated that a total political, economic, social, and cultural revolution was being carried out under the harshest conditions. The new rulers were revolutionary in every sense of the word. Their goal was not simply overthrowing Lon Nol or ousting "American imperialism" but total change of the society and even of the personalities and values of the Cambodian people.[23] Prime Minister Pol Pot stated the reasons for the need for total revolution in September 1977:

[22] Cady, p. 695.

[23] See Timothy Michael Carney, *Communist Party Power in Kampuchea (Cambodia)*, Data Paper No. 106, Southeast Asia Program (Ithaca, N.Y.: Cornell University Press, 1977).

During the pre-communist era Cambodia was a satellite of imperialism, of U.S. imperialism in particular. This means that Cambodia was not independent, did not enjoy freedom, was in the state of being half-slave and half-satellite of imperialism. In general it was an imperialist satellite, but in particular, it was a satellite of U.S. imperialism. Thus, though in form it was independent and neutral, in essence it was not, since its economy was under the blanket of U.S. imperialism and its culture and lifestyle were influenced by imperialism. This was most obvious among the ruling class. We thus considered such a society as being a satellite of imperialism or a semicolonial country.[24]

The revolutionary doctrine emanates from a tightly disciplined party vanguard called "the organization" (Angka). Angka saw itself as the leader of the oppressed workers, farmers, and poor and lower-middle-class peasants against the feudal, imperialistic, capitalist, reactionary, and oppressor classes represented by former regimes:

> The Communist Party of Kampuchea and the Government of Democratic Kampuchea who suffered cruelly from the barbarous acts of the imperialists, expansionists and reactionaries in the cause of their history and who fought in concern with the oppressed and exploited peoples in the world, stand resolutely and always on the side of the oppressed peoples in the world.[25]

The Cambodian Communist party has strengthened its control in a number of ways. It first attempted to legitimize its rule by a new constitution and by announcing elections. The formal process of changing Cambodia into a "people's democracy" began in December 1975, when the new constitution was promulgated and the document changed the name of the nation to Democratic Kampuchea. The monarchy was dissolved and all private enterprise was expropriated. The GRUNK regime was dissolved on 7 April 1976, following "elections" in which 98 percent of the eligible voters "chose" representatives to the national assembly. Pol Pot emerged as the unrivaled leader in his

---

[24] Pol Pot's speech, 27 September 1977, KCP Anniversary Meeting, *Foreign Broadcast Information Service* (Asia and Pacific), IV, no. 192 (October 4, 1977), p. 26.

[25] "Communist Party Secretary Pol Pot's Speech," *Peking Review*, no. 41 (October 7, 1977), p. 26.

positions of prime minister and Communist party secretary general.

Pol Pot is a pseudonym for Saloth Sar, a leader of the Cambodian Communist movement who had disappeared in 1963. Very little is known about his activities since then, except that he was elected Communist party secretary in 1963, 1971, and 1976. The Communist party did not proclaim its leading role in the takeover of Cambodia until October 1977, when Pol Pot spoke in China. The party leadership feared that such a disclosure could rally anti-Communist resistance before the party had total control.

When the Communist party went public, Pol Pot denied any Vietnamese involvement in its establishment, despite the fact that the party, 27 years later, is an outgrowth of the Vietnamese Lao Dong party. Pol Pot, however, in an attempt to shore up the nationalist image of the party, claimed that the Communist party of Kampuchea was born in 1960 when 21 members, all Cambodians, secretly assembled.

More important than any new constitutional provisions for enhancing the regime's power were the government's draconian measures to silence all potential voices of opposition and to reduce to impotency every person believed to be allied to the former ruling groups. The means to this end included strict discipline, total control, terror, and isolation from "unpure" societies. One policy was to evacuate every person from the major cities to the countryside. At first it was believed that the new government feared mass starvation in Phnom Penh and other cities because of the limited supply of rice. It was thought also that the government feared renewed bombing by the United States against Cambodian cities and that the confusion of the new government during the takeover period caused soldiers to overreact to orders. The actual reason for the evacuations, however, was internal security and the need to rid the country of "spies," "imperialists," and "enemies." Pol Pot enunciated this view:

> One of the important factors for Cambodia's successes after April 1975 is the evacuation of the city residents to the countryside. This was decided before victory was won, that is, in February 1975, because we knew that before the smashing of all

> sorts of enemy spy organizations, our strength was not strong enough to defend the revolutionary regime. Judging from the struggles waged from 1976 and 1977, the enemy's secret agent network lying low in our country was very massive and complicated. But when we crushed them it was difficult for them to stage a comeback. Their forces were scattered in various cooperatives which are in our own grip.[26]

The evacuation led to thousands of deaths and the separation of family members. No one was allowed to meet in a group. In this way the government could assure that opposition forces could not meet together.

The party leaders also purged persons who in any way were related to the Lon Nol regime or who were believed to harbor even the slightest "bourgeois" values. An estimated one million persons have been executed since April 1975—an act of genocide that has few parallels in history—to rid the country of its "worst elements" (thus strengthening the Communist party's rule) and to set the scene for a "dictatorship of the proletariat."

Prime Minister Pol Pot has explained that contradictions still exist in Cambodia and must be eradicated, contradictions that stem from the remaining vestiges of class divisons:

> In our new Cambodian society there also exist such life-and-death contradictions as enemies in the form of various spy rings working for imperialism and international reactionaries are still planted among us to carry out subversive activities against our revolution. There is also another handful of reactionary elements who continue to carry out activities against and attempt to subvert our Cambodian revolution. These elements are not numerous, constituting only 1 or 2 percent of our population. Some of them operate covertly while others are openly conducting adverse activities. These counterrevolutionary elements which betray and try to sabotage the revolution are not to be regarded as being our people. They are to be regarded as enemies of Democratic Cambodia, of the Cambodian revolution and of the Cambodian peo-

[26] Pol Pot's Press Conference in Peking, New China News Agency, October 3, 1977, *BBC Summary of World Broadcasting,* October 4, 1977, quoted in Karl Jackson, "Cambodia 1977: Gone to Pot," *Asian Survey,* 18, no. 1 (January, 1978), p. 77.

ple. We must thus deal with them the same way we would with any
enemy, that is, by separating, educating and coopting elements
that can be won over and corrected to the people's side, neutraliz-
ing any reluctant elements so that they will not undermine the
revolution, and isolating and eradicating only the smallest possible number of these elements who are cruel and who deter-
minedly oppose the revolution and the people and collaborate
with foreign enemies to oppose their own nation, their own people and their own revolution.[27]

Further enhancing the Communist's rule was the policy of
collectivization and total restructuring of the economy. All Cambodian entrepreneurs lost their businesses and fortunes when
the regime stopped the use of currency and nationalized private
businesses. The family unit was replaced by collectives of up to
1,000 households who eat and work together. Khmer Rouge
troops enforced harsh rules and made sure no one resorted to
the bourgeois values of privatism, hierarchy, individualism, and
the nuclear family. The collectives allowed the regime to watch
over every aspect of the life of every person, thereby precluding
antirevolutionary activity.

Pol Pot in his September 1977 speech to the Communist party
placed the role of the collectives in a more positive light:

> The collective cooperatives of the peasants throughout the
> country, which were founded in 1973 amid the air war waged by
> U.S. imperialism, are strengthened and expanding themselves
> both in quality and quantity. These cooperatives have successfully
> trained, experimented and strengthened themselves and have
> successfully experienced and served the revolutionary movement
> in all fields since 1973. During the war, they were the source of
> manpower for the army, the economy, transportation and other
> fields. Since the war, they have assumed the tasks of increasing
> production, improving the people's livelihood with total indepen-
> dence, sovereignty and self-reliance, and supporting and feeding
> the people who were newly liberated on 17 April 1975. Each of
> these cooperatives constitutes a small collective society, which is a
> brand new community where all kinds of depraved cultural and

[27] From Pol Pot's Speech at 27 September 1977 KCP Anniversary Meeting,
p. H28.

social blemishes have been wiped out. This new, sound, equal, harmonious collective society with all the facilities for livelihood, such as food, health services, culture and education, is being consolidated and developed.[28]

Refugees reported that the society was rigidly organized into separate groups of adult men, adult women, the elderly, children six to 15 years of age, and older teenagers. Families were said to share a roof only in the periods in which their members' communal groups happened to work in the same place. Refugees reported that only small quantities of food (twice a day) were available for communal workers. No schools were open and no money was in circulation. Buddhist temples were turned into rice-storage buildings.

Under Pol Pot, Cambodia became one of the most closed societies on earth. The political and economic life of the Cambodians opened up slightly following the Vietnamese invasion. Buddhism once again was practiced, shops were opened in Phnom Penh and featured a wide array of goods, and money was reintroduced into the economy. The totalitarian nature of the previous regime was lifted so that terror and force were no longer the primary means to assure conformity.

Vietnam controlled the major policymaking bodies and insisted that Cambodian foreign relations follow the Vietnamese line. Some 150,000 Vietnamese troops in Cambodia assured that no popular uprisings or demonstrations occured. There was tragic irony in the fact that the Vietnamese dominated People's Republic of Kampuchea was an oppressive regime which came to power through aggression, and simultaneously a regime which protected Cambodia from the ravages of the genocidal Khmer Rouge.

VIETNAM

Vietnam shares with other Southeast Asia nations a long tradition of military involvement in politics. The nation's great hero, Emperor Gia Long, commanded huge armies that brought

[28] Ibid., p. H30.

about the unification of Vietnam within its present boundaries in 1802. This military dominance was curtailed when the French colonized Vietnam in the late 1800s and Frenchmen took over the highest positions. Although the French planned to establish a Vietnamese national army, their defeat by Germany and the Japanese occupation of Vietnam in World War II kept them from carrying out this plan.

When Ho Chi Minh declared the independence of Vietnam in 1945, the Vietminh (Vietnam Independent League) was the only effective Vietnamese fighting force—an alliance of nationalist and Communist groups that had formed a program in September 1941 that called for the expulsion of the French and Japanese and establishment of an independent Vietnamese republic. The leadership of the Vietminh, which was avowedly Communist, established a fighting force near the China border, in relative safety from the French, and Vo Nguyen Giap was appointed to build up the force. By June 1945, much of the northern area of Vietnam was controlled by the Vietminh, who rapidly filled the void left by the French defeat. They were in undisputed control when Ho Chi Minh formed his first government and proclaimed Vietnam's independence.

The French decision to reconquer their former colony catapulted Vietnam and France into a war that lasted eight years. The Vietminh became the primary anti-French force. Joseph Buttinger observes that

> the evidence that the Vietminh leaders were talented, energetic, and devoted can be ignored only at the risk of failing to grasp the reasons for their success. Their propaganda reached every corner of the country; they mastered the art of organizing great masses openly and clandestinely both in their territory and in French-controlled regions; they battled starvation and overcame the crippling shortages of agricultural tools and essential drugs. The tasks that faced them were gigantic. At the beginning of the war they possessed virtually no means of transportation, no heavy weapons, not a single plane, and they themselves had destroyed most of the roads, railroads, and bridges to block the French. Their soldiers had no shoes, their children no clothing, they had no soap with which to wash the one garment they owned, and their diet was not varied enough to sustain soldiers and civilians in the

tremendous effort demanded of them. That the Vietminh ultimately won the war stands as a truly extraordinary achievement.[29]

Not all Vietnamese supported the Vietminh during the war for independence. The French established an anti-Communist Vietnamese national army under French leadership, but this army never experienced the "glorious victories" of its Vietminh brother. Its history was one of defeats and subordinate status under the French.

When Vietnam became independent and was temporarily partitioned into two military sectors as a result of the 1954 Geneva Conference, the southern military force consisted of about 250,000 soldiers. The southern-based army was factionalized, poorly trained, and in poor morale. In contrast, the Vietminh forces, who had withdrawn north of the 17th parallel in accord with the Geneva Agreements, were unified and supported by the overwhelming majority of Vietnamese as the true and legitimate independence force.

Ngo Dinh Diem became premier of South Vietnam in 1954. His anti-Communist policies and superb manipulative skills eventually led the southern army to support his regime. The United States began an aid program that each year became more militarily oriented. The top military leaders found that support for Diem assured them rapid promotions and access to more resources. Military officers were reluctant to move against Diem for fear of losing American aid.

But after several years of rule by Diem, more and more South Vietnamese began to perceive his administration as repressive. The military were especially concerned by Diem's inability to deal effectively with the rising insurgency of the National Liberation Front. It was not the Communists, however, who overthrew Diem, but a group of dissident army officers. Diem's policy of placing loyalists in the highest command positions eventually backfired when independent-minded generals found their advancement blocked. Diem's incompetence caused even

---

[29] Joseph Buttinger, *Vietnam: A Political History* (New York: Praeger, 1968), p. 333.

his ostensibly loyal followers to side with the dissidents when they made their move in November 1963.

The military's largest stumbling block in mounting a successful anti-Diem coup was the United States. The coup leaders sought assurance from the American ambassador, Henry Cabot Lodge, that the United States would not sabotage their endeavor and would continue to provide aid to the successor regime. When those assurances were given, the military made their move.

Post-Diem Vietnam was characterized by administrative incompetence, instability, and personal rivalries. The many army regimes that came to power failed to understand the fundamental needs of the South Vietnamese:

> [The generals] had done nothing beyond executing a coup, a change of government accompanied by some uninspired political reforms, such as the lifting of the most absurd and vexing restrictions on freedom imposed by the Diem regime. But they were totally devoid of constructive political ideas and took no measures to organize the country's anti-Communist nationalists; and though they were generals, they did not even have a military plan for dealing with the growing force of the Communist-led insurrection. Of the need for drastic social reforms they remained so completely unaware that the words "land reform" were never even uttered.[30]

The 12 changes of government between the fall of Diem in 1963 and the Communist victory in 1975 were largely a result of rivalry among the leading generals. The sole goal of these governments and their major supporter, the United States, was a military victory over the Viet Cong and the North Vietnamese. American support for the South Vietnamese military rulers was embarrassing because it was not compatible with claims that the struggle was between Communist dictatorship and South Vietnamese freedom. To mitigate that difficulty, the Americans persuaded the military rulers to hold elections to legitimize their rule. Even though the 1967 elections were controlled by the military and took place only in government-held areas, the army

---

[30] Ibid., p. 475.

leaders won only 35 percent of the votes. Because the elections did not achieve their purpose, only massive United States intervention (reaching a peak of 500,000 soldiers in 1968 and $25 billion per year expenditures) allowed the military to retain power until the end of the struggle in 1975.

Postindependence political dynamics in North Vietnam differed substantially from those in South Vietnam. In 1954, after the victory over France at Dienbienphu, Ho Chi Minh alone enjoyed universal acceptance as the legitimate leader of a united Vietnam. However, the rulers in South Vietnam reneged on the Geneva Conference's provision for elections in all of Vietnam in 1956 as a prelude to reunification. Twenty-one years of war followed the Geneva Conference, before reunification was finally achieved.

In contrast to the south, where the rulers had limited and unpredictable control over the citizenry, the north was ruled in a highly centralized and disciplined manner, with the government exercising virtually total control over every aspect of life. The Vietnam Workers' party (Lao Dong), renamed the Communist party of Vietnam in 1976, was the primary policy-making body. Communist party control extended throughout the north, down to the lowest administrative levels. The centralized nature of the regime was an outgrowth of a system of overlapping functions. In the top echelons of government, a small number of the highest-level officals concurrently held seats in the Communist party politburo. For example, Ho Chi Minh was simultaneously president of the nation and chairman of the party's Central Committee and politburo.

These overlapping responsibilities ensured that the party could check all levels of government for ideological purity. Even the army, which has long had a major role in the North Vietnamese government, was infiltrated with Communist party leaders. In contrast to the south, where the military ruled supreme from 1963 to 1975, the army in the north has been subordinate to the state.

The Communist party established cells at all levels of administration, including villages, schools, religious bodies, factories, and youth and minority groups. The leaders of the cells acted as cadre members who regularly reported to upper party echelons about the performances and support of the people under their responsibility. The party hierarchy was so tightly organized that the nation's rulers could mobilize the citizenry instantaneously. In essence, the government acted as the administrative arm of the party. A central task of the North Vietnamese government was to develop the society's economy. The centralized nature of the regime was manifest in the mobilization of the populace in industrialization plans and rapid agricultural collectivization. The pace of the forced changes in 1956 led to a peasant uprising against certain "extremist" government leaders. Ho Chi Minh stepped back temporarily and instituted a period of repression against dissidents. The Communist government subsequently continued its collectivization program, so that by 1960 more than 80 percent of the arable land was collectivized, and state cooperatives performed services previously provided by small businesses.[31]

The second major task of the Democratic Republic of Vietnam was to reunify the partitioned country. Ho Chi Minh's government had considerable resources in the south as well as the north. Many southerners had fought against the French in the Vietminh under the leadership of t' e Communist Lao Dong party. The party's southern organizational structure remained intact after the Geneva Accords. This structure became the base for the "people's war," a guerrilla war that was initially southern-based but eventually came under the control of the North Vietnamese government. By 1960 the Lao Dong party central committee was concentrating on political action to gain its objectives, stressing the corruption, repression, and reactionary policies of the Diem regime in the south. The "people's war" later moved toward military and terrorist activities, including the assassination of village leaders. The DRV armed forces did not become directly involved in the south until 1965, after the United States had escalated its participation in the war.

The policies of "liberating" the south and "building socialism" in the north required a maximum effort and extraordinary resources. At the same time, the north suffered manpower losses in industry and agriculture as United States bombing

[31] Cady, p. 313.

missions over the north increased. Despite the tremendous toll inflicted upon the north, the dual policies of socialist construction and southern liberation continued concurrently up to the 1973 Paris Peace Accords. With the end of the American bombing, the North Vietnamese put their major efforts into building socialism in the north.

The person who laid down the broad outlines of DRV government policy was Ho Chi Minh. Following his death on 3 September 1969, his overwhelming presence was no longer available to assure party unity. A number of disagreements arose regarding the importance of internal economic recovery and development versus prolonged guerrilla warfare in the south, and the degree to which Vietnam's best interests were served by a Soviet or Chinese alliance.

North Vietnam had not concerned itself with political succession because Ho Chi Minh had ruled since independence was declared. A form of collective leadership emerged that included Le Duan, party first secretary and party politburo member; Truong Chinh, chairman of the National Assembly and party politburo member; Pham Van Dong, premier and party politburo member; and Vo Nguyen Giap, vice premier, minister of national defense, and party politburo member. None of these persons had the towering influence of Ho. Le Duan, who was pro-Soviet, was principally concerned with the liberation of the south, while Truong Chinh focused on strengthening socialism within the DRV along Maoist lines. Despite differing views on priorities, the collective leadership has carried out policies that point to a high degree of unity.

When victory was achieved by the north in 1975, the DRV government first proposed that a separate government be allowed to exist temporarily in the south before reunification took place. Both the north and the south requested United Nations membership. The Provisional Revolutionary Government was to hold power in the south until economic conditions there were suitable for reunification.

However, by the end of 1975 the government decided to move toward immediate and complete unification, with emphasis on building a socialist state in the south. The DRV government planned April 1976 elections to choose a national assembly made up of representatives from throughout the nation. In the transition stage, military management commissions were set up in the south to administer law and order. Suspected dissidents and former South Vietnamese government officials were sent to reeducation camps. The separate goals of socialist construction and liberation of the south were merged into one when the country was reunited following the Communist victory. The northern leaders were faced with the task of implementing socialism in the south, rebuilding the north's economy, and simultaneously establishing a new administrative system. The first task, implementing socialism, required collectivization of the farms and nationalization of all businesses. For the first two years, the government chose a more pragmatic policy of transforming private industry and agriculture through joint state-private enterprise and mutual aid teams of peasants acting over an extended period, rather than a policy of doctrinal purity that would necessitate immediate and complete economic transformation.

The pragmatic thrust of the government after April 1975 reflects a long-held strategy in the DRV that synthesized Soviet and Chinese experience and adapted Marxist-Leninist doctrine to the conditions of the Vietnamese revolution. As Ho Chi Minh put it in a speech in 1951:

> Disregard for the peculiarities of one's nation while learning from the experiences of the brother countries is a serious mistake, is dogmatism. On the other hand, undue emphasis on the role of national peculiarities and negation of the universal value of the great basic experiences of the brother countries will lead to grave revisionist mistakes.[32]

The regime's decision to move cautiously reflected the desire to avoid arousing hostility and to minimize economic dislocation during the transitional period before the government had total control. Moreover, no one, including the North Vietnamese themselves, had predicted how quickly the Thieu regime in South Vietnam would collapse. In *Great Spring Victory*, a book-

[32] Ho Chi Minh, *Selected Works*, Foreign Language Publishing House, Hanoi, 1960, IV, 253–54, quoted in William J. Duiker, "Ideology and Nation-Building in the Democratic Republic of Vietnam," *Asian Survey*, XVII, no. 5 (May, 1977), p. 418.

length memoir, a prominent general in the north stated that the Communist victory came far sooner than government officials had planned or predicted. The new government, which did not have ample time to plan adequately for immediate reunification, decided to wait one year after the military victory to hold elections to choose the 492-member National Assembly.

The 25 April 1976 election was the first in a united Vietnam since 1946 when Ho Chi Minh called for National Assembly elections following the Japanese occupation. Close to 99 percent of the eligible voters over 18 years old voted for 249 national assemblymen in the north and 243 in the south. The massive turnout reflected the mobilizing capacity of the new administration and the perception of the South Vietnamese that their voting card was equivalent to an identification card. The voters had a choice of candidates representing similar positions. The assembly was to be a unified bloc, with "no conflicting viewpoints or opposition organizations." The list of candidates in the south included leading members of the Lao Dong party, the National Liberation Front, and the Provisional Revolutionary government of the Republic of South Vietnam. In the north, candidates represented the top positions of the administration, including Prime Minister Pham Van Dong, first secretary of the Community Party Le Duan, and Truong Chinh, chairman of the Standing Committee of the National Assembly.

In a detailed discussion of the All-Vietnam National Assembly, Tai Sung An noted:

> The 492 deputies elected to the all-Vietnam National Assembly included 80 workers (16.26%), 100 peasants (20.33%), 6 handicraftsmen (1.22%), 54 military men (10.97%), 141 political cadres (28.65%), 98 intellectuals (19.92%), and 13 religious representatives (2.64%). Among these deputies were 129 women (26.22%), 127 young people (27.84%), 72 members of non-Vietnamese ethnic minorities (14.63%), and 29 labor and armed forces heroes (0.06%).[33]

[33] Tai Sung An, "The All-Vietnam National Assembly: Significant Developments," *Asian Survey*, XVII, no. 5 (May, 1977), p. 434.

The newly elected National Assembly emphasized the dominance of the north over the south by agreeing to the following:[34]

1. The reunified country of Vietnam took the name Socialist Republic of Vietnam (SRV), thereby replacing the Government of the Democratic Republic of Vietnam and the Provisional Revolutionary Government of the Republic of South Vietnam.

2. The old DRV flag became the new national flag of the SRV.

3. Hanoi was chosen the capital of the SRV.

4. As of July 2, 1976, the nation was formally reunified.

5. Saigon was officially renamed Ho Chi Minh City.

6. Pending a new constitution, the SRV will be organized on the basis of the DRV's 1959 constitution.

7. Ton Duc Thang, Truong Chinh, and Pham Van Dong were elected respectively as president, chairman of the Standing Committee of the National Assembly, and premier. Vo Nguyen Giap was named defense minister.

8. A new administrative map was created which divided the country into thirty-five provinces (vs. sixty-one previously) and renamed all the provinces in the south.

Le Duan, the Communist party secretary, noted in the major policy statement that the whole of Vietnam had entered the stage of socialist revolution. He stressed that the south must immediately abolish the comprador bourgeoisie and the remnants of the feudal landlord classes and undertake the socialist transformation of private capitalist industry and commerce, agriculture, handicrafts, and small trade through appropriate measures. His call for nationalization and complete control over the means of production and distribution was indicative of the regime's increasing confidence about its power and its perception of the citizenry's willingness to acquiesce to these policies.

The All-Vietnam National Assembly follows the precedent of the preceding five National Assemblies (elected in united Viet-

---

[34] Adapted from ibid., pp. 435–37; and Douglas Pike, "Vietman During 1976: Economics in Command," *Asian Survey*, XVII, no. I (January, 1977), p. 38.

nam in 1946 and in North Vietnam in 1960, 1964, 1971, and 1975) in rubber-stamping decisions made by the Vietnamese Communist party politburo.

The second major event since April 1975 was the convening of the Fourth National Congress of the Vietnamese Workers' party in December 1976. The congress was even more significant than the Sixth National Assembly session since the Communist party makes the crucial political and economic decisions for the nation. This Fourth Congress (the others were in 1935, 1951, and 1960) set forth the national leadership, party ideology, and an economic development plan for the entire country.

Membership in the Vietnam Workers' party, renamed the Communist party of Vietnam (CPV), rose from 800,000 in 1966 to 1.8 million in 1985. The politburo, which has been the major policy-making body, essentially retained the same members. The congress admitted several "big mistakes," particularly in the agricultural sector, called for a redoubling of efforts, and provided for elections to "people's councils" at the provincial, municipal, and district levels, to be held from May to June 1977. As in the election to the National Assembly, candidates were carefully screened to assure ideological orthodoxy. The purpose of the elections was to generate a sense of unity and participation rather than to allow a choice among alternative programs and ideas.

The congress also adopted a Second Five-Year Economic Development Plan (1976–80) that emphasized technology and education as the bases for rapid economic growth. A massive literacy program was launched throughout the nation. One of the major economic problems faced by the government was high unemployment in Ho Chi Minh City. During 1977, an estimated 700,000 unemployed persons in the city were resettled in "new economic zones" (NEZ) on newly reclaimed land. Despite the movement of so many persons to rural areas, the city still had 500,000 jobless citizens in a total population of 3.2 million. The New Economic Zones were also a means to increase agricultural production in formerly uninhabited areas, although in 1978 there was no clear evidence that production had grown. Prime Minister Pham Van Dong attributed the failure to achieve the production goals in the NEZ to "ideological shortcomings."

The NEZ represents an extraordinarily ambitious effort to restructure Vietnamese society, indeed to reshape the entire social face of Vietnam. Eventually, if pursued to completion, one out of every two Vietnamese will find himself living somewhere else and doing something new. A vastly changed set of social relationships will result. The NEZ program ultimately could have a more profound effect on Vietnam than any other event in the 20th century.[35]

It is difficult to assess the support from southerners for the new Communist government. Refugees report that living conditions have deteriorated for many and that a repressive and arrogant bureaucracy has already stifled economic growth. Most journalists who have visited Vietnam since April 1975 report that at least half the populace in the south is wary and even hostile toward the new government. To counteract this resistance the government set up "reeducation camps" to indoctrinate dissidents. An estimated 2.5 million Vietnamese have gone to these camps and, following "rehabilitation," have been released.[36] Some 30,000 persons are political prisoners. Further corroborating the view that many southerners oppose the government is the fact that 500,000 persons have fled to other nations since April 1975.

In contrast to the situation in Cambodia, the Vietnamese have moved more slowly than many predicted. The bloodbath perpetrated by the Communist rulers in Cambodia has no parallel in Vietnam. The Vietnamese have not attempted to undermine the family structure, nor have they desecrated Buddhist temples. Vietnam has encouraged trade and established diplomatic relations with almost all nations, except the United States, whereas Cambodia has restricted its diplomatic relations to a few nations. The Vietnamese invasion of Cambodia and the Chinese incursions into North Vietnam have drained needed resources from the Vietnamese society. Moreover, the exodus of the influential Chinese entrepreneurs from Vietnam has undermined the strength of the economy. The program to nationalize the industrial and agricultural sectors in the south has met with resistance. These problems have brought about increased government repression as the Communist regime consolidates its power.

LAOS

Because Laos is a relatively weak nation with a small population its political policies and procedures have been dictated by other nations. Traditionally, Vietnam and Thailand have had the greatest impact on Laotian political affairs, but after World War II the United States became the paramount power, with almost total control over every aspect of Laotian political life.

Because of United States intervention, right-wing anti-Communist regimes have ruled Laos for the past three decades. As early as 1949 the United States promoted a friendly government in the French-sponsored Royal Laotian government. Heavy-handed interference by the Americans and Thais precipitated the organization of the Pathet Lao, a left-wing nationalist group that became the major insurgency force and later the core of the Communist government.

In 1954, when the Pathet Lao was making significant headway in large areas of the Laotian countryside, the United States sponsored a coup by the anti-Communist Phoui Sananikone against Premier Souvanna Phouma, who was considered too much a neutralist by American government leaders. The coup failed but Souvanna Phouma was put on notice that left-wing or neutralist policies were considered intolerable by the United States. When a right-wing government emerged in 1955, the United States immediately began a $45 million annual aid program.

The United States and Thailand were disappointed when Souvanna Phouma, the neutralist, returned to power in 1955 following elections. The United States temporarily refused to continue subsidizing the Royal Lao Army while Souvanna Phouma ruled, in order to encourage an army revolt against his administration. Even though Souvanna Phouma refused Pathet Lao involvement in his cabinet following the May 1958 elections, which gave a majority of seats to the Pathet Lao and its allies, the United States still did not trust him. Hence the United States maneuvered to oust Souvanna Phouma and replace him with a right-wing government.

The United States used its economic leverage to assure friendly rule in Vientiane. The Laotian military was totally financed and controlled by the American military mission. Moreover, the United States insisted that certain military leaders (including Phoumi Nosavan) be named to the cabinet, despite the fact that the right wing had no representation in the elected National Assembly. The government became a client of American interests. To keep opposition to American intervention to a minimum, the CIA was given primary responsibility for clandestine measures to assure continued pro-American rule. American involvement, however, was not sufficient to keep Souvanna Phouma from returning to power to establish a neutralist government acceptable to the right-wing military and the Pathet Lao, and he increasingly came under the influence of American diplomats. He eventually was considered "tolerable" by the Americans, after he gave permission to the United States to bomb Pathet Lao areas secretly.

At the same time, the CIA supported a secret army of Meo (Hmong) hill tribesmen to fight against the Pathet Lao. This force, under the leadership of Vang Pao, was totally subsidized and run by the CIA. The Meo became the most important fighting force against Pathet Lao troops.

Souvanna Phouma dropped his neutralist position and in 1964 requested United States bombing missions over Pathet Lao areas of control. These missions' annual cost is estimated at $2 billion. More tons of bombs were dropped on Laos per capita than on any nation in history, and fully one-third of the population was forced out of its homes and became refugees. The bombing missions were carried out from 1964 to 1973 for three reasons: (1) to strengthen the anti-Communist government in Vientiane, (2) to demolish the Pathet Lao infrastructure, and (3) to interdict soldiers from North Vietnam.

American involvement in Laos became so great that one scholar noted:

> It is indisputable that the impact of United States intervention on Laos itself has been crushingly total and pervasive. Laos' capacities are so minute that it has not been able to deflect the enormous

interventionary power of the United States. The Royal Lao Government is so dependent on the United States' purse strings that the U.S. establishment in Vientiane has become the real government of Laos.[37]

Only the massive bombing of Pathet Laos-held areas and American financial subsidizing of the government and military kept Souvanna Phouma in government. When this ended, the Pathet Lao moved to unify and control the entire country. By December 1975 the United States no longer could exert influence on the Lao People's Democratic Republic.

Like Vietnam and Cambodia, Laos is ruled by the Communist party. The Lao People's Revolutionary party (LPRP) had directed the war against the Royal Lao government from caves and did not emerge as the leader of the revolutionaries until after the Communist takeover in December 1975. Almost nothing is known about the organizational structure of the LPRP, although, as in most Communist parties, policy is made and implemented by the party politburo. Leading the politburo is Kaysone Phomvihan, secretary general of the party and prime minister. Also in the politburo is Prince Souphanouvong, Souvanna Phouma's half brother and president of the LPDR. Souvanna Phouma, who was named "adviser" to the government, died in 1984. The Lao Patriotic Front, at one time the ostensible revolutionary group, has apparently been integrated into the LPRP.

The major strength of the new government is its discipline, doctrine, and unity. The party practices democratic centralism, requiring unanimous support of all decisions made by the leadership. The new leaders have led spartan lives for years and are not yet corrupted by the perquisites usually available to government leaders. During the consolidation of power after 1975 there was no evidence of factionalism among the top leaders.

The new government proclaimed that Laos would pursue a goal of independent, self-reliant socialism. The means to this goal were to be more similar to those in Vietnam than in Cambodia, with emphasis on gradual collectivization and encourage-

[37] Usha Mahajani, "U.S. Intervention in Laos and Its Impact on Laotian Relations with Thailand and Vietnam," in *Conflict and Stability in Southeast Asia,* eds. Mark W. Zacher and R. Stephen Milne (Garden City, New York: Anchor, 1974), p. 270.

ment of outward migration from urban areas (mainly Vientiane) to the countryside. However, a devastating drought in 1976 and 1977 reduced the rice harvest by 40 percent nationwide, forcing the government to import food. Self-sufficiency in agriculture was enjoyed by prewar Laos, despite the almost complete absence of irrigation facilities or mechanization. Laos, in contrast to Cambodia, has requested and accepted aid from various international organizations.

The new government moved quickly to eradicate "the worst vestiges of bourgeois society" by banning nightclubs, massage parlors, and dance halls. Crime, drug addiction, and prostitution have been suppressed. A concerted effort was made to increase the number of young people in schools and to lower the rate of illiteracy.

Whereas the United States dominated the Royal Lao government up to 1973, North Vietnam or, after 1975, the Socialist Republic of Vietnam became the dominant external power. Vietnam retained a force of about 40,000 troops in Laos and gradually increased its economic influence, at least partially because Thailand initially refused to allow imports and exports into and from Laos. The fact that the port of Haiphong in Vietnam became the only outlet for Laotian goods provided Vietnam with leverage and influence over Laotian policies. References to an Indochina federation by the Vietnamese raised the specter of Laos losing its autonomy to the far more powerful Vietnam.

The collectivization program and the government's attempt to "reeducate" thousands of Laotians made the populace wary of the new regime. Reports of arrogant bureaucrats and repressive rules and regulations were brought out by the estimated 300,000 refugees who have fled Laos. By 1978 the soft approach was reported to have hardened against dissidents. Kaysone Phomvihan's government announced it held 40,000 people in "reeducation" camps, giving Laos the distinction of having more political prisoners per capita than almost any other country.

By the mid 1980s most of those 40,000 detainees had been freed, although Amnesty International estimated that 6–7,000 political prisoners remained in 1984. More pragmatic policies were set forth at the Third Congress of the Lao Peoples' Revolutionary Party in 1982. The loosening of government control over the economy, along with the introduction of agricultural technology, resulted in larger crop output and self sufficiency in rice for the first time since the revolution. These new policies reflected the views of the Soviet Union and Vietnam, the two nations which controlled policymaking in Laos.

PHILIPPINES

From July 1946, when the Philippines became an independent nation, to September 1972, when President Ferdinand Marcos declared martial law, the Philippines was considered the showcase of democracy in Southeast Asia. The political system was based on the American-sponsored 1935 constitution, which featured the separation of powers and a bill of rights. Executive functions were carried out by the president, who was chosen by direct popular vote for a four-year term. The president could be reelected once only. His role as leader of one of the two major political parties, head administrator of the cabinet and civil service, commander-in-chief of the armed forces, chief dispenser of patronage, and leading patron in the ubiquitous patron-client relationship network made him the dominant political personality and power. His power to supervise local government policies and projects and to determine budget allocations for rural development projects further enhanced his political leverage.

However, constitutionally and in practice, the president shared power with the bicameral legislature. The Senate, consisting of 24 persons, was elected from the nation at large for six-year terms. The 104-member House of Representatives was chosen in single-member districts for four-year terms. All adults, over 21 and literate, were eligible to vote. The legislature had the power to initiate and pass on all laws and the president had veto power. Scions of the wealthiest families in the Philippines dominated the Senate.

The Supreme Court was the third pillar in the system of separate powers. The court's members were appointed by the president for life terms (or until age 70), assuring them some degree of independence. On numerous occasions the court has struck down executive decisions and legislative laws on constitutional grounds.

During the democratic period (1946 to 1972), the two major

political parties played a political role not altogether different from that played by the Democrats and Republicans in the United States. The primary function of the Liberal and Nacionalista parties was to rally support for particular personalities rather than to set forth a coherent political ideology adhered to by the party members. Indeed, the most striking element of the party system in the Philippines was the degree to which supporters and candidates switched party labels. The two parties did not stand for a particular set of political beliefs, nor did they represent a particular class of people. However, they *did* help assure a regular changeover in the presidency and legislative body. Until Marcos was reelected president in 1969, no incumbent president had managed to serve more than one term.

On the surface, it appears that during the first 26 years of independence the Philippines could properly be referred to as a democracy. Carl Landé, a leading scholar of Philippine politics, carried out a study to determine the ways in which the Philippine political system could be considered democratic and the ways in which it fell short of the democratic ideal. He measured the Philippine political process against the following criteria:[38]

> 1. Free competition between rival aspirants for control of the key positions in government and between rival substantive proposals for the conduct of government.
>
> 2. Important policy-making positions in government collectively responsible to the electorate for their conduct of public affairs.
>
> 3. Political influence distributed widely among the country's citizens.
>
> 4. Political influence distributed equally among these citizens.

Landé shows that in many respects there was lively competition among parties and candidates for office, and diverse proposals for governmental action. Throughout this period the margin of victory in most elections was narrow, and neither

---

[38] Carl H. Landé, *Leaders, Factions, and Parties, The Structure of Philippine Politics,* Southeast Asia Studies Monograph No. 6 (New Haven, Connecticut: Yale University Press, 1964), p. 108. The following paragraphs draw closely from Landé's monograph.

party was able to take its hegemony for granted. Although voters were able to choose between parties, they were not able to choose between fundamentally different types of parties; the candidates were also indistinguishable in terms of background and policy preferences. Landé concludes that while there was considerable competition between rival aspirants, there was not a corresponding competition between substantive proposals for the conduct of government.[39]

Landé also points out that party unity and discipline were practically nonexistent, making it impossible for the electorate, after the elections, to hold someone accountable for particular policies. More important than the Liberal bloc or the Nacionalista bloc in the Congress was the sugar bloc or tobacco bloc, both of which cut across the two major political parties. Even the program of the president was a personal program, rather than a program of his party, and party members may or may not have agreed with his program. In any case, their approval was secondary.

Landé shows that while the Philippine political system failed to provide responsible party government, it fulfilled another criterion of a democratic political system: wide distribution of political influence. The narrow margin by which most candidates won office gave the voter a good deal of leverage at election time. The intensity of competition among candidates led them to extremes to gain votes, including outright payments. Persons such as village leaders, who might have influence over a bloc of voters, had considerable bargaining power in their dealing with national party leaders. In that sense, the Philippine political system was responsive to the people's needs.[40]

The wide distribution of political influence was not paralleled by a marked equality of distribution. On the contrary, certain elites, known as patrons, had far more bargaining power than ordinary villagers who were their clients. A disproportionate share of the dispensed benefits went to the upper classes.[41] In sum, the "democratic period" in the Philippines in some respects

---

[39] Ibid., pp. 198–210.
[40] Ibid., pp. 114–16.
[41] Ibid., pp. 117–18.

met the criteria for democracy and in others fell short of the democratic ideal. In any case, the structures of government fundamentally changed when President Marcos abrogated the 1935 constitution and took all powers to himself in September 1972.

Marcos' proclamation of martial law was accepted by the majority of Filipinos as a necessary step in bringing stability to a nation under siege. Most Filipinos also realized that Marcos was halfway through his second term of office and constitutionally precluded from running again. Most believed that martial law would be temporary, until the new constitution was approved.

In an objective report by the International Commission of Jurists in August 1977, Marcos' martial-law proclamation was found to be "a proper exercise of the presidential power in the circumstances existing at that time." The jurists also determined that there was no convincing evidence that the continuation of martial law and the almost total suspension of civil and political liberties were still justified four years after their introduction. Accordingly, they concluded that "the present government is now employing the power granted to it by the constitution not primarily to protect the nation from 'invasion, insurrection, or rebellion or imminent danger thereof, when the public safety requires it . . . ,' but rather to perpetuate the personal power of the president and his collaborators and to increase the power of the military to control Philippine society."[42]

Although martial law was declared according to provisions of the 1935 constitution, four months prior to the declaration Marcos had convened a constitutional convention to draft a new constitution, presumably based on a parliamentary rather than presidential model. The convention had not yet reached consensus on a number of issues, specifically those transitory provisions that provided total power to the executive (Marcos) during the interim period. Marcos' declaration of martial law silenced the voices opposed to those provisions. Public debate terminated, newspapers closed, and members of the opposition were detained. Two months after martial law began, the constitutional

---

[42] William J. Butler, *The Decline of Democracy in the Philippines* (Geneva: International Commission of Jurists, 1977), p. 46.

convention approved the new constitution, which called for a parliamentary form of government, led by a prime minister, and included the transitory provisions allowing the interim president (Marcos) to decide when to convene the interim national assembly and providing him with power to make and execute all laws until he convened the assembly.

The constitution was to be approved or disapproved by a mass plebiscite. Marcos, however, through a series of decrees, refused to hold such a plebiscite, and instead announced creation of People's Assemblies (called Barangay) to act as consultative bodies. These assemblies were convened in each *barrio* and asked to vote on the new constitution by a show of hands. Military and civilian officials monitored the results in each barrio. About 90 percent of the Barangay assembly members raised their hands. The lack of secrecy in voting caused the International Jurists to conclude that the vote could not be considered a true expression of the will of the people.[43] Nevertheless, Marcos promulgated the new constitution on 17 January 1973. Simultaneously, he declared the continuation of martial law. The Philippine Supreme Court could not achieve a majority statement that the new constitution had been properly ratified and was in force. Neither, however, could the court achieve enough votes to declare that the new constitution was not in force. Hence the court concluded that there was no judicial obstacle to the new constitution's being considered in force.

President Marcos refused to call for an Interim National Assembly until April 1978. During the intermittent five years, he ruled according to the transitory provisions that gave him the powers of the president (according to the 1935 constitution), an interim martial-law dictator, and the prime minister (according to the 1973 constitution). To provide legitimacy to his regime, Marcos instituted five referenda, all of which turned out a 90 percent vote in favor of his continued tenure. Press censorship of all criticism of the government, jailing of dissidents, lack of freedom of assembly and speech, absence of a secret ballot, and control of ballot-counting by government officials raised questions about the validity of the referenda.

[43] Ibid.

The most controversial referendum took place 6 August 1978, when the citizenry voted for members of the Interim National Assembly (Batasang Pambansa). The assembly had only limited powers, since Marcos could still issue decrees that had the force of law, and he could veto any law passed by the assembly. Despite the lack of power accorded the assembly, the election aroused a great deal of interest in Manila, where an opposition slate was allowed to run against Marcos' New Society Movement.

The opposition was led by former Senator Benigno Aquino, Marcos' chief political rival, who had been imprisoned since martial law began. His circumscribed campaign was carried out from his jail cell. Leading the Marcos faction in Manila was Imelda Marcos, the president's wife and governor of the metropolitan Manila area. Clearly, the opposition had no hope of gaining control since the most seats it could win were 21 of the 200-seat assembly. It sought a "moral victory," but was only partially successful. The international press condemned the fraud that accompanied election procedures, and the opposition claimed victory, despite President Marcos' claim of a sweep in Manila for his candidates. After the election he arrested opposition members and put more restrictions on political activity.

The president's skill was exemplified in his administration of local elections held 30 January 1980 for mayors, governors, and local-level councilors. His call in December 1979 for elections the next month was unexpected and caught the opposition unprepared. The president's New Society Movement was well organized and financed, and mobilized to contest virtually every seat available. However, the opposition parties, at odds whether to boycott the elections entirely, were factionalized, financially insolvent, and circumscribed by restrictive election laws. The result was a massive New Society victory including wins in 69 of 73 governorships and over 1,450 of 1,560 mayoral races.

The New Society sweep resulted from the party's superb organization and resources and the opposition's lack thereof. New Society candidates were incumbents who used the trappings and organizational base of their positions to amass votes. The entire local-level bureaucracy was mobilized and in some areas was indistinguishable from the New Society's organization. The opposition itself was fragmented. The Liberal and Laban parties who had contested elections in the 1978 Interim National Assembly boycotted the local elections although a few party members ran as individuals. The boycott stemmed from Marcos' decision to limit the campaign to 30 days in order "to conserve" in the words of the Commission on Elections, "the gains of the New Society and shield them from erosion by the return of the Old Society political practices which are certain to happen if the campaign period is long and protracted." The most famous opposition leader, Aquino (who was subsequently allowed in May to go to the United States for a heart bypass operation) was in prison during the election and was himself barred from running by the election code enacted 18 December 1979 by the government-controlled Interim Assembly.

Marcos' New Society was authoritarian. He suppressed political activity and institutions, including political parties; he centralized power in the hands of close family associates, including relatives of his wife; he clamped down on every opposition group to assure the perpetuation of his power. One author has characterized the New Society as "Philippine corporatism":

> The leaders of the New Society, after having destroyed the political institutions of the precoup regime, have used authoritarian state power to proceed to construct new institutions, not only for the political sphere of public life but for the economic and social as well. In each sector the new institutions have decidedly corporatist characteristics: competing groups are forced to merge under state sponsorship; labor is coerced into "cooperating" with management and the government in building the economy; private associations are integrated under a formula of a single peak body for each profession, economic function, or social activity; . . . disciplined "harmony" is decreed as the basis for building the New Society along with "developmentalism"; the military is accorded new honor, respect, and power; and massive public information programs are directed towards socializing the population into the values of the new order.[44]

The persons or groups that gained the most from this corporatist structure were the elites who chose to ally with Marcos, and

---

[44] Robert B. Stauffer, "Philippine Corporatism: A Note on the New Society," *Asian Survey*, XVII, no. 4 (April 1977), p. 406.

family members who reaped fortunes from their close ties. About three to four percent of the population constituted this group. The military also gained immensely, with increased budgets and a more prominent role in political affairs; between 1972 and 1975, national defense outlays rose from 13.4 to 28 percent of the total budget.[45] Before 1972 the armed forces, numbering 55,000, were among the smallest and least political in Southeast Asia; in 1978 they numbered 160,000. Foreign investors supported the coup because of the increased stability it promised and because of the liberalized foreign investment guidelines that were announced after martial law. The largest group of supporters, however, were those who acquiesced to the regime because of a fatalistic view of politics and life or a realistic assessment of the regime's strength and their own lack of power.

Marcos found that authoritarian governments cannot automatically resolve a society's problems. Significant groups in the Philippines continued to oppose Marcos and his regime. An estimated one percent of the population engaged in rebellion against Marcos' rule. About 15 percent of the population refused to grant legitimacy to the regime but stopped short of active resistance. Politically aware peasants, workers, students, clergy, middle-class professionals, and landlords composed this group.[46]

Several groups in the Philippines were especially critical of the martial-law regime. Elements of the Catholic church's leadership criticized Marcos for human rights violations. Their opposition was muted, partially because Marcos had the power to require taxation of church-owned school property; nevertheless, clergy and lay persons worked among the poor to help them resist government programs inimical to their well-being.[47] In 1978, 246 Catholic priests, nuns, and lay workers faced trials on charges of sedition.

The New People's Army (NPA) is the military component of the Communist party of the Philippines. Growing armed insur-

---

[45] David Wurfel, "Martial Law in the Philippines: The Methods of Regime Survival," *Pacific Affairs*, L, no. 1 (Spring, 1977), p. 21.

[46] Ibid., p. 9.

[47] Kit G. Machado, "The Philippines in 1977: Beginning a 'Return to Normalcy'?" *Asian Survey*, XVIII, no. 2 (February, 1978), p. 296.

gency was related to the nation's broader political and economic problems. Depressed economic conditions, weak and ineffective local government administration compounded by budgetary shortfalls, a perception that the central government under Marcos did not respond to the people's basic social and economic needs, lax and inequitable dispensation of justice, and instances of abuse of citizens by military forces, all contributed to support for the NPA, which projected itself as a group of idealistic political social reformers.

In 1985 the U.S. government estimated that the NPA had a meaningful presence in about two-thirds of the country's provinces, and had moved into urban centers. Both the number and scale of armed encounters with the armed forces was growing. The U.S. Central Intelligence Agency stated that within three years Communist guerrillas would achieve military parity with the Philippine army. That projection was slightly less than that given to a congressional committee by a Defense Department spokesman who estimated that the guerrillas could achieve parity within five years. This estimate was noteworthy since the NPA had no major leaders with mass appeal, no appreciable foreign support, and outdated weapons that were stolen or bought from the military.

Following her takeover of the government, President Aquino moved quickly to grant amnesty to all political prisoners including leaders of the Communist party. She set forth a program calling for a ceasefire and a national reconciliation. Thousands of guerrillas proclaimed their support for the new government. NPA leaders announced a willingness to work with the new government but demanded an end to U.S. bases and major land reform before giving their full support. The fall of Marcos undermined the strength of the Communist movement by removing the major target of their wrath.

One of Marcos' major problems during the five-year period of martial law was the Muslim rebellion in the southern Philippines. The rebellion, led by the Moro National Liberation Front (MNLF), caused some 10,000 deaths and left the economy of the southern islands in chaos. Adding to the problem was the fact that Libya supplied arms and funds to the MNLF. The MNLF struggled against the Marcos government's perceived attempt to "Christianize" the Muslims and take away their traditional land.

Every attempt at resolving the conflict through negotiations failed.

The New Society did not fundamentally change the central role of factionalism, patronage, and elitism as the core of politics in the Philippines. The steps toward normalization, taken by Marcos when he allowed the Interim National Assembly as well as local elections, and when he announced the "lifting" of martial law to occur in January 1981, temporarily improved the image of the New Society in the world but did not significantly change the authoritarian political order. The Philippine government continued to be based on personalism rather than institutional structures. Every facet of policymaking was determined by Marcos himself or his closest confidants. Whereas the other Southeast Asian nations had more or less successfully institutionalized the regimes in power, through the Communist party or the military, for example, politics in the Philippines remained the politics of Marcos.

The Philippine government can be described as clientelist, a form of societal organization in which political life centers on relationships that are largely person to person, informal, hierarchical, and reciprocal. Because the Philippines was under authoritarian rule from 1972 to 1986, and because the pre-martial law institutions were rudimentary, interest groups, political parties, the legislature, and other formal institutions of government have been weak and supplanted by clientelist relationships. Government institutions such as the army and bureaucracy played an important role, but the heart of Philippine politics has been in the interplay among and within patron-client groupings that pervade these groups, as well as the entire society from the president down to the peasant in the barangay. Political life in the Philippines has consisted of constantly changing coalitions of clientele groups (sometimes within the flimsy framework of political institutions) that serve as the basis both for the articulation of mass interests and for government control over the people.

Patron-client ties are connected with networks and larger group structures that extend throughout Philippine society. The stability of this kind of personalistic politics depends on the capacity of patrons to hold on to their clients and the clients' ability to meet the needs of their patrons. The relationship generally maintains the client in his dependent position, relative to the superior or patron, because the client is more in need of the patron's resources than the patron is in need of the client's resources.

The need for patrons to provide resources to their clients has been a major cause of corruption throughout Philippine society. Public office has been used for private gain and for the support of clients. Because the Philippines is an underdeveloped nation, the central government has been the major institution to provide resources to patrons to assure the loyalty of subordinates. As President Marcos attempted to extend his power and support, corruption increased.

Clientelist systems rely neither on rational allocations of resources nor on market forces nor on any other universal criteria of need. Accountability to the public becomes secondary among the rulers in determining who gets most of what there is to get. In clientelist regimes, the first priority is to perpetuate the power of those who already rule.

Clearly, the stability of such a regime depends greatly on the capacity of individual rulers to meet the needs and expectations of their followers. Although in most Third World societies the majority, lower socioeconomic classes do not have high expectations about their ability to influence or control government policymaking, in the Philippines, where there is a history of political involvement by all classes, expectations are high. Thus, following the Aquino assassination when President Marcos lost his supreme capacity to control resources, not only his clients, but the entire society, began to question the legitimacy of the political system. In the clientelist Philippine society, societal legitimacy was linked with the capacity of individual patrons and, above all, with the supreme patron, President Marcos.

Personalistic politics requires access to resources that can be used to reward clients for their loyalty and support. Prior to martial law, the economy was concentrated in the hands of a few olilgarchical families. After 1972, however, President Marcos moved to dismantle the fiefdoms of these rich families and to take control of their resources, either through state monopolies or private corporations dominated by his own associates. Because both the state and the new oligarchy have made major policy errors and have not used resources effectively, the economy of the Philippines underwent serious structural problems, culminating in the worst fiscal crisis of any of the non-Communist Southeast Asian nations. Because the crises emanated from the clientelist structure established by President Marcos, his adversaries claimed that any solution to the crises required a fundamental restructuring of the polity and the political leadership of the Philippines.

The most comprehensive and objective analysis of the Philippine economy was published in 1984 by the school of economics at the University of the Philippines. In great detail and with extensive documentation, the report showed that Marcos himself, by means of hundreds of presidential decrees and letters of instruction, was responsible for the crisis. The Philippines faced a $26 billion foreign debt in default; disastrous declines in industry and agriculture production; falling wages and increasing unemployment; the flight of capital; high inflation; severe undernourishment; a rich-poor gap greater than any other nation's in the area with 40 percent of the population living in poverty (60–70 percent in the least developed regions); and a negative economic growth. The cliche about the rich getting richer and the poor poorer was an accurate representation of the Philippines under Marcos.

These crises, each severe but, ensemble, a disaster, were all the more shocking when compared to the pre-martial law period or to other Asian nations with comparable resources. In the 1950s, nations such as Taiwan and South Korea were far behind the Philippines in terms of natural resources. In 1965 the value of Philippine exports was four times that of South Korea. By 1982, the exports of South Korea were four times the exports of the Philippines. Just two decades ago, Taiwan specialized in clothing and footwear. In 1983, it sold computers, telecommunications equipment, and electrical products to the United States amounting to $11.2 billion, more than twice the total value of Philippine exports for the same year.

The school of economics report analyzed three possible explanations for the Philippines' economic debacle: (1) external circumstances, affecting all developing countries, over which the leadership had no control; (2) mismanagement by the Marcos administration; and (3) unforeseen events, including the assassination of Aquino in 1983. The conclusion was that while external difficulties were certainly a reason for the crisis, the major explanation was the economic policies of the Marcos government. The Aquino assassination tore the already weakened fabric of the economy. The report declared that the policies that led to the crisis were rooted in political imperatives, suggesting that the leadership would abandon them only with difficulty.

The recession in the developed countries during the late 1970s and early 1980s, and the increases in the price of OPEC oil brought havoc to the Philippines. However, Thailand, with similar resources, population, economic development, and oil resources, managed to escape severe crisis. Thailand came out of the period without substantial foreign debt and with excellent growth rates, about seven percent per year. The Philippines, on the other hand, emerged with the largest foreign debt of any nation in Southeast Asia and with the lowest growth rates, averaging only three percent.

The major characteristic distinguishing the Marcos policies from premartial law times, and from Thailand, was the concentration of economic power in the government and small factions loyal to the president. This expansion of government in financial markets and in granting monopoly privileges to a favored few paralleled the more centralized system of government. To assure support from his clientele, Marcos not only borrowed heavily, both domestically and internationally, but accelerated government spending. These expenditures, in turn, generated inflation and the overvaluation of the peso.

The Aquino assassination exacerbated the crisis of confidence, not only among domestic entrepreneurs but also among foreign banks, which refused to renew financing. The result was that international reserves fell drastically and many local businesses went bankrupt. Some 2,134 companies closed down in 1984, more than double the 1983 figure. Inflation averaged 50 percent in 1983 and 1984, compared to Thailand's single digit inflation. These difficulties led to a reduction in private consumption, as consumer prices trebled between 1972 and 1983. The real monthly earnings of salaried workers in 1980 were 93.2 percent of the 1972 level, while that of hourly wage workers was only 86.7 percent. Earnings of lower paid workers deteriorated more rapidly than those of the better-paid. The real wage of skilled laborers in Manila in 1980 was only 63.7 percent of its level in 1972 while that of the unskilled was even lower, 53.4 percent.

The clientelist nature of Philippine society was most obvious in the president's granting of monopoly privileges to selected followers, especially in the coconut and sugar industries, which together affect almost half the country's population. Eduardo Cojuangco, the president's close friend (and, ironically, the cousin of Corazon Aquino), was given control over virtually every phase of the coconut industry. He dominated the crushing and milling of coconut meat, the export of coconut oil, and financial operations under the United Coconut Planters' Bank, the only bank allowed to participate in the industry. Marcos' decrees provided Cojuangco exclusive rights to import and export resources connected with the coconut industry. He was allowed to expropriate private property and to control credit. When the world market for coconut oil decreased, Cojuangco and his associates kept their profits high by lowering their prices to millers who in turn lowered prices to farmers. Cojuangco became one of the richest men in the Philippines, largely due to his clientelist contacts with the president.

In the mid-1970s, President Marcos established a monopoly that effectively nationalized both domestic and export sugar trading. He placed the monopoly under the control of his former fraternity brother, Roberto Benedicto. The result was a disaster for sugar planters and workers who suffered from severe malnutrition as thousands were laid off because of plummeting production. Benedicto was given power to seize sugar mills he found were not meeting contractual obligations at the same time he owned sugar plantations that were competing with those he "policed."

During Benedicto's reign, the price of sugar abroad fell drastically. After the price dropped, sugar farmers were not getting the world market price. The cost of production was greater than the price paid to the planters because the sugar barons cut the wages of the workers in response to the drop in sugar prices. Moreover, corruption was rampant within the monopoly with unauthorized funds going to associates of Benedicto. In 1985 the sugar crisis in Negros was serious enough that Communist insurgency threatened the island's security.

President Marcos not only decreed monopoly privileges to his clientele but assured them lucrative contracts and immunity from loss. A close friend, Rudolfo Cuenca, was provided contracts that made him the richest construction company owner in the Philippines. Cuenca's Construction and Development Corporation was awarded the contracts for almost every major construction project including highways, a new international airport, the landfill in Manila Bay, and the first lady's cultural buildings. Poor management led to the bankruptcy of his company but the government bailed out the corporation. This support of a crony by Marcos is a classic example of the clientelist emphasis on the use of public funds for private gain.

The clientelist concept helps explain Marcos' great power as well as his downfall following the 7 February 1986 elections. By placing his clients (cronies) in key positions Marcos ruled through these personal ties, dispensing favors and gifts in return for total loyalty. He controlled the army through his cousin and confidant General Fabian Ver. Close friends and relatives were given control over major industrial and agricultural monopolies, banks, and the mass media. Bureaucratic officials were indebted to Marcos for their positions. Yet, despite his domination of key institutions, Marcos lost all power following the extraordinary events surrounding the 1986 election.

Patronage ties depend on the capacity of patrons to meet the needs of their clients. As the economy declined, fewer resources were available to Marcos and corruption became a principal means to dispense favors. Eventually, the enormity of corruption at all levels of the society drained the nation's resources and undermined Marcos' control over those groups left out of the patronage system.

In clientelist societies, patrons have closer control over their immediate followers than those lower in the network. While Marcos demanded and received total loyalty from his closest cronies, the Filipino masses were never totally under his control. When the economy collapsed, those hurt most seriously were the peasantry and workers who were already poor and who now faced even more severe deprivation. Their loyalty to the regime became tenuous as shown by the massive shift of allegiance to candidate Aquino during the 1986 election.

The fall of Marcos is also explained by his inability to meet the expectation that patrons are respected as well as generous. The 1983 assassination of Senator Aquino undermined the perception of the president's authority. That event, and the belief in the president's complicity, began the unraveling of his power as his credibility plummeted. His involvement in the fraudulent elections of 1986 and his refusal to recognize Aquino's election victory were interpreted as brazen acts of a man who would use any means to keep power, including cheating, lying, fraud, intimidation, and murder. When evidence showed that he lied about his real estate holdings abroad and his alleged war heroism, he became a pitiful caricature of moral authority. He became the object of scorn and jokes, much as the first lady had been previously. The Catholic church's condemnation of Marcos and the first lady further undermined his moral authority.

During the campaign, it became clear that Marcos' health had deteriorated rapidly and many expected him to die imminently. He was not able to walk and had to be carried to his rallies by his aides. His poor health undermined the loyalty of his clients who found themselves attached to a dictator who had not only lost respectability and legitimacy but who was dying. Military leaders in particular saw that their long-term interests would not be served by their ties to Marcos.

In addition to being the nation's supreme patron, Marcos was intertwined in a complex set of patron-client ties with the United States government. The role of the United States in Philippine affairs has been large since the period of colonial rule. Although Marcos used the U.S. military bases in the Philippines as leverage, he nonetheless was dependent on American support for his regime. For 20 years the United States had provided economic and military aid to the Marcos government and had publicly endorsed his rule. Before the 1986 elections Marcos' support of U.S. bases and his anti-Communist ideology were more important factors in determining American policy than was the refusal to reform his administration, the abuse of human rights, and the abrogation of democratic-constitutional rule.

Under President Reagan, the U.S. government saw Marcos as part of the problem, but also, necessarily, as part of the solution to bringing about reform. The State Department noted that the United States did not want to remove Marcos from power to destabilize the government. Instead, they wanted to persuade Marcos to reform his administration and prepare eventually for a peaceful transition of power.

Throughout 1985 President Reagan dispatched a number of

high ranking diplomats and personal envoys to the Philippines to pressure Marcos to reform his administration and to bring legitimacy to the government by holding elections. Marcos' decision to call elections was the result of U.S. prodding and his own belief that he could easily win a new six-year term.

During the election campaign, however, the Reagan administration shifted its view of which candidate would best serve the interests of the United States. Marcos' deteriorating health, his inability to control NPA insurgency, the nation's economic debacle, his waffling on the issue of retaining the U.S. bases, and the clear surge of mass and church support for Corazon Aquino convinced President Reagan that a victory by Marcos would not necessarily be in U.S. interests. Members of the House of Representatives and Senate denounced Marcos' usurpation of office and moved to cut off military and economic aid.

As the evidence mounted that Marcos had committed gross fraud and had no intention of giving up his power to the legitimate victor, Corazon Aquino, the Reagan administration publicly rebuked him. Through direct and indirect diplomacy the U.S. position was made clear: Marcos could not rule illegitimately. When Defense Minister Enrile and General Ramos rebelled against Marcos and the military no longer took orders from the president, the United States received approval from Aquino to provide safe passage for Marcos from Malacanang. The U.S. Air Force provided Marcos and his entourage with aircraft to fly to Hawaii.

Marcos' clientelist ties collapsed when he lost his resources, moral authority, and his major patron, the United States, and when simultaneously an alternative leader arose who symbolized qualities opposite to those of Marcos. Corazon Aquino, the martyred wife of a nation's hero, was accepted with a religious fervor as a symbol against corruption, greed, and tyranny. She was not an ordinary politician easily demolished by the president's control over the society. She stood above the political fray, a saint in the minds of many, and unreachable.

When Aquino set forth her political and economic program and campaigned tirelessly throughout the archipelago, she overcame the concerns of many about inexperience. When she refused to bow to Marcos' claim of victory, and launched a peaceful and steadfast campaign of civil disobedience, she alleviated concern about lack of resolve and strength.

Clientelist dictatorships eventually fall as they become obsessed with the task of holding on to their followers, and become paranoid about potential usurpers, trusting no one but a small body of cronies. Such leaders become isolated and dependent on self-interested sycophants who provide them with information they want to hear. They are no longer open to new ideas and believe they are indispensible to the survival of their nation. Marcos succumbed to the inevitable and surrounded himself with a handful of "loyal" friends who attempted to convince him that he must stay in power not only for his sake and that of the nation, but for the sake of his loyal followers. Even on his last day in the Philippines, 25 February 1986, he attempted to follow the advice of his wife and cronies to launch a counterattack against the military who had sworn allegiance to Aquino.

President Aquino faced overwhelming political and economic problems bequeathed to her by her predecessor. Marcos' followers dominated the bureaucracy, major monopolies, and rural government. Poverty, unemployment, inflation, and corruption pervaded the nation. In many ways, the Philippine situation paralleled that of Thailand in October 1973 when a student-led revolt succeeded in overthrowing the Thai military dictatorship. The euphoria in the Philippines was reminiscent of the exhilaration felt following the military's downfall in Thailand.

Because the economic and political problems of the two nations were parallel, the Aquino government would find little solace from the Thai experience. The "democratic" period in Thailand lasted only three years before the military regrouped and retook power. The civilian-democratic government in Thailand had not been able to meet the rapidly rising expectations of the people following their "liberation" from tyranny. The established bureaucracy remained entrenched, corruption shifted to new groups, the new leadership began to factionalize, and the poor remained poor.

The jubilation felt in the Philippines subsided as the hard realities were faced. The clientelist system proved difficult to dismantle. Because the new government was pressed to meet the rising expectations expeditiously, there were pressures to cut through red tape, to bypass the proper structures, and to rule by decree. That process, in turn, revivified the former rulers who pointed to the new leaders' authoritarian and extra-constitutional procedures. To build democracy, instill meaningful reform, and dismantle old structures ensemble is a formidable task requiring patience, constraint, skill, balance, tenacity, and luck.

MALAYSIA

The governmental institutions of Malaysia reflect the heritage of British colonialism. The 1957 constitution calls for a federal system with a strong central government based on parliamentary rule. The "paramount ruler" of Malaysia is the Yang di-Pertuan Agong, who, unlike most hereditary monarchs, is elected on a rotational basis (according to seniority) for a term of five years from a group of the nine Malay state rulers. The paramount ruler's powers are not dissimilar from those enjoyed by the British monarch.

In 1983 Prime Minister Mahathir proposed constitutional amendments to prevent the king (paramount ruler) from delaying legislation through his veto power or from declaring a state of emergency. However, the hereditary rulers (sultans) of the nine federal states refused to accept the amendments and the king would not sign the act. Because the role of the rulers is considered a matter of great sensitivity, the Malaysian people were not informed about the constitutional crisis until the matter came to a head. A major crisis was averted when a compromise agreement was reached that partially limited the king's powers on the question of his veto prerogative. The sultan of Johore was elected king in 1984.

The chief political leader of Malaysia is the prime minister. He must be a member of the lower house of the Parliament and command majority support. Since 1957 the succession of prime ministers has proceeded smoothly. Alliance party leader Tunku Abdul Rahman was succeeded in 1970 by his heir apparent, Deputy Prime Minister Tun Razak, who in turn was succeeded by Deputy Prime Minister Datuk Hussein Onn in January 1976.

The Malaysian government features a bicameral Parliament, including a Senate (Dewan Negara) and House of Representatives (Dewan Ra'ayat). The upper house has 58 members, 26 elected and 32 appointed by the paramount ruler upon recommendation of the prime minister. Senators hold office for six years. The lower house has 144 elected members, with 24 representing Sarawak, 16 representing Sabah, and 104 representing the Malay peninsula. Representatives serve five years unless the parliament is dissolved. The constitution also calls for a separate and independent judiciary.

The principal dynamic of Malaysian political life can be capsulized in one word: communalism. The religious, linguistic, cultural, economic, and political features of Malaysia are determined by, and coincide with, the ethnic makeup of the nation. The three major ethnic groupings in Malaysia are the Malays, with 46.8 percent of the population; the Chinese, with 34.1 percent; and the Indians, with 9.3 percent. The Malays consider themselves the *bumiputera,* which literally means "sons of the soil." All others are deemed sojourners or aliens who have no roots in Malay culture and tradition.

The Malays and Chinese have a stereotyped mirror image of the other, which stems from and results in mutual prejudice. In his excellent study of the Malaysian bureaucracy, Milton Esman summarized the views of Malays and Chinese toward each other.[48] The Malays regard themselves as scrupulous in their dealings with others and with their family members; they see themselves as more concerned with the quality of human relationships and less with material acquisition. In contrast, they tend to see the Chinese as aggressive, acquisitive, unscrupulous in their business dealings, insensitive in human relationships, ritually unclean, and politically suspect.

The mirror image, according to Esman, is exemplified by the Chinese view of themselves as hardworking, progressive, competitive, and faithful to their family. They view themselves as loyal to Malaysia and, indeed, largely responsible for the nation's high economic growth rate. To the Chinese, the "typical Malay" is lazy and superstitious, without motivation for hard work or personal advancement.

The result of these stereotypical images is a lack of communication among the two ethnic groups (except among intellectuals

---

[48] Milton J. Esman, *Administration and Development in Malaysia* (Ithaca, N.Y.: Cornell University Press, 1972), pp. 20–22.

and government officials in the cities). For the most part, the two groups live totally separate existences, with contrasting religious and cultural beliefs that limit interaction. The differences between the two groups are so great that Esman concludes that "any expectation of integration or the development of an integrative identity in the foreseeable future is pure rhetoric or fancy."[49]

The communal character of Malaysian life influenced the nature of political structures and behavior even before 1957, when Malaya became independent. The British colonialists favored the bumiputera in government administration and, at the same time, encouraged the Chinese and Indians in business pursuits. When Britain and Malaya were negotiating independence, the two parties agreed to retain the essentially Malay features of government with Malay political dominance, while guaranteeing that no legislation would jeopardize Chinese economic interests.

The major institution for expressing Malay sentiments was the United Malay Nationalist Organization (UMNO), created in 1946 to oppose British plans for the Malayan Union (which would have weakened Malayan rights by taking power away from the traditional rulers). Subsequently, the Chinese and Indian political and economic leaders created their own parties. In the local government elections in Kuala Lumpur in 1952, the leaders of the Malayan Chinese Association (MCA) and UMNO discovered that by supporting each other's candidates they could assure electoral victory. Their success persuaded them to institutionalize the arrangement under the title "Alliance party." In 1955 the Malayan Indian Congress (MIC) joined the Alliance.

All three parties gained from the Alliance formula to embody the legitimate interests of each ethnic group it represented. The formula required that each of the three groups accept the basic societal division: the Malays dominate the political sphere, while the Chinese and Indians dominate the economy. By negotiations that provided concessions to the three parties on a variety of issues and required avoidance of "extreme demands," the Alliance formula worked. As long as the three parties perceived

[49] Ibid., p. 23.

their interests as best served by the intercommunal organization, the Alliance flourished. In each election up to 1969 the Alliance party won overwhelming victories.

The party benefited from the leadership of Tunku Abdul Rahman, who was the single person most responsible for Malaya's independence. Rural Malays accepted Rahman as the person who could best maintain the continuity between traditional Malay rule and the modern political institutions of the postindependence period. In addition, the considerable financial resources of MCA, a party led by the wealthiest entrepreneurs in Malaya, allowed the Alliance party to campaign more effectively than any other party.

The strength of the Alliance party—that is, the formula calling for concessions and moderate demands by each communal group—was also, paradoxically, its major weakness. For many who were not part of the establishment, the Alliance did not meet important needs, and disruptive pressures intensified. For example, the younger generation of Chinese, who were born in Malaya, demanded full equality rather than the partial equality negotiated by older MCA leaders with the UMNO leaders. Malays and Chinese protested against the Alliance party's complacency and refusal to stand up more forcefully for the rights of the ethnic populations.

Opposition parties attempted to exploit the Alliance weaknesses by appealing to ethnic interests and grievances. The principal opposition party was the Pan-Malayan Islamic party (PMIP), which emphasized traditional Malay rights, Malay nationalism, and state support for Islam. The major Chinese opposition party was the Democratic Action party (DAP), which grew out of the People's Action party in Singapore. DAP took a much stronger stand than MCA on equal rights for all citizens, without special rights for any group. In the 1969 elections the Alliance party lost a number of seats to the opposition. Riots followed and the country was placed under martial law for 21 months.

The May 1969 riots vividly showed the problems inherent in the Alliance. To offset these weaknesses, Prime Minister Tun Razak formed coalitions with other parties, including those traditionally opposed to the Alliance. By the end of 1972 Razak had formed a National Front (Barisan Nasional) of political parties "dedicated to a united Malaysia." At first the coalition was based only at local levels but eventually encompassed the nation. After two years of martial law and a period of flux as the government sought identity and stability, the Front proved able to bring about communal peace and effective administration.

The National Front had its first opportunity to prove its effectiveness in August 1974, when parliamentary elections were held. The Front was made up of the three Alliance components, as well as the Gerakan Rakyat Malaysia, Parti Islam, People's Progressive party, Sabah Alliance, and the Sarawak United People's party.[50] The Democratic Action party stayed out of the Front. Tun Razak determined the number of seats to be allocated to each party within the Front and decided which candidates would campaign. The strategy was successful; the Front won almost 60 percent of the vote and 135 of the 154 parliamentary seats. The opposition DAP won only nine seats. Political stability and continuity was thus temporarily guaranteed, with the Front dominating the office of prime minister and parliament.

Similarly, in the March 1978 general election, the National Front won 131 of 154 parliamentary seats, and in the 1982 election, the Front claimed 132 of 154 seats. The 1986 election provided the National Front with more than two-thirds of the parliamentary seats. Within the Front are multiple cleavages and interests which must be taken into consideration when planning policy. The Front's domination of national politics is not tantamount to dictatorship. Vigorous political debate and compromise help assure that diverse interests are taken into consideration.

Politics in Malaysia is fragile because of the constant threat of communal eruption. The rise of Islamic fundamentalism has been especially troubling to the Chinese and Indian minorities who fear their rights will be repressed if an Islamic state is proclaimed.

SINGAPORE

Its island nature and ethnically Chinese population are distinctive attributes that make Singapore unlike any other

Southeast Asia nation. Since 1959 the country has been dominated by one party, the People's Action party (PAP), which in turn has been led by a single personality, Lee Kwan Yew. In contrast to its neighbors, Singapore has enjoyed two decades of stability and rapid economic growth within the formal framework of parliamentary democracy and an informal framework of paternalistic authoritarian rule.

The formal structures of government are based on the British model. The prime minister is accountable to the parliament and must command its support. The informal dynamics of politics in Singapore revolves around the PAP and its leader. PAP was founded in 1954 by a group of nationalist politicians who desired an end to British colonial rule. To achieve this, the party drew on the collective strengths of Communists and democratic socialists.

When PAP assumed power in 1959, the Communist-non–Communist alliance broke down, resulting in the establishment of the left-wing Barisan Sosialis (Socialist Front) party. As leader of the now dominant democratic socialist faction of the party, Prime Minister Lee Kwan Yew presided over the merger in 1963 of Singapore with Malaya to form Malaysia. The union proved unworkable and in August 1965 Singapore was formally expelled and became an independent island republic.

By winning every parliamentary seat in the 1968, 1972, 1976, and 1980 elections, PAP became the only effective party in Singapore. A number of factors help explain the continued dominance of PAP over every facet of political life in Singapore. First, the parliamentary legislation set forth by Lee Kwan Yew emphasized social and political discipline which significantly limited any political opposition. Rigid rules restraining the political activities of oppositions groups have been instituted, newspapers circumscribed, suspected Communists arrested, and rights of habeas corpus abrogated. PAP resigned from the Socialist International in 1976 when the Dutch Labor party submitted a memorandum claiming that Singapore was run by totalitarian policies and methods counter to the principles of social democracy and that pro-Communist political prisoners were being detained unlawfully.

> Autonomous trade unions have been smashed. All the conventional channels for debate and dissent, opposition parties, trade unions, the press and education institutions, have been

suppressed and the population pacified by the use of an elaborate network of area control organizations and the Special Branch (secret police).[51]

This exaggerated critique notwithstanding, PAP has kept potential opposition parties from mounting an effective campaign. Although the leaders of PAP accept in principle the concept of a critical competitive opposition, they do so as long as that opposition remains weak. The weak commitment to an active opposition is reflected in a public speech by Foreign Minister S. Rajaratnam, when he noted that

> an opposition party consisting of bums, opportunists, and morons can endanger democracy and bring about chaos, disorder, and violence. . . . Equally a one-party parliament can safeguard democracy and bring about peace, progress, and prosperity. . . . If you forget theory and look at the hard facts you will discover that though the People's Action Party has been in power for 12 years, its greatest achievements in promoting the welfare of the people were under a one-party parliament.[52]

To consolidate its rule, PAP has mobilized the civil service to carry out its programs. To many Singapore citizens PAP is synonymous with the state itself. The phenomenal economic growth in Singapore that touched virtually every person during the 1960s and '70s was perceived to be a PAP accomplishment. For example, a massive housing program significantly affected 40 percent of the population in the decade 1960 to 1970, and will affect 80 percent by 1980.[53] With its clean sweep of the parliamentary seats in the past four elections, PAP was transformed from a mere political party into a national, state institution. One-party rule became institutionalized by a majority vote of the electorate. For many Singapore citizens, a vote against PAP was tantamount to a vote against Singapore. The election of two opposition candidates in the 1984 general elections only partially undermines this assertion.

[51]"Memorandum Recommending Expulsion of the People's Action Party of Singapore from the Socialist International," in *Socialism That Works: The Singapore Way*, ed. C. V. Devan Nair (Singapore: Federal Publications, 1976), p. 250.

[52]Quoted in Chan Heng Chee, *The Dynamics of One Party Dominance: The PAP at the Grass Roots* (Singapore: Singapore University Press, 1976), p. 228.

[53]Ibid., p. 29.

Further obliterating the distinction between the party and the state has been the formation of Citizen Consultative Committees (CCC) that ostensibly act as liaison bodies between local community leaders and party and government officials. In fact, CCC is an important arm of PAP for the purpose of disseminating information and inculcating national values to local constituencies. CCC leaders are chosen by and responsible to PAP. PAP leadership has used the CCC to mobilize the masses in support of party programs.

PAP dominance results to a great extent from the leadership of Lee Kwan Yew. Prime Minister Lee is brilliant (first in his class at Cambridge University), energetic, and motivated. He is the consummate pragmatist, concerned with effective and efficient results. He can be ruthless, as when he ordered political adversaries to be imprisoned. At the same time, he eloquently and passionately speaks about democracy in Singapore. He takes credit for the fact that Singaporeans enjoy the second highest standard of living in Southeast Asia. Although he describes himself as a socialist, he has permitted capitalism to flourish in Singapore and he is strongly anti-Communist. He has coopted intellectuals and youth into PAP, thereby defusing their possible opposition.

Lee Kwan Yew has stressed that his authoritarian and paternalistic government is based on the best interests of the people and is congruent with Chinese political tradition. Paternalistic government is seen as "family government." Chan Heng Chee writes that, according to Confucian political philosophy,

> family virtues are transformed into political virtue. . . . So long as the ruler fulfills the conditions of his rule he holds the political stewardship entrusted to him by Heaven but should he deviate from the Mean, calamities would visit the nation and the authority of the ruler will be taken away because of his misgovernment.[54]

From 1959 to 1986 the PAP has sufficiently fulfilled the basics of benevolent government—peace and prosperity—to retain the support and deference of the overwhelming majority of Singaporeans.

[54] Ibid., p. 231.

BRUNEI

The political dynamics of Brunei are different from that of the other Southeast Asian nations. All power resides in the hands of the sultan, a hereditary monarch, who controls all aspects of life in Brunei. His access to virtually unlimited oil revenues, and his willingness to use these revenues for development projects, have helped provide support and legitimacy from all sectors of the society.

The Cabinet and top level bureaucratic positions consist of members of the royal family. There have been no elections since 1970 when opposition party victories convinced the sultan, Sir Muda Hassanal Bolkiah, to revert to an absolute monarchy. In 1986 the 40 year old sultan and his close family members ruled in the style of classic potentates complete with fabulous palaces. At the same time, the sultan oversaw a vast welfare and development program, and employed half the workforce of the entire nation in the bureaucracy. High level bureaucratic positions have been reserved for Sunni Muslim Malays.

The nation's unique economy, a result of vast oil reserves, makes Brunei's political dynamics different from the agriculturally based economies of most of the other Southeast Asian nations. The government's capacity to meet the needs of the people is clearly greater given the unlimited financial resources available to the government. Moreover, the small territory and population of Brunei make governing far easier than in the large and more diverse Southeast Asian countries such as the Philippines and Indonesia, where the island-nature of these nations reduces communications, unity, and stability.

7
Problems and Prospects in Southeast Asia

Southeast Asia is beset by a number of problems, both internally and externally induced, that significantly affect the prospects for the ten nations of the region.

INTERNAL CONSIDERATIONS

The first problem which has a major bearing on the region's future is pervasive poverty. The standard of living is low for the overwhelming majority of Southeast Asian inhabitants. One traditional indicator of material well-being is per capita income. As Table 1 (pages 4–5) shows, in 1986 that indicator varied from U.S. $140 in Laos to $22,000 in Brunei with most of the Southeast Asian nations at the lower end of the scale. The same indicator for Japan in that year was $9,714.

At the aggregate level, the absolute poverty of Southeast Asia as a region becomes clear when its 1985 total GNP of $69 billion is compared to Japan and the United States. The United States GNP was more than 14 times the combined figure for all of Southeast Asia, and the Japan GNP was five times the total.

The nations of Southeast Asia (with the obvious exceptions of Brunei, Malaysia, and Singapore) rank among the poor nations of the world. Within Indonesia, Thailand, and the Philippines, the 40 percent of the population lowest in income receives less than 17 percent of the total income.[1] It is this 40 percent whose

---

[1] Cited in Soedjatmoko, "Perceptions of Social Justice in Southeast Asia," *Questioning Development in Southeast Asia,* ed. Nancy Chang (Singapore: Select Books, 1977), p. 88.

level of life is so poor as to threaten permanent damage to their health and potential for human growth. In fact relative inequality within any one nation of the region has become greater, even while per capita income increases. This crisis has not yet been adequately faced.

A more optimistic view can be formulated by comparing per capita income figures today with those ten years ago. The ASEAN states have tripled their per capita income levels within the decade and have diversified their economies so that agriculture now accounts for a far smaller percentage of the gross national product. Virtually every social-political indicator for ASEAN (life expectancy, infant mortality, number of doctors, literacy) shows an increase in the citizens' standard of living compared with ten years ago.

The reasons for the inequality of wealth in Southeast Asia can be traced to the traditional societies themselves and to the colonial era. The elites of the society lived in the urban centers and tended to neglect the periphery while feathering their own nests and those of their urban clients. The imperialist nations similarly developed only those sectors of the economy which increased their own profits and interests. At the present time, the governments of non-Communist Southeast Asia continue to practice the economics of a dual society: priority to the urban industrial centers with an expectation that resources will eventually trickle down to the masses. For many decades the rural people have fatalistically accepted this inequity. As communications improve throughout the countryside and as the populations become more and more urbanized, however, the perceptions and expectations of the people change. What the rural people once considered as acceptable may no longer be so.

Economic development is closely tied to population trends. As Table 1 indicates, the population of each Southeast Asian nation is expected to double in the next 28 (Vietnam and Philippines) to 64 (Singapore) years. An increasingly higher percentage are under 15 years of age, so that future demands on public services cannot possibly be met if economic growth rates continue as at present. The primary cities are becoming crowded. Insufficient services have caused gigantic slums in almost every capital city. As cultivable land becomes even more scarce, thousands of rural farmers will continue to stream to the cities looking for nonexistent jobs. The region's pernicious poverty, exacerbated by rapid population growth, remains the principal problem affecting every aspect of Southeast Asian life, including the viability of the sociopolitical systems themselves.

A second problem affecting the prospects for Southeast Asia is the continuing pattern of authoritarian rule. The traditions of Hinduism found in Burma, Thailand, Cambodia, and Laos, and the tradition of Confucianism found in Vietnam, laid the foundation for centralized, hierarchical rule. Colonial rule strengthened those elite groups who had the most to gain by collaborating with the European colonialists. Even in the contemporary period neither the bureaucrats nor general masses share cultural values, attitudes, and beliefs that are conducive to flourishing nonauthoritarian rule. The values tend to emphasize dependence, nonparticipation, deference to authority, and preference for dictatorship in times of crisis. Hence, even in Malaysia and Singapore, which have democratic governments, the level of support for democracy is mostly formalistic.

The armies of contemporary Southeast Asia have been most successful in gaining and retaining power. The armies' control over weapons, their material and moral support from the United States, their claim to purity in contrast to the civilian government's reputation for corruption and ineptness, their hierarchical organization, westernized values, and reputation as the leaders of the independence movements, explain their preeminent position. Yet army rule in Vietnam and Cambodia was overthrown in 1975 and in Thailand a student-led revolt sent the military leadership into exile in 1973. Both General Suharto in Indonesia and Ne Win in Burma resigned from the military to become civilian leaders. Indeed, each of the military governments in Southeast Asia represents a variant on the general pattern of military rule by including civilian technocrats and bureaucrats. Pure military rule no longer appears to be the only viable authoritarian mode. The Communist governments in Indochina clearly represent an alternative model of centralized rule.

For the most part authoritarian governments are isolated from the large masses of the people. Their perspective tends to be urban and self-interested. Their purpose is to perpetuate their rule rather than to mobilize the nation's resources for the inter-

ests of the many. Such rule is inevitably self-defeating and destabilizing as particular factions in power struggle to strengthen
their rule against potential coup leaders. Because centralized
sovereign state systems have existed for centuries in Southeast
Asia, one can assume they will remain for the near future at
least. Thus far, there is little evidence that these governments
are moving to improve significantly the lives of the large majority of their citizens nor are these governments insisting on a
more equitable distribution of the nation's resources.

REGIONAL AND GREAT POWER CONSIDERATIONS

All the Southeast Asian nations, including even Burma despite
its concerted effort to achieve non-alignment in an isolationist
context, are buffeted by regional and world powers. In 1975 the
Southeast Asian region witnessed a change of dramatic propor-
tions as the nations of Vietnam, Laos, and Cambodia became
Communist ruled. The non-Communist nations regarded the
change with varying degrees of shock. In response to this drastic
change the remaining non-Communist nations moved to
strengthen the alliance to assure some semblance of a balance of
power. The Association of Southeast Asian Nations (ASEAN),
founded in 1967 by the governments of Thailand, the Philippines, Singapore, Malaysia, and Indonesia, served as a vehicle
for strengthening their shared resistance to communism.

Initially ASEAN was concerned with accelerating economic
growth, social progress, and cultural development. The primary
means to these ends have been to break down trade barriers, to
expand exports, and to call for a joint commodity price stabilization scheme to protest against world price and market variations
for important crops. By emphasizing economic programs and
avoiding political issues, ASEAN has remained both non-
controversial and passive. After the change in government in
Indochina the ASEAN members met at Bali in February 1976 to
affirm political as well as economic cooperation and to secure
respect for Southeast Asia as a "Zone of Peace, Freedom, and
Neutrality." However, such declarations thus far have been more
rhetorical than substantive and the Association remains primarily a body for economic cooperation and periodic consultation.

The Indochinese states view ASEAN as a front group for American "imperialism" despite the attempts by ASEAN members to have the three Communist nations join the alliance. ASEAN has agreed not to include a military dimension, although Vietnam's invasion of Cambodia and support of internal Communist insurgency in Thailand have raised questions of whether or not ASEAN as a collectivity should confront such intervention. In spite of the protestations of neutrality by ASEAN members, the governments in Hanoi, Phnom Penh, and Vientiane perceive ASEAN to be a substitute for the defunct SEATO military alliance and an anti-Communist puppet of American militarism.

Nationalism is the major reason Southeast Asian nations have had difficulty establishing groups such as ASEAN. Two ingredients of nationalism are sovereignty and separateness, neither of which is conducive to the idea of regionalism. The history of Southeast Asia is the history of violent struggles for power among the various ethnic groups living in the area. For example, the Thais, Burmese, Cambodians, and Vietnamese have continually engaged in warfare for territorial aggrandizement. Except in times of warfare, interaction among the various societies was infrequent, so that no patterns or habits of cooperative endeavors developed. Moreover, the great ethnic, linguistic, religious, and cultural diversity in Southeast Asia narrows the scope of potential regional coordination. At present regionalism is not a salient factor affecting Southeast Asia's political prospects.

Despite these problems, ASEAN has experienced significant strengths that make it one of the most vibrant regions of the world. Economically, ASEAN has become a showcase of successful economic development. The member nations have become a major international economic force because of their natural resources, strategic location, immense market, active trade, and stable governments.

The Communist victory in Vietnam and the subsequent reunification of the nation have brought about an entirely new power configuration in Southeast Asia. For the first time in the postindependence era a single Southeast Asian state has become a dominant and potentially hegemonic power. Moreover, the Socialist Republic of Vietnam, in the name of revolutionary ideology, has called for the masses throughout the region to join in a revolutionary struggle against the forces of oppression. Hence, the leading military and political power of the region has aligned itself against the "status quo" forces represented by Indonesia, Thailand, Malaysia, Singapore, and the Philippines.

The potential power of Vietnam is clear. With 60 million people, the country is the second largest in Southeast Asia after Indonesia, and the Communist bloc's third largest. More importantly, Vietnam has some one million soldiers in the People's Army of Vietnam (PAVN), making it the fourth largest military force in the world. Vietnam's military strength is greater than the combined totals of the ASEAN members. In addition, Vietnam boasts a 1½ million militia which can be immediately mobilized. More than $5 billion of United States weaponry, including artillery, tanks, and planes captured at the end of the Vietnam War, makes the Vietnamese army far superior to the combined forces of the non-Communist Southeast Asian powers. Having recently fought and won a protracted war, the Vietnamese army is the best trained and most experienced in Southeast Asia.

Above and beyond its military capacity, Vietnam is led by stable leadership with full control over the countryside and an ability to mobilize the population at will. That fact in and of itself makes Vietnam unique among the Southeast Asian nations and provides it with a significant power advantage. In addition, the Hanoi government has articulated a revolutionary ideology which proclaims the inevitability of socialist rule for Third World nations, and, in particular, Southeast Asian nations. When the advantages of a superior military force, cohesive leadership, and a revolutionary ideology are seen ensemble, it becomes easier to understand the degree of concern expressed by ASEAN members toward the ambitions of Vietnam.

However, to point out the fact of military superiority is not to say that Vietnam will engage in direct or indirect intervention in the affairs of other non-Communist Southeast Asian nations. One possibility is that Vietnam will now concentrate its energies on establishing socialism in its southern half, rebuilding the devastated infrastructure in the entire country, and consolidating its power over Laos and Cambodia. As long as Vietnam sets a high priority on economic reconstruction, a task which could take several decades, the Communist government is less likely to seek regional hegemony. Vietnam's request for technical aid from the West supports the view of those who believe that Vietnam's domestic development is more important to the government than exporting its revolution at the present time.

Those who argue that Vietnam will act on the momentum it has going stress the fact that Vietnam has already stationed large numbers of troops in Laos thereby paving the way for armed aggression against Thailand. The argument also emphasizes the antipathy of the American government and people to becoming bogged down once again in an Asian quagmire. It is clear that no American president will look favorably on intervention especially to deal with problems of insurgency. If Vietnam perceives the American commitment to be of low priority, the Communist government may decide to aggress, on the assumption there will be no American response.

Vietnam's future role vis-à-vis the other Communist nations in Southeast Asia is difficult to assess. Historically, the Laotian Communist party has been dependent on the Vietnamese Communist party for ideological and material support. In 1986 an estimated 40,000 Vietnamese soldiers were stationed in Laos ostensibly to "maintain law and order," to help build up the nation's economic infrastructure, and to provide security along the Laotian border with Cambodia and Thailand. The presence of these troops has led some analysts to view Laos as no more than a "supplicant satellite, if not outright colony" of the Socialist Republic of Vietnam.[2] The Vietnamese desire to establish an Indochinese Union has led Laotian nationalists to fear annexation of Laos into a federation which, given the small population and military weakness of the country, could lead to the absorption and eventually the disappearance of Laotian society.

Vietnam's relations with Cambodia must be seen in a historical context. The common Communist ideology shared by these two nations has not erased three centuries of enmity due to traditional Vietnamese expansionism. In the 19th century Cambodia was forced to accede to France's colonialism to halt the process of dismemberment at Vietnamese hands. More recently, Cambodian hatred for the Vietnamese was manifested in the quasi-

---

[2] Donald E. Weatherbee, "U.S. Policy and the Two Southeast Asias," *Asian Survey*, XVIII, No. 4 (April 1978), p. 410.

official program against the Vietnamese minority living in Cambodia in the early 1970s following the overthrow of Sihanouk. Thousands of Vietnamese were summarily killed by Cambodians.

Following the Communist victories in the spring of 1975 both Cambodia and Vietnam carried out raids against the other's border towns. Diplomatic relations were broken off in December 1976 and 60,000 Vietnamese became refugees, fleeing to their homeland. The causes for the border clashes are not clear although they do reflect the historical adversary relationship. One theory suggested that Hanoi was purposely attempting to undermine Cambodian stability to prepare for a Vietnamese-supported coup d'etat against the Pol Pot government, a coup which would have brought to power a pro-Vietnamese Cambodian administration.

A second theory was that the Cambodian government was deliberately provoking an armed conflict in order to mobilize the masses in support of the new Communist government. By proclaiming an outside threat to the sanctity of Cambodian territory the new regime was able to strengthen its nationalist credentials. The Cambodian government claimed that following the Communist victory in 1975 Vietnamese troops remained on Cambodian soil. From the point of view of Cambodian leaders the border war was necessary for the very survival of the nation. One difficulty in assessing the motives of the Cambodian leadership, if border problems are at the core of the dispute, is the lopsided nature of each country's military strength. It seems unlikely that Cambodian leaders would deliberately go to war against Vietnam given the fact that Vietnam's 600,000 trained troops and sophisticated weaponry could overwhelm Cambodia's relatively unarmed army of 90,000 with ease. Indeed, the Vietnamese invasion of Cambodia required only several weeks to accomplish its goal of setting up a puppet government.

The Cambodian-Vietnamese dispute has also been interpreted as a "proxy war" fought by surrogates of China and the Soviet Union. Because China has provided aid to Cambodia and the Soviet Union has supported Vietnam, the argument is made that the two world powers are deliberately provoking confrontation for the purpose of increasing their own self-interest and potential control over insurgent movements and governments throughout Southeast Asia. This interpretation sees Cambodia and Vietnam as pawns of major powers rather than as independent nations. However, there are historical precedents to the rivalry which suggest that more was at stake in these border wars than competition between the major Communist powers.

Relations among the Southeast Asian nations have been complicated by the flood of refugees fleeing Vietnam, Cambodia, and Laos. Since the 1975 Communist takeover, almost two million persons have left the repression and hunger they saw as unending in each of the three nations. Having managed to endure harrowing escapes by land and sea these refugees were further subjected to suffering when they reached the shores of nations that made clear the refugees were not welcome. By 1980, after Vietnam had reduced the flow of refugees, the crisis of the boat people seemed manageable although still serious. The movement of starving Cambodians into Thailand, however, remained a stark reminder of the continuing incapacity of some Southeast Asian nations to cope with the most basic needs of the people.

For the past four centuries European colonial powers, beginning with the Spanish and later the Americans in the Philippines, the Dutch in Indonesia, and the Portuguese in Malacca, played a crucial role in Southeast Asian societies. The colonial period was followed by the Japanese interregnum when Japan, itself a great power during World War II, succeeded in occupying every Southeast Asian nation. The Japanese period brought about fundamental changes in the political life of the region and set the scene for the struggle for independence. Following the war, the European powers attempted to regain their colonies, but after long bitter wars, most notably in Vietnam and Indonesia, the colonialists were forced out. It appeared as if Southeast Asia was to be free of outside military-political involvement for the first time in centuries. However, with the massive American intervention into Vietnam, the involvement of the great powers proved to be a continuing reality in Southeast Asia.

The American defeat in Vietnam made Southeast Asia politically and militarily less a priority for the United States in the 1980s. Whereas the United States in the 1970s was the paramount military power in Southeast Asia, its role in the 1980s was far less significant as national security issues centered on relations with the Middle East, China, Latin America, and the Soviet Union. The rapprochement between China and the United States and between China and ASEAN decreased Washington's security concerns about China's threat to Southeast Asia.

On the other hand, U.S. foreign policy did not simply write off the region. The United States maintained military bases in the Philippines as a countervailing power to the Soviet Union's use of the Vietnamese base at Cam Ranh Bay and continued to provide significant military and economic aid to ASEAN and support for ASEAN foreign policy stands. Because 30 percent of U.S. trade ties were with ASEAN and investments there totaled $10 billion, the economic significance of ASEAN to the United States increased.

The most controversial U.S. role in Southeast Asia concerned the use of Subic Bay Naval Base and Clark Air Base which the United States viewed as essential to its own as well as Asia's security. The bases have provided facilities for the collection of intelligence, for logistical supplies (from the Pacific to the Persian Gulf), for protection of sea lanes extending from the Indian Ocean and South China Sea to Japan, and for counterbalancing Soviet forces deployed in Vietnam.

The controversy stemmed from the view of many Filipinos that the bases, while important to U.S. strategic interests, did not serve Philippine interests. In June, 1983 the United States and the Philippines signed a memorandum extending the base agreement until 1991 with the United States agreeing to pay the Philippines $900 million in aid. Following the 1986 election campaign, President Aquino promised to retain the bases until 1991 and then submit a referendum to the people on the future of the bases.

The ASEAN states as well as China supported the bases as a balance to growing Soviet military strength in the region. The Chinese government warned the region's leaders "not to let the Soviet tiger in the back door while driving the U.S. wolf out the front." However, the political and economic problems in the Philippines along with rising nationalist sentiments and a belief that the Philippines itself was not threatened by any outside power, left the future of the bases in question. In 1986 the Reagan administration was studying alternative sites in the Pacific in case the bases were closed.

ASEAN governments have taken the lead in foreign policy issues affecting the region. The United States followed the ASEAN view that Vietnam constitutes the major threat to the region. To buttress its support, the United States provided the ASEAN governments with over $400 million in economic and military aid in 1984 alone, and used its influence to support ASEAN's stand against representation in the United Nations for the Heng Samrin regime in Cambodia.

The Soviet Union's role in Vietnam since the Communist takeover is perceived by the ASEAN states as destabilizing and potentially threatening. Soviet domination of Vietnam, Laos, and Cambodia has provided a base for expansion in Southeast Asia. The development of a naval base at Cam Ranh Bay has been particularly troubling to ASEAN, Japan, the United States, and China, who view the Soviet military build-up in Vietnam as a major security threat. The Cam Ranh base provides potential Soviet control over the vital waterways of the Pacific Ocean, South China Sea, and Indian Ocean which are deemed indispensable for American trade, access to oil by Japan, and the security of ASEAN. Soviet goals in the area have included the use of waterways for the Soviet Pacific fleet between the eastern ports of Russia and the Indian Ocean, and the containment of Chinese expansionism. Soviet relations with ASEAN states have been tense because of ASEAN's perception that the Vietnamese threat is made possible through Soviet aid and encouragement.

China's role in Southeast Asia continues to depend on its relations with the Soviet Union and its concern about a united Vietnam in alliance with the Soviets. Cambodia under Pol Pot was China's only close ally in Southeast Asia. When the Pol Pot government was overthrown, the Chinese viewed the Vietnamese invasion as a bid by the Soviet Union for regional dominance. To "punish" Vietnam for its invasion, and to show the Soviet Union that China was not a paper tiger, the Chinese themselves invaded the northern provinces of Vietnam. The invasion ended in a stalemate.

Critics of China's foreign policy in Southeast Asia note that China's military pressure on Vietnam's border provided legitimacy to the Soviet troops stationed in Vietnam and Cambodia. Although a strong Vietnam, independent of Soviet pressures, is in China's best interests, Chinese policy toward Vietnam has actually moved Vietnam closer to the Soviet Union through its aid to the Cambodian rebels, its treatment of Vietnam as the major adversary, and its close ties to the United States. These critics note the contradiction in China's professed support for popular regimes and its support for the hated Pol Pot and his guerrilla rebels.

China's main aims in Southeast Asia under the more pragmatic post-Mao leadership have been to contain Soviet expansion, develop closer economic ties with ASEAN, assure an independent Cambodia free from Vietnamese occupation, and to keep Southeast Asia from being dominated by any one superpower. Thus, there exists a clear coincidence of interests by China and the United States toward Southeast Asia.

Japan's war-time goal of a Greater East Asia Co-Prosperity Sphere was shattered after Japan's defeat in World War II. Just 40 years later, Japan became the major economic power in Southeast Asia. The animosities and suspicions of the Southeast Asians, all of whom had been occupied by the Japanese during the war, gradually subsided in the post-war era as Japan set forth a foreign policy renouncing a military role and proposing massive aid projects in Southeast Asia. Forty percent of the foreign aid received by ASEAN has come from Japan.

Japan has clear security interests in Southeast Asia because of the vital seaways in the region that link Japan with its supply of oil from the Persian Gulf. Almost 80 percent of Japan's oil needs go through the Straits of Malacca and the South China Sea. To secure these seaways Japan has supported the presence of U.S. bases in the Philippines, especially since the Soviet Union began to use naval facilities at Cam Ranh Bay. Japan has depended upon the United States for military security in Southeast Asia, while emphasizing its own complementary economic development role as an important ingredient of security in the region.

Twenty-eight percent of ASEAN exports are purchased by Japan (15 percent by the United States), and 22 percent of Japanese exports go to ASEAN. ASEAN provides Japan with significant and strategic raw materials and in return purchases Japanese industrial products. Southeast Asians refer to the "Honda revolution" in their countries; few Southeast Asian villagers are without some Japanese products in their home and the city streets are crowded with Mazda, Toyota, Honda, Yamaha, Isuzu, and Mitsubishi vehicles.

Because the ASEAN states have opted for an export-led development strategy, they are increasingly dependent upon their major trade partners, Japan and the United States. The economies of ASEAN are dependent on open access to Japanese and American markets. Protectionist sentiments in both countries have raised tensions and expressions of nationalism and self-reliance within Southeast Asia. The close economic ties have become a two-edged sword providing development benefits to Southeast Asia as well as assuring dependency on the great powers.

PROSPECTS FOR SOUTHEAST ASIA

In the 1970s, the prospects for stability, peace, and development in Southeast Asia seemed bleak. The Communist regimes in Vietnam, Laos, and Cambodia were economically devastated and politically repressive, the United States appeared unwilling to play a role in the region after its defeat in Indochina, and the non-Communist ASEAN governments were ruled by authoritarian leaders. Malaysia was still tense from the ethnic riots of 1969, Indonesia was reeling from the effects of the 1965 Gestapu coup and the subsequent bloodbath against the indigenous Chinese, and Thailand's experiment with democracy ended in 1976 with the resurgence of the military and a harsh regime. In the Philippines martial law ended democratic rule, while in Burma the military continued isolationist and socialist policies that have kept the nation in poverty up to the present. Singapore's economic growth rate was high but questions were being raised about the authoritarian leadership and loss of traditional values as modernization was thrust upon the city state. A decade ago Brunei was still colonized by the British.

In the mid 1980s, with few exceptions, the nations of Southeast Asia have experienced an economic dynamism within the context of political stability. Indonesia, Malaysia, Singapore, and Thailand have achieved remarkable economic growth rates under steady leadership. Thailand, for example, has posted annual growth rates of about seven percent, with a declining birth rate, and a stable political system without a successful coup d'etat since 1977. At the same time Communist insurgency has been controlled through judicious governmental policies, and there is no direct threat to the nation's sovereignty.

The Vietnamese occupation of Cambodia was the major regional crisis in the 1980s. None of the superpowers involved had any incentive to end the stalemate. The Soviet Union viewed the occupation as a means to keep Vietnam dependent and to reduce China's role in the area. China saw the occupation as tying down Soviet resources in a protracted conflict. China's attempt to improve relations with ASEAN was strengthened by their parallel policies toward Cambodia.

The United States also viewed the stalemate with equanimity. U.S. policy followed that of ASEAN and China and was designed to limit Soviet influence in Southeast Asia at no cost to the United States. The ASEAN states were content to follow Thai policy because of Thailand's status as a "front-line" state. With no incentive to end the crisis, the fate of Cambodia remained in abeyance. The refusal to recognize the Vietnamese supported government and the policy to aid rebel forces did not appear to have any impact on the Vietnamese. On the other hand, the Vietnamese have not been able to institutionalize their rule or dislodge the resistance sufficiently to guarantee the continuation of the pro-Vietnamese regime.

Hence, the Soviet sponsored Vietnamese occupation of Cambodia has stabilized much of Southeast Asia in unexpected ways. As a result of fear of a Soviet foothold in the region, China forged closer ties with the ASEAN states, no longer supported insurgency in ASEAN, and established trade and aid ties throughout the region. Moreover, the occupation of Cambodia drained Vietnam's economic and military resources to such an extent that the nation was no longer capable of aggressing against ASEAN.

In the mid 1980s, a direct threat to ASEAN sovereignty from the Soviet Union, China, or Vietnam was no longer a major concern. The ASEAN states looked to the United States as a major ally, although Southeast Asia moved away from American center stage. This movement reflected the American view that ASEAN enjoyed sustained economic growth and development, political stability, and security from outside intervention.

The one exception to this optimistic prognosis was the Philippines which, until February 1986, was the least stable of the Southeast Asian nations. Events during the 1986 election made clear that Marcos' rule was illegitimate and contrary to the will of the Filipino people. However, the severe problems faced by President Aquino and the high expectations that the new administration could solve these problems forthwith have threatened the nation's prospects.

The Indochina states presented a different kind of problem for Southeast Asia. The continued occupation of Cambodia and Laos by Vietnamese troops brought stability in the short run but could eventually escalate tensions regionally and bring about renewed superpower intervention. Cambodia remained a pawn of larger powers, a "sideshow," of concern only in tactical and strategic terms to its adversaries and allies.

In Vietnam, the eventual demise of the old revolutionary leadership could bring into power a more pragmatic administration much like that in China. New leadership could carry out less doctrinaire and rigid economic policies and a movement away from dependence on the Soviet Union. Until then, the prospects are poor for dynamic growth and the reduction of repressive measures now deemed necessary in the transition to a socialist regime.

In the 1980s Southeast Asia ceased to be of paramount interest in American foreign policy. Except for the assassination of Senator Aquino and the presidential elections in the Philippines, few events have occurred in the region that have made the headlines in American newspapers. The region was viewed as an economic and political success story and therefore of less concern than the world's crisis areas.

The future of Southeast Asia is inextricably tied to the policies of the great powers. At the same time Southeast Asian nations are moving in the direction of greater national resilience and self-reliance. There is a growing belief that the prospects for each individual country inevitably rest on that nation's internal capacity to meet the needs of the people and to assure a higher standard of living and justice for all. Despite progress toward these idealistically stated goals, some of the area's leaders have continued to opt for authoritarian rule as the means to increase governmental capacity. The political background, political culture, and political dynamics of the region have provided the basis for elite rule.

The cultural richness stemming from the great diversity within Southeast Asia makes generalization difficult. Each nation must find its own balance between the requirements for growth and stability, authority and freedom, regional interdependence and nationalism, and modernization and cultural integrity. Each nation must solve the problem of the wide gap between the haves and the have-nots. In the mid-1980s, the prospects for achieving these goals in much of Southeast Asia are favorable.

Selected Bibliography

Below is a list of basic books on contemporary Southeast Asian politics. Readers of this book who desire up-to-date analysis of politics in Southeast Asia should consult current issues of the following journals: *Asian Survey, The Journal of Asian Studies, Pacific Affairs,* and *Far Eastern Economic Review.* The January and February issues of *Asian Survey* feature articles which summarize the major political events of each Southeast Asian nation during the preceding year.

GENERAL

Bastin, John, and Harry Benda. *History of Modern Southeast Asia.* Englewood Cliffs, New Jersey: Prentice-Hall, 1968.

Butwell, Richard. *Southeast Asia: A Political Introduction.* New York: Praeger, 1975.

Chawla, Sundershan, Melvin Gurtov, and Alain-Gerard Marsot, eds. *Southeast Asia Under the New Balance of Power.* New York: Praeger, 1974.

Fifield, Russell.. *The Diplomacy of Southeast Asia 1945–1958.* Hamden, Connecticut: Archon Books, 1968.

Golay, Frank, R. Anspach, M.R. Pfanner, and E. Ayal. *Underdevelopment and Economic Nationalism in Southeast Asia.* Ithaca, New York: Cornell University Press, 1969.

Gordon, Bernard. *The Dimensions of Conflict in Southeast Asia.* Englewood Cliffs, New Jersey: Prentice-Hall, 1966.

Kahin, George McT., ed. *Governments and Politics of Southeast Asia.* Ithaca, New York: Cornell University Press, 1964.

Kearney, Robert N., ed. *Politics and Modernization in South and Southeast Asia.* Cambridge, Massachusetts: Schenkman Publishing Company, 1975.

Mauzy, Diane K., ed. *Politics in the Asean States.* Kuala Lumpur: Marican and Sons, 1984.

McAlister, John T., Jr. ed. *Southeast Asia, The Politics of National Integration.* New York: Random House, 1973.

McCoy, Alfred. *The Politics of Heroin in Southeast Asia.* New York: Harper and Row, 1972.

Morrison, Charles E. *Japan, the United States and a Changing Southeast Asia.* New York: The Asia Society, 1985.

Pauker, Guy J., Frank H. Golay, and Cynthia H. Enloe. *Diversity and Development in Southeast Asia, The Coming Decade.* New York: McGraw-Hill, 1977.

Pye, Lucian W. *Southeast Asia's Political Systems.* Englewood Cliffs, New Jersey: Prentice-Hall, 1974.

Scott, James C. *The Moral Economy of the Peasant, Rebellion and Subsistence in Southeast Asia.* New Haven, Connecticut: Yale University Press, 1976.

Shaplen, Robert. *Time Out of Hand: Revolution and Reaction in Southeast Asia.* New York: Harper and Row, 1969.

Smith, Roger M., ed. *Southeast Asia: Documents of Political Development and Change.* Ithaca, New York: Cornell University Press, 1974.

Steinberg, David J., ed. *In Search of Southeast Asia.* New York: Praeger, 1971.

Tilman, Robert O., ed. *Man, State and Society in Contemporary Southeast Asia.* New York: Praeger, 1969.

Waddell, J.R.E. *Southeast Asian Politics.* New York: John Wiley and Sons, 1972.

Williams, Lea E. *Southeast Asia, A History.* New York: Oxford University Press, 1976.

Zacher, Mark W., and Robert Stephen Milne, eds. *Conflict and Stability in Southeast Asia.* Garden City, New York: Anchor, 1974.

BURMA

Butwell, Richard. *U Nu of Burma.* Stanford: Stanford University Press, 1963.

Cady, John. *The United States and Burma.* Cambridge, Massachusetts: Harvard University Press, 1976.

Leach, Edmund. *Political Systems of Highland Burma.* London: Bell, 1954.

Pye, Lucian W. *Politics, Personality, and Nation Building: Burma's Search for Identity.* New Haven, Connecticut: Yale University Press, 1962.

Silverstein, Josef. *Burma: Military Rule and The Politics of Stagnation.* Ithaca, New York: Cornell University Press, 1977.

CAMBODIA

Armstrong, John P. *Sihanouk Speaks.* New York: Walker, 1964.

Leifer, Michael. *Cambodia: The Search for Security.* New York: Praeger, 1967.

Sihanouk, Prince Norodom. *My War with the CIA.* New York: Pantheon, 1973.

Smith, Roger M. *Cambodia's Foreign Policy.* Ithaca, New York: Cornell University Press, 1965.

INDONESIA

Anderson, Benedict R. O'G. *Java in a Time of Revolution, Occupation and Resistance, 1944–1946.* Ithaca, New York: Cornell University Press, 1972.

Benda, Harry J. *The Crescent and the Rising Sun.* The Hague and Bandung: Van Hoeve, 1958.

Brackman, Arnold C. *The Communist Collapse in Indonesia.* New York: Norton Publishers, 1969.

Brackman, Arnold. *Indonesian Communism, A History.* New York: Praeger, 1963.

Dahm, Bernard. *Sukarno and the Struggle for Indonesian Independence.* Ithaca, New York: Cornell University Press, 1969.

Emmerson, Donald K. *Indonesia's Elite, Political Culture and Cultural Politics.* Ithaca, New York: Cornell University Press, 1976.

Feith, Herbert. *The Decline of Constitutional Democracy in Indonesia.* Ithaca, New York: Cornell University Press, 1962.

Feith, Herbert and Lance Castles, eds. *Indonesian Political Thinking, 1945–1965.* Ithaca, New York: Cornell University Press, 1970.

Hughes, John. *Indonesian Upheaval.* New York: David McKay, 1967.

Jackson, Karl D., and Lucian W. Pye, eds. *Political Power and Communications in Indonesia.* Berkeley: University of California Press, 1978.

Kahin, George McT. *Nationalism and Revolution in Indonesia.* Ithaca, New York: Cornell University Press, 1952.

Legge, J.D. *Sukarno, A Political Biography.* New York: Praeger, 1972.

Lev, Daniel. *Islamic Courts in Indonesia: A Study in the Political Bases of Legal Institutions.* Berkeley: University of California Press, 1972.

Liddle, William R. *Ethnicity, Party, and National Integration: An Indonesian Case Study.* New Haven, Connecticut: Yale University Press, 1970.

Liddle, William R., ed. *Political Participation in Modern Indonesia.* New Haven, Connecticut: Yale University, Southeast Asia Studies, 1973.

McVey, Ruth T. *The Rise of Indonesian Communism.* Ithaca, New York: Cornell University Press, 1965.

Vittachi, Tarzie. *The Fall of Sukarno.* New York: Praeger, 1967.

Weatherbee, Donald E. *Ideology in Indonesia: Sukarno's Indonesian Revolution.* New Haven, Connecticut: Yale University Press, Southeast Asia Studies, 1966.

Wertheim, W.F. *Indonesian Society in Transition: A Study of Social Change.* The Hague: Van Hoeve, 1959.

LAOS

Adams, Nina, and Alfred McCoy, eds. *Laos: War and Revolution.* New York: Harper and Row, 1970.

Dommen, Arthur. *Conflict in Laos: The Politics of Neutralization.* New York: Praeger, 1971.

Kiernan, Ben and Chanthou Boua, eds. *Peasants and Politics in Kampuchea: 1942–1981.* New York: M.E. Sharpe, Inc., 1982.

Langer, Paul F. and Joseph J. Zasloff. *North Vietnam and the Pathet Lao, Partners in the Struggle for Laos.* Cambridge, Massachusetts: Harvard University Press, 1970.

MALAYSIA

Bedlington, Stanley S. *Malaysia and Singapore: The Building of New States.* Ithaca, N.Y.: Cornell University Press, 1978.

Enloe, Cynthia. *Multi-ethnic Politics: The Case of Malaysia.* Berkeley: University of California Press, 1967.

Esman, Milton. *Administration and Development in Malaysia.* Ithaca, New York: Cornell University Press, 1972.

Means, Gordon. *Malaysian Politics.* New York: New York University Press, 1970.

Milne, R.S. and Diane K. Mauzy. *Politics and Government in Malaysia,* 2nd edition. Singapore and Vancouver: Times Books International and University of British Columbia Press, 1980.

Ness, Gayle D. *Bureaucracy and Rural Development in Malaysia.* Berkeley: University of California Press, 1967.

Roff, William R. *The Origins of Malay Nationalism.* New Haven, Connecticut: Yale University Press, 1967.

Tilman, Robert O. *Bureaucratic Transition in Malaysia.* Durham, North Carolina: Duke University Press, 1964.

Von Vorys, Karl. *Democracy Without Consensus. Communism and Political Stability in Malaysia.* Princeton: Princeton University Press, 1975.

THE PHILIPPINES

Abueva, Jose V., and Paul P. de Guzman, eds. *Foundations and Dynamics of Filipino Government and Politics.* Manila: The Bookmark, Inc., 1969.

Buss, Claude A. *The United States and The Philippines.* Washington, D.C.: American Enterprise Institute; and Stanford: Hoover Institute on War, 1977.

Esperitu, Socorro C., and Chester L. Hunt, eds. *Social Foundations of Community Development: Readings on the Philippines.* Manila: R.M. Garcia, 1964.

Grossholtz, Jean. *Politics in the Philippines.* Boston: Little, Brown, 1964.

Hollnsteiner, Mary R. *The Dynamics of Power in a Philippine Municipality.* Quezon City: University of the Philippines, Community Development Research Council, 1963.

Kerkvliet, Benedict. *The Huk Rebellion, A Study of Peasant Revolt in the Philippines.* Berkeley: University of California Press, 1977.

Kerkvliet, Benedict. *Political Change in the Philippines: Studies of Local Politics Preceding Martial Law.* Honolulu: The University Press of Hawaii, 1974.

Landé, Carl. *Structure of Philippine Politics: Leaders, Factions, and Parties.* New Haven, Connecticut: Yale University, Southeast Asia Studies, 1965.

Muego, Benjamin N. *The Philippines Under Martial Law: A Spectator Society?* Athens, OH: Ohio University Press, 1983.

Rosenberg, David A., ed. *Marcos and Martial Law in the Philippines.* Ithaca, N.Y.: Cornell University Press, 1979.

Steinberg, David Joel. *The Philippines: A Singular and Plural Place.* Boulder, CO: Westview Press, Inc., 1982.

SINGAPORE

Bellows, Thomas J. *The People's Action Party of Singapore: Emergence of a Dominant Party System.* New Haven, Connecticut: Yale University, Southeast Asia Studies, 1970.

Chan, Heng Chee. *The Dynamics of One Party Dominance: The PAP at the Grassroots.* Singapore: Singapore University Press, 1976.

George, T.J.S. *Lee Kwan Yew's Singapore.* London: Andre Deutsch, 1973.

Josey, Alex. *Lee Kuan Yew.* Singapore: Asia Pacific Press, 1968.

THAILAND

Akin Rabibhadana. *The Organization of Thai Society in the Early Bangkok Period 1782–1873.* Ithaca, N.Y.: Cornell University Southeast Asia Program Data Paper No. 74, 1969.

Ayal, Eliezer B., ed. *The Study of Thailand.* Athens, OH: Ohio University Center for International Studies, Southeast Asia Series, No. 54, 1978.

Darling, Frank. *Thailand and the United States.* Washington, D.C.: Public Affairs Press, 1965.

Girling, John L. S. *Thailand: Society and Politics.* Ithaca, NY: Cornell University Press, 1981.

Likhit Dhiravegin. *The Bureaucratic Elite of Thailand.* Bangkok: Thai Khadi Research Institute, Thammasat University, 1978.

Morell, David and Chai-Anan Samudavanija. *Political Conflict in Thailand: Reform, Reaction, Revolution.* Cambridge, MA: Oelgesclager, Gunn and Hain, 1981.

Moore, Frank J., and Clark D. Neher. *Thailand: Its People, Its Society, Its Culture.* New Haven, Connecticut: Human Relations Area Files, 1974.

Neher, Clark D. *Modern Thai Politics, From Village to Nation.* Cambridge, Massachusetts: Schenkman Publishing Company, 1976 (second edition, 1979).

Phillipps, Herbert P. *Thai Peasant Personality: The Patterning of Interpersonal Behavior in the Village of Bang Chan.* Berkeley: University of California Press, 1965.

Potter, Jack M. *Thai Peasant Social Structure.* Chicago: The University of Chicago Press, 1976.

Riggs, Fred W. *Thailand, The Modernization of a Bureaucratic Policy.* Honolulu: East-West Center Press, 1966.

Siffin, William J. *The Thai Bureaucracy: Institutional Change and Development.* Honolulu: East-West Center Press, 1966.

Skinner, G. William. *Chinese Society in Thailand: An Analytical History.* Ithaca, New York: Cornell University Press, 1957.

Turton, Andrew, Jonathon Fost and Malcolm Caldwell, eds. *Thailand: Roots of Conflict.* Nottingham, U.K.: Spokesman, 1978.

Wilson, David A. *The United States and the Future of Thailand.* New York: Praeger, 1970.

Wilson, David A. *Politics in Thailand.* Ithaca, New York: Cornell University Press, 1962.

Wit, Daniel. *Thailand: Another Vietnam?* New York: Charles Scribner's Sons, 1968.

VIETNAM

Buttinger, Joseph. *A Dragon Defiant.* New York: Praeger, 1972.

Fall, Bernard. *The Two Vietnams.* New York: Praeger, 1966.

Fitzgerald, Frances. *Fire in the Lake.* Boston: Little, Brown, 1972.

Halberstam, David. *The Making of a Quagmire.* New York: Random House, 1965.

Kahin, George McT. *Intervention: How America Became Involved in Vietnam.* New York: Alfred A. Knopf, 1986.

Kahin, George McT. and John W. Lewis. *The United States in Vietnam.* New York: Dial, 1969.

Lacouture, Jean. *Ho Chi Minh: A Political Biography.* New York: Random House, 1969.

Lacouture, Jean. *Vietnam: Between Two Truces.* New York: Random House, 1966.

McAlister, John T., Jr. *Vietnam: The Origins of Revolution.* New York: Knopf, 1969.

The Pentagon Papers. The Senator Gravel Edition. 4 volumes. Boston: Beacon Press, 1971.

Pike, Douglas. *Viet Cong: The Organization and Techniques of the National Liberation Front of South Vietnam.* Cambridge, Massachusetts: MIT Press, 1966.

Raskin, Marcus and Bernard Fall, eds. *The Vietnam Reader.* New York: Vintage Books, 1966.

INDEX

ALSO OF INTEREST
FROM SCHENKMAN BOOKS: